GROGAN'S
COMPANION TO DRINK

GROGAN'S
COMPANION TO DRINK

PETER GROGAN

Virgin BOOKS

2 4 6 8 10 9 7 5 3 1

Published in 2010 by Virgin Books, an imprint of Ebury Publishing
A Random House Group Company

The Random House Group Limited Reg. No. 954009

Addresses for companies within the Random House Group can be found at www.randomhouse.co.uk

A CIP catalogue record for this book is available from the British Library

Typeset by Palimpsest Book Production Limited,
Falkirk, Stirlingshire

Printed in the UK by Butler Tanner and Dennis Ltd

ISBN 9780753522226

For the Mrs Grogans

Contents

Introduction

It may be that my spectacles are rosé-tinted but it seems to me that I am fortunate to live in a golden age of peace, progress and prosperity. This is reflected brilliantly in the half-full glass of anybody in this sceptred isle whose interest in the subject of alcohol ever extended beyond the immediately utilitarian one of drunker, faster, cheaper – for, truly, we've never had it so good.

Here's a very modern story. The makers of Tyrrells rather fine potato crisps sold their business to a private equity company for a lot of money in 2008. It being a thoroughly modern deal, the purchasers didn't want the muddy stuff – the fields-full of top-quality spuds, the shed-loads of tractors – they just wanted the name . . . the *brand*. This left the Chase family with the problem of what to do with a rather fine arable farm. Two years later at the prestigious San Francisco World Spirits Competition, the winner of the award for the 'World's Best Vodka' was announced to be a new, English one, made from potatoes and called Chase.

Innovative and imaginative behaviour like this is by no means uncommon among the officers and crew of the good ship UK Booze. British brewing has convulsed these forty-odd years since the birth of the Campaign for Real Ale among beer drinkers feeling themselves at risk of slipping beneath the waves of tasteless, gassy 'keg'. Of the ten biggest-selling beers in 2010 – mostly tasteless, gassy lagers – only one is made by a British-owned company but there are, meantime, 700-odd (some very odd) craft brewers, mostly in rosy-cheeked health – a higher number per head of population than anywhere else can boast. They can barely muster a tasteless or a gassy liquid between them and their brews take only minimal trouble to find.

As one of the great crossroads of wine since before Bordeaux was Blighty: the UK has had the most diverse and dynamic market in the world for many years. The bar inches ever upwards – even the biggest sellers are not to be dismissed out of hand (not if the names Don Cortez, Lazki Rizling or Hirondelle have any meaning for you, at any rate). More exciting is the new breed of ambitious young winemakers emerging around the world who, taking the huge leaps forward in the science of the thing as givens, now seem able to make what is recognisable as 'fine wine' in every detail except that of the place in which it is made . . . and, more importantly, the price. Some of them make me wonder if the sacred sites of wine will have much more than symbolic significance in a generation's time.

Most exciting of all are the people who are selling these wines. For another new breed is springing up, this time of independent, quality-fixated merchants who appear to be thriving in the ready-made and willing constituency of increasingly sophisticated and demanding (but still reticent) British drinkers. It's not a big surprise that many of them also choose to sell some of their favourites among those thousands of craft beers . . . and maybe a handful of the dozen or so top-quality gins that have emerged in the last few years . . . or the flavour-packed, saccharine-free mixers that set them off to their best advantage. I could go on . . .

The one thing missing in this Arcadian picture has been a book to bring together and present all this abundant diversity to a wide and willing audience. There's no shortage of coverage of the individual subjects but booze writers tend to stay in their boxes, leaving a yawning gap for a single source of information for, say, how to optimise that world's best vodka in the ultimate Bloody Mary (no celery salt? . . . then no Bloody Mary, as far as I'm concerned); to list the key ingredients in a Pimms (on no account forget the mint – but basil works a refreshing treat too); for a pithy tutorial on how the hierarchy of the wines of Bordeaux is structured (what are people on about when they refer to a 'first growth' or a 'cru bourgeois?'); or for a round-up of all those Polish beers now on the shelves (they're mostly terrific. By the way, the biggest seller, Zywiec, is pronounced something like 'zuh-VEE-etch'). My hope is that this book will plug that gap.

So, a golden age indeed, and one in which a minimum of effort – made miniscule by the exigencies of the interwebby – enables proud British piss-pots to propel themselves into the position of drinking like their kings and their queens. And all this for the price just of . . . drinking.

How to Use This Book

This is not an encyclopaedia. Whether it is merely an *omnium gatherum* or a gallimaufry is not for me to say. Hopefully, it will prove to be some sort of *vade mecum* but – indisputably – it is an alphabetical book about booze.

The subject matter is treated generically and/or geographically (and hopefully not always idiosyncratically) such that, for example, a commercial product such as Dubonnet is covered under the most relevant heading of the type or group of drink(s) which define(s) it – in this case vermouth. However, as one of the comparatively rare cases of commercial synecdoche in which a proprietary brand – think Hoover or Biro – becomes better known than the category of which it forms part, the Dubonnet cocktail does deserve its own listing.

Some subjects are rather longer than others and the biggest categories of all – wine and beer – have been sub-divided by nation or, in a few cases, continent. Very large books have been written about even the smallest of the great French wine regions and my attempt has been to stuff, stick, splice and shoe-horn as much detail as I possibly can into the space allowed and I have seen off with a stick any editorial attempt to smuggle out a single sentence.

What are now known as the 'international' grape varieties – the ones people have heard of (and the ones seen most often on labels) – are listed separately whereas the lesser-known ones feature under the regions where they flourish. As such, and in all cases, if you don't find what you're looking for straight away, check the detailed index at the rear.

Look in vain for a formal vintage chart. Technical advances have – with the odd exceptions like Italy and the Rhône in 2002 – made the 'bad vintage' virtually a thing of the past while in the southern hemisphere, vintages have always been less variable anyway. Meanwhile, the hype that surrounds stellar years like 2000, 2005 and 2009 in Bordeaux and 2007 in the southern Rhône risks undermining the whole idea of merchants offering a disinterested comparison of vintages.

The small selection of cocktail 'standards' that has been included could never be perfectly formed but hopefully the basics of an illimitable subject – one mixologist's Bullshot is the next one's bullshit – have been covered.

I have given an idea of approximate prices of wines from individual producers with a handy codification in which they are allotted between one and three pictographic wine bottles. [1] represents a wine that can be had for the price of between one and two bottles of the average wine sold in the UK in mid-2010, which was a fiver less a few bob. (All the wines listed in the 'Drink Like A King' boxes are in this category.)

For reasons of space I have only been able to list a few of the biggest and best producers in any region – and finding the best producers, in wine as in every material aspect of life, is the key to everything – and the symbol represents the price-level of their simplest offering. The fact, for example, that a Burgundy winemaker's basic *Bourgogne Rouge* can be had for a shade less than a tenner doesn't mean that their best wines will be priced even in double digits.

[2] represents producers whose 'entry-level' wines cost approximately two to three times that average-bottle price while [3] indicates those whose wines cost in excess of that sum, sometimes multiply so, and, as such, no minimum price is implied.

As prices for beers and spirits vary far less widely – wildly even – than those for wine, they are not included in the system (although I have noted one or two eye-watering recent prices for some of the listed producers' bottlings of their oldest malt whiskies).

Peter Grogan
August 2010

alcoholics anonymous algeria absinthe abv acapulco additives aghioritiko agioritiko aglianico albariño alvarinho

alvarinho alcohol alcopops algeria aligoté americano anis angel's tit appellation controlée apple martini arinto

argentinian wine arinto arneis arrack australian wine

AA (Alcoholics Anonymous) – a salutary starting-point, in case one should get carried away with what follows. Conceived by Bill 'W' in 1934 on a rainy night in Akron, Ohio – and who, in truth, might not succumb to strong drink on a rainy night in Akron, Ohio? – 'the club' now has around two million members belonging to about 100,000 groups throughout the world. Iceland has one for every 1,250 people (the highest), while Britain has the same ratio of pubs per head of population – a much more sensible idea. The 'Twelve Steps' – although it sounds like an Aussie Chardonnay – is in fact the core programme of the 'fellowship', which strives to maintain the anonymity of its adherents and encourages sober members to mentor new ones via one-to-one sponsorship. The first step requires the subject to recognise rock bottom and their powerlessness over alcohol; the final step exhorts them to carry the message of AA to other alcoholics. Controversy surrounds the quasi-religious terminology used by the organisation and its insistence that total abstinence is the only solution; however, their results are impressive (at least they have been for a few members of my family).

Aberfeldy – the flagship distillery (Highland) of Dewar's whisky (itself owned by Bacardi and the biggest-selling Scotch whisky brand in the USA). Unusually, markets just two single malts: a twelve-year-old and a twenty-one-year-old.

Aberlour – speyside distillery making a range of classy single malts including excellent cask-strength A'bunadh, arguably the best of the Pernod Ricard-owned whiskies and particularly popular in France.

Abona – I know next to nothing about this small, demarcated wine region in the south of Tenerife (nor, indeed, had I ever heard of it until happening upon the fact that within Abona lies Europe's highest vineyard, at over 1500m). I have never tasted any of its wines and – as none are apparently available in the UK – I am unlikely ever to do so without going to some trouble. Were you to develop a fondness for them, remember never to say, 'Oh, yes, I do like Abona.' There are hundreds of little appellations like this dotted around the wine world, many of which have within them at least some conscientious producers whose output would be deserving of attention had we but world enough, and time. My apologies, then, both to those producers and to those inquisitive, wine-loving souls who've recently holidayed in the south of Tenerife.

absinthe – (aka *la fée verte* – the green fairy), a highly alcoholic (50–75% abv), foul-tasting grape-spirit-based liqueur originating from Switzerland, flavoured with wormwood (*artemisia absinthium*), anise, fennel, etc. Its notoriety among the demi-monde of fin-de-siècle Paris, a consequence of its highly alcoholic nature rather than the hallucinogenic properties that continue to be erroneously attributed to it, nonetheless led to a ban in Europe and the USA in

1915. (After a decent interval, replacements appeared in the guise of what we know as anis and pastis – including that of the original absinthe producer, Pernod – minus the wormwood, in the 1920s.)

Nerdism seems to accompany consumption of the modern versions from producers such as La Fée, François Guy, Pontarlier and Trenet, produced first in the Czech Republic in the early 1990s but now widespread, and the contemporary absinthe bore is more likely to be found in the suburbs banging on about the superiority of his method of preparation than baying at the moon in the Place Pigalle. (Poured over a cube of sugar held by a perforated spoon resting across the rim of a small, stemmed glass; ignited and, when the sugar has melted, topped up with water to taste). If you must, try using the Jade brand made by the obsessive American Ted Breaux, who creates his absinthe to original specifications using nineteenth-century equipment at the Combier distillery in Saumur.

abv – acronym for 'alcohol-by-volume' the most sensible of the various systems for measuring alcoholic strength, as the percentage of the volume of liquid that equates to pure alcohol. Most beers are in the range 3.5–6% abv; still wines 8–15% abv; fortified wines 17–22% abv; and most spirits 35–50% abv.

Acapulco – five parts light rum, two parts each lime juice and egg white, one part Triple Sec and simple syrup to taste shaken with ice, strained from a convenient clifftop in to a cocktail glass and garnished with a sprig of mint.

additives – a list of additives as long as your arm is allowed in the ingredients of beers, wines and spirits. Some are necessary for regulating acidity and sweetness or as preservatives (sulphur dioxide, also known as sulphite, is ubiquitous and essential to prevent oxidation in wine). Various types of clay, egg white, milk products and isinglass (made from the swim bladders of fish) are used for fining (clarifying) and filtration – they don't sound very nice but they do the job and are not present in the finished product. The line is blurred between necessary additives and those used to disguise defects and alter the apperance of a product and though it is easy to say the fewer the better there is seldom any indication on labels of what has been used.

African beer – love is all around, says the song, and so is beer. Good beer, too – unto the four corners of Africa where East African Breweries' famously elephantine Tusker, Brasseries du Maroc's Casablanca, Namibia Breweries' estimable Windhoek, and Nigerian Breweries' Star – sometimes using sorghum in the mash – slake some serious thirsts.

Aglianico – aristocratic red-wine grape variety and one of the best of Campania, a region of southern Italy, where it makes their best dinner-party reds. A double-decant an hour ahead helps (as does a fine roast beast on the table).

Airén – unspectacular white grape, the most widely planted of any variety (the equivalent of every square inch of Surrey) in Spain, and therefore, by acreage, the world (with some three-quarters of a million acres), making a sea of Spanish brandy and an ocean of Valdepeñas, which can be perfectly decent with a nice bit of fish on a southern Costa. Gradually being supplanted by more characterful varieties – could be 'goodnight Airén'?

Alabama Slammer – shake equal parts sloe gin, amaretto and Southern Comfort with two parts fresh orange juice and ice and strain in to a highball glass. Or not.

Albariño/Alvarinho – graceful white-grape variety of north-western Spain and northern Portugal, where it makes enigmatic, aromatic wines that have a Viognier-esque perfume about them with perhaps some smoky, oily Alsace Pinot Gris thrown in for good measure. Before the late 1990s Albariño seldom made it out of the lush green, fjord-scape of Galicia's Rias Baixas (try 'ree-ash by-shas') appellation, where all Spanish stereotypes are redundant: them Gallegos are Celts, right down to the kilts and the bagpipes, and Celts everywhere would feel at home in the Galician rain – all 60 annual average inches of it, which requires everything to be kept off the damp ground including the vines that are trained up tall granite posts. Traditionally a highly prized – but moderately priced – local secret, the cat is now well and truly out of the bag and arguably Spain's best white wine is ubiquitous. It is also being planted in the USA, where its popularity has surged rapidly. Preferably drunk young, on its own or with some pre-dinner salted almonds in order not to miss the subtlety, but most nonetheless have enough body to partner fish and *mariscos* (and enough acidity to hold their own should such things arrive in a dairy-based sauce).

alcohol – (from the Arabic *al-kohl*), any of a series of volatile hydroxyl compounds made from hydrocarbons by distillation, of which one – C_2H_5OH (aka ethanol, ethyl alcohol) – is the subject of this book.

alcohol dehydrogenase – aka ADH, an enzyme found in the liver and stomach, where it breaks down alcohol (and without which its consumption would not be possible). Lower levels occur in people of Asian descent and this is thought to be responsible for their higher levels of alcohol intolerance and 'Asian flush'. Lower levels also occur in women generally, but especially those from Essex.

alcohol-free beverages – happily, the nature of this book precludes much discussion of such vileness, such dross. Rather drink your bathwater, or even your own waters. If you must, one or two of the 'beers' (Clausthaler, Buckler) are relatively inoffensive and with 'spinning cone' technology, the 'wines' have improved somewhat. But if you're going alcohol-free, not much beats a spicy Virgin Mary or the clean taste of cranberry juice.

alcoholism – best defined for me by a close relative as his 'morbid and insatiable craving for alcohol'; however, the spectrum of qualifying behaviours is broad, very broad. Many more millions would be defined as suffering from it by exceeding 'guidelines' for safe consumption than would be referred to as 'functioning alcoholics', though a non-functioning one is fairly easy to spot. It is undoubtedly a physical addiction and withdrawal symptoms can be severe even if judged only by the alternate substances people will consume in attempts to satisfy their cravings. Much debate relates to whether it is an affliction, a genetic inevitability or a choice. A consumption that exceeds the individual's ability to deal with it either physically, psychologically or circumstantially is the common element but if the 'problem drinker' is recognised early, preferably by themselves, then – through intervention, moderation or abstinence – they can most often be kept from the park bench.

alcopop – sweet, fizzy drinks in which the taste of alcohol is masked have always been around and, whether proffered by unscrupulous manufacturers in pursuit of profit or by unscrupulous individuals in pursuit of gratification of the flesh, they are often aimed at impressionable girls. In the 1970s Cherry B, Pony and Babycham worked well, as well as Snowball, and it is instructive to bracket them all as direct precursors of today's alcopop. The popular ones manufactured by the largest vodka and rum brands are sudsy with flavours of bubblegum, bubble bath and boiled sweets and so disgusting even park-bench winos steer clear.

Algeria – of massive importance to the French wine trade in the middle of the last century with a million acres of vines providing bold reds to beef up all sorts of blended wines. The market plummeted after independence and in the early 1970s they were sending a billion bottles per year to the USSR. Production has fallen by ninety-five per cent and under a stricter Islamic regime more than half of grape production is destined for the fruit bowl.

Aligoté – unobtrusive white-grape variety that would be much better known and regarded if it were not thought of as the Cinderella grape of Burgundy, perpetually in the shadow of Chardonnay and Pinot Noir. It has its own appellation (and its own base in the village of Bouzeron) and makes appetising wines with good acidity; best sipped on their own on golden summer evenings. It's the wine the French mix with a little Crème de Cassis to make Kir.

Americano – pour equal parts sweet vermouth and Campari over ice in a rocks glass and finish with a splash of club soda and an orange (or lemon) twist. (Devised by Gaspare Campari and the first drink consumed by James Bond in the original Ian Fleming novel, *Casino Royale.*) Adding an equal part of gin makes it a Negroni.

Angel's Tit – layer one part each white crème de cacao, cherry liqueur and single cream in a chilled liqueur glass, garnished with a maraschino cherry in the middle (at which point the name will become self-explanatory and mock the American bowdlerization to Angel's Tip).

anis – (aka anise, anisette, pastis, raki, arak, ouzo); loose group of alcoholic beverages popular around a great swathe of the Mediterranean and which have in common the fact that they are aniseed-flavoured. Some are effectively flavoured vodkas; other sweetened versions are liqueurs. France's leading brand, Pernod (see absinthe p. 4) is dry and less alcoholic than pastis, which is flavoured with both star-anise and liquorice. Spanish anis (Mono, Chinchón) is sweet or dry (dulce or seco). French anisette liqueur (Brizard) is sweetened and similar to Sambuca in Italy. Usually served diluted with water (anywhere from 1:1 to 5:1). A rough Greek ouzo was responsible for one of my worst ever hangovers, although sleeping on a sandy beach facing windward didn't help. The inevitable mouthful of sand and a steep climb back up to the bar where mein host informed me: 'It's still fermenting in your stomach', finished me off.

appellation contrôlée (AC) – in full, appellation d'origine contrôlée (AOC) the French term for a demarcated region of production, originally for wine (the first was for Châteauneuf-du-Pape in 1923) but now covering all manner of comestibles from cheeses to chickens. Portugal's Douro claims to have had the first such system, devised in 1756; however, Hungary classified their vineyards in 1700 and

Tuscany's Carmignano had a go in 1716 and they both also claim the original honours. It's the French term that has stuck and I use it rather than 'controlled appellation' which sounds daft (especially in the US – there is very little control of anything in the Appalachians, as anyone who has watched the film *Deliverance* will know).

Most national systems are based on the French model and the regulatory authority will not only demarcate the geographical area but also stipulate which grape varieties may be used, maximum yields, parameters for alcohol content and so on; in general, the smaller and more prestigious the region, the more hoops must be jumped through.

Fundamentally such systems are best thought of as having a purpose similar to the UK Trades Description Act and are designed to protect consumers from unscrupulous producers. Conversely, narrowness restricts the output of scrupulous producers – to the extent that some of the best wines in Europe have to call themselves *vin de pays* or *vino da tavola*.

Apple Martini/Appletini – the cider of the gods is made with two parts gin (or vodka) stirred with one part apple schnapps and poured in to a chilled cocktail glass.

aquavit/akvavit/akevitt – it's vodka really, from Denmark (Aalborg), Sweden (Absolut, OP Anderson), Norway (Linie) and Finland (Finlandia, as if), but let's play along as it was probably the original version. All distilled from potatoes, flavoured with caraway and usually one or more of fennel, dill, aniseed, cumin and bitter orange.

Ardbeg – peatiest and smokiest of all of Islay's peaty, smoky whiskies, its long story, which started in 1815, reached its most dramatic chapters only in the late twentieth century: having lost money for many years the distillery was mothballed in 1981 and after spasmodic attempts to breathe some water-of-life back into it over the next decade and a half it was finally bought by Glenmorangie in 1997, when full production resumed. If the award of the *Whisky Bible*'s 'World Whisky of the Year 2008' makes misty-eyed, *Whisky Galore*-style fantasies cloud the judgement it should be remembered that Glenmorangie was itself acquired by LVMH in 2004 and the cockles of the hearts most warmed by this story are corporate ones.

Argentinian wine – Argentina is the biggest producer among South America's winemaking countries (and fifth in the world), with a long and proud history of viticulture and distinctive, signature red (Malbec) and white (Torrontés) grape varieties, both of which can be excellent value. As elsewhere in South America, vines were introduced by thirsty European invaders in the sixteenth century and the Spanish also established the first irrigation systems, which remain vital – in one form or another – to successful winemaking. Low rainfall and long, sunny summers combine with a third factor: cool nights at the altitude of the winemaking regions – the highest in the world at between 700 and 1400m – to complete a unique climatological recipe. The result is that Argentina's reds (especially Malbec) have a freshness and complexity that other 'New World' producers have emulated. The dry growing conditions mean the vines develop deep roots to draw up all sorts of flavourful minerals; the cool nights at altitude also prevent the development of those baked smells and flavours that used to be common in wines from the other side of the Andes.

Malbec has done more to establish Argentina's standing in the world of wine than all other factors combined. The grape, native to

Cahors in south-western France, where it still flourishes, appears to have found its ideal home in Argentina. Its meaty, almost bloody character makes it the perfect foil for the country's other stand-out product in the food and drink department – beefsteak – and the search for the perfect meat-and-Malbec match is something of a national obsession.

As elsewhere in the New World, leading producers tend to make rather over-extracted, unbalanced luxury cuvées – perhaps with the intention of impressing wine critics and judges, to the extent that the 'basic' wines have almost invariably been preferable. Argentine Malbec can produce complex, age-worthy wines on a par with, for example, top *Cru Bourgeois* claret, and, as such, can be among the best value wines in the world. Originally from north-western Italy's Piedmont region, Argentina's other natural red resource is Bonarda, a grape that until now has been underexploited (Colonia la Liebres [1], Dante Robino [2] or El Retiro [3]).

The distinctive white-grape Torrontés (pronounced with the emphasis on the final syllable) is related to Muscat and there's certainly a family resemblance in the flowery, grapey aromas and frequently orangey palate. Neither Torrontés nor Muscat is a variety for making grand *Vins de Garde* but for producing substantial wines that are perfumed – sometimes intensely so – both are adaptable to food matching.

A plethora of international grape varieties thrive in Argentina: Cabernet Sauvignon; Merlot; Tempranillo and – reflecting the large number of Italian families who settled in the country – Sangiovese and Barbera. Syrah, in particular, is worth checking out among the reds. Of the whites, Pinot Grigio, Semillon and Chenin Blanc show the most potential along with some cool, classy Chardonnays, especially from Tupungato.

Geographically the Mendoza region is where it all happens. It accounts for seventy per cent of wine production and the Andes provides the cooling influence that keeps the wines fresh, a lesson that has been learned elsewhere. A varied region in terms of terrain, with vineyards at altitudes ranging from 700–1,700 metres, and of climate, Mendoza is itself divided into a number of sub-regions. The Uco Valley in the south, and especially the Tupungato area within it, and Luján de Cuyo – and its sub-divisions of Pedriel, Agrelo and Vistalba – are where some of the best wines are made. Way up to the north the region of Salta has, at over 3,000m what are believed to be the world's highest vineyards. San Juan to the south is the second-biggest producer and the vine action goes on southwards, in a small way, right down into Patagonia. Brief mention should be made of the country's average annual consumption, which peaked at a heroic ninety litres per head during the darkest days of the 1960s and 1970s but is now less than half that amount.

DRINK LIKE A KING
with ...

Bianchi
Catena
Colonia Las Liebres
Las Hormigas
Luigi Bosca
Nieto Sentiner
O Fournier
Pulenta
Renacer
Michel Torino

... FOR THE PRICE OF JUST DRINKING

Argentina remains a keen but nervous newcomer on the world stage: whilst growing, exports still account for only twenty per cent of production. Producers bring to their wine a seriousness of intent normally reserved only for the tango. Having seen the potential, however, investors have arrived from all corners – to an extent that most of the high-profile new ventures are at least partly in foreign hands: Moët et Chandon (who have been making large quantities of very good 'champaña' for local consumption since the 1960s at Bodegas Chandon 1); Portugal's biggest producer, and maker of

Mateus Rosé, Sogrape with Finca Flichman [1]; arguably the world's most influential wine consultant Michel Rolland with his Clos de los Siete [2]; and Pierre Lurton of Bordeaux-legend Château Cheval Blanc is producing Cheval de los Andes [3] with LVMH subsidiary Terrazas de los Andes [1]. And these are just the biggest names. Meanwhile, at the other end of the corporate scale, Fairtrade-accredited producers – notably the La Riojana [1] cooperative – appear to be thriving respectably in a fiercely competitive market.

*GET A HANDLE...

ARGENTINA PROVES THAT BIG NEW WORLD REDS (ESPECIALLY MALBEC) CAN HAVE FRESHNESS AND COMPLEXITY. THE COOL NIGHTS AT ALTITUDE PREVENT THE WINES DEVELOPING THE BAKED SMELLS THAT USED TO PLAGUE SOUTH AMERICAN WINES AND THE DRY GROWING CONDITIONS MEAN THE VINES DEVELOP DEEP ROOTS THAT DRAW UP ALL SORTS OF FLAVOURFUL GOODIES.

Of the old guard of producers, include Norton [1] (now owned by the Swarovski bangle family); Etchart [1] (by Pernod Ricard); Flichman [1] (by Sogrape); Weinert [1] and Schroeder [2], only the latter two remain in private hands but all still produce good wines – funny about all those German names though. The price/quality ratio is enviable across the board – from entry level (Bianchi [1], La Esperanza [1], Graffigna [1], Las Moras [1], Michel Torino [1], Nieto Senetiner [1], Schroeder [1], Chile's Concha y Toro-owned Otra Vida [1], Zuccardi [1]) through Sunday-best bottles (Alta Vista [1], Altos las Hormigas [2], prime mover Nicolas Catena [2], Colomé [2], Don Domenico [2], Gougenheim [1], Luigi Bosca [1], O Fournier [1], Pulenta [1], Renacer [1], Santa Ana [1], Trapiche [1],Viñalba [1] and Susana Balbo – another prime mover) to the very top, where the wines have chilled out admirably from the rather overwrought efforts of a few years ago (Achaval Ferrer 2, Alicia 2, Benegas 2, Bressia 2, Don Cristobal 1492 2, Viña Cobos 2).

Arneis – upwardly mobile white-grape variety of Piedmont in northern Italy, enjoying a new silky, peachy, dinner-party-food-friendly lease of life after nearly becoming a footnote. Arneis has two eponymous DOCs in the Langhe and Roero areas.

arrack – booze was probably first formed in a gourd of palm sugar left out in the rain into which the right little speck of yeast landed, setting off a spontaneous fermentation. Whoever looked at it the next morning and wondered why their breakfast was bubbling should have stopped there. But they had a sniff . . . and then a sip – at which point all their instincts should have said, 'Eeeuw!' But the person who started it all (I suspect a direct ancestor of mine) thought, 'Mmmm, you know, that's really not bad,' and then took a second sip – the first ever booze-up. Similar drinks are still made by primitive peoples in Java, Borneo, Sumatra, South London and Sweden, where it has evolved into what they call Punsch.

Arran, Isle of – one of Scotland's newest distilleries – and the only one on Arran – began production in 1995. The ten-year-old won lots of friends, as have all the bells-and-whistles 'expressions' but the fifteen-year-old is still in the cask as I write.

Artillery Punch – into a large bowl mix ten parts each bourbon, red wine and strong black tea; five parts each dark rum and orange juice; two parts each apricot brandy and gin; one part each lemon juice and lime juice and chill before adding ice and slices of lemon and lime. Serve (but don't try this at home) by gathering your guests around the bowl and dropping a cannonball into the mix from a decent height.

Asian and Australasian beer – the beatitudes of beer brook no boundaries or borders and Australians (Coopers, Gage Roads, Malt Shovel, Matilda Bay) and New Zealanders (DB, Emerson's, Mac's, Tuatara, Twisted Hop) are now brewing good stuff that exposes the insipid big brands (VB, Foster's, Tooheys). In Tahiti twenty years ago I was paying more for each beer (Hinano) than for my bed – but how many beds can you sleep in? The standards of south-east Asia are not to be sniffed at in Singapore and Malaysia (Asia Pacific Brewery's Tiger has good bite), Indonesia (Multi Bintang, Bali Hai) and Thailand (Boon Rawd's Singha).

If conjuring the image of a condensation-covered bottle of Indian UB Group's Kingfisher and the motto on its label 'Most Thrilling Chilled!' makes other people want to drink some as much as I do then the future funding of flamboyant owner Vijay Mallya's IPL cricket and Formula 1 motor-racing teams is assured. Next door, Sri Lanka makes it on to the grid as well with Lion Brewery.

Thirsty, de-stressing Japanese have enough post-work steam to make one of their beers, Asahi, the world's tenth biggest and it's a relief they're doing less of the 'dry' beer thing, which turns all the sugar to alcohol and takes the taste away with it – and making proper beer (Hakusekikan, Hitachino Nest, Ise Kadoya, Kinshachi, Kirin, Yoho Brewing).

I have felt at home with the beer I've had in every Chinese restaurant I've ever been into anywhere in the world – Tsingtao – pronounced 'ching dow' – but have yet to try Snow, which is on everybody's lips indoors and which will soon be the biggest beer brand of all – and that's sno' joke.

Assyrtiko – svelte white-grape variety of Greece making mineral-rich wines such as those of Gaia, Hatzidakis, Sigalas, on Santorini; in Thrace with Biblia Chora and on Halkidiki with Tsantalis. All a good bet to help you wash down the meze platter.

Australian wine – it all seemed to come so easily to Australia. The basic premise was simple: big, pure-fruit flavours + oak = happiness. The results – 'Sunshine-in-a-Bottle' Chardonnays and blackcurrant fruit gum Cabernet Sauvignons – charmed the throats of millions for whom wine had hitherto been for posh people. 'Chuck another prawn on the barbie . . .'

Thankfully, though, despite all the climate-defying science, the march of the international grape varieties and the global reach of the big producers and their supra-national brands, every major wine-producing country remains uniquely itself, with its unique set of advantages and its unique set of challenges.

Australia's biggest natural advantages are a climate that has only recently shown signs of being science-defying and a huge variety of terroirs in which an amazingly diverse portfolio of grape varieties can thrive and sometimes excel. These resources, combined with the natural pragmatism, optimism and enthusiasm for hard work of the inhabitants, have – in twenty years – propelled Australia from being a viticultural backwater to being the fourth-largest exporter of wine, now sending over a billion bottles annually out in to the world. Furthermore, that well-known Aussie wanderlust – as expressed in the form of 'flying winemakers' – has now, in turn, taken Australian winemaking principles and practices into every corner of planet vino.

Australia has long been wine-waiter in chief to the UK, putting on our tables more than one in five of the bottles we opened at the end of the noughties. Second-placed USA would need a forty per cent increase in sales to catch up. Meanwhile, the Yanks themselves have overtaken us Limeys as Australia's biggest customers, accounting for thirty per cent of their exports. So 'no worries' then?

Well, yes and no. Unlike the earliest British consumers of Australian wine we are not a captive market.

More than any wine region except California, with which it has so much in common, Australia requires us to make an invidious distinction between the cheap agro-industrial product (the mass-produced 'beverage wine' of the supermarket own-labels and the now overfamiliar proprietary brands) and the much smaller production of something finer and more cherishable that, until somebody comes up with a better term for it, is hard to avoid calling 'fine wine'. Australia's long-term future is in moving upmarket as worldwide competition to supply wine to the entry-level market hots up and lower-cost countries (and you can forget South America and South Africa here – we're talking about China and India) start to rain on Australia's parade. It may be two-way traffic, though, as Asia may be Australia's biggest market.

Australian wine is very democratic – the best wines share the same genes as the crowd-pleasers, they're made of the same stuff but the essence of many producers' top wines such as Rosemount's Show range [2], Hardy's Eileen Hardy wines [3], Brown Brothers' Patricia and many of Penfolds' labels – at least as far as reds are concerned – is in their sheer concentration. Part of the impetus for making these dense, heavily extracted wines is the popularity of wine competitions. I once sat next to a leading Australian winemaker at a dinner to promote his multi-award-winning flagship range. After tasting through them, alongside his mid-range wines, our first course arrived and I noticed that he, like me, chose one of the latter to drink with it. After mustering a little Dutch courage I asked him if just possibly the showboaters might not be a fraction over-the-top? 'Sure they are, but that's what you've got to do if you want to win prizes,' he smiled. 'They're not for drinking.'

Australian viniculture began in 1788 with Captain Arthur Phillip – founder of Sydney – and then abruptly stopped when his vines failed. Later, in the 1820s, commercial production got under way and the industrious James Busby did the first methodical work, trying out nearly 700 different vine varieties. Penfolds, founded in 1844, is the oldest winemaker, maker of the iconic Grange and arguably the best in Australia. Busby laid good foundations – Australia is the only southern hemisphere country with anything like a truly European diversity of established grape varieties and styles.

DRINK LIKE A KING With ...

- Andrew Peace
- Brookford
- Broken Shackle
- Cranswick
- Grant Burge
- Marktree
- One Chain
- Runamok
- St. Hallett
- Trentham Estate

... FOR THE PRICE OF JUST DRINKING

The Big Three of those varieties are Shiraz with thirty per cent of plantings, Chardonnay with twenty-five per cent, and Cabernet Sauvignon with twenty per cent, and the remaining twenty-five per cent comprises just about every grape you can think of. As people look more for subtlety and complexity rather than power, Rhône-style GSM (Grenache, Shiraz, Mourvèdre) and Shiraz-Viognier blends are the new big things in reds. Some growers of cooler-climate Shiraz are beginning to label it Syrah to reflect its lighter, peppery Rhône-like qualities in contrast to the familiar booming, medicinal styles from the warmer areas.

Finding one's way to the good stuff is difficult: there's no up-itself *cru* system operating here, just regional and sub-regional Geographical Indication (GI). Supra-regional South-Eastern Australia is not exactly exclusive: it covers ninety-five per cent of the wine-growing areas' output yet some solid wines – Banrock Station, McGuigan, Yellow Tail – do very good business under its designation, as do some tyros such as Andrew Peace [1], Brookford [1], One Chain Vineyards [1], and Runamok [1], Some Young Punks [2] (you should see the names of their wines), and Griffith Park [1] for fizz. Finding some of the best stuff has been made easier by the formation in 2009 of Australia's First Families of Wine, an alliance of some of the larger, high-quality independent firms.

Most of the biggest firms have bought up numerous companies, many of which offer good – even very good – value, depending on the waxing and waning madness of the discounting moon. Constellation Brands, for example, is more recognisable (in Australia) as Hardy's [1] and Banrock Station [1] – all 4,000 acres of it; Fosters' offspring include Penfolds [1], Lindemans [1], Wolf Blass [1] and Rosemount [1]; Pernod Ricard's Jacob's Creek is the biggest French-owned wine brand (!); Lion Nathan has Petaluma [2], Stonier [2] and Mitchelton [2]; Casella is better known as the phenomenon that is Yellow Tail [1]; busy Australian Vintage is resolving its identity crisis and, apart from its McGuigan [1] brand, is a humungous provider of supermarket own-brands and 'private brands' as well as supplying millions of cases of wine made under contract for some of its biggest competitors – they're all there, side by side, on the shelf.

The 'consolidation' process now appears to have peaked and Fosters and Constellation have sold some of their smaller subsidiaries. It seems a good omen that an old, established firm like Clare Valley's Leasingham [2], gobbled up by Hardy's, who were themselves then taken over by Constellation, is now back in the private hands of Tim Adams [2]. The surviving mid-size independents (Brown Brothers [1], Peter Lehmann [1], Cranswick [1]) have long offered an excellent price/quality ratio and it seems too that the big firms' mid-tier ranges (Hardy's Oomoo [2], Penfolds' Thomas Hyland [2] and Jacob's Creek's Three Vines [1]) are intended to emulate (and compete with) them as they plot their path away the from heavy-handed, and heavily discounted, over-oaked Chardonnay and overly alcoholic, medicinal Shiraz.

Oz broke all the rules. It blew a gale of fresh air through the stuffy world of European winemaking. The Aussies grew what they wanted, they irrigated, they trucked grapes hundreds of miles to make the blends they wanted. It looks as if they're now starting to break a few of their own rules to keep Matilda waltzing.

As the corporations ponder their future a new breed of highly trained, fleet-footed and – above all – cool winemakers are developing a new style of Aussie wine that is gaining ground at the viral speed of the internet. Mac Forbes, Giant Steps/Innocent Bystander, Two Hands, Ben Glaetzer, Ten Minutes by Tractor are just a few of the names at the forefront. The country's cool-climate winemaking areas – Heathcote, Geelong, Mornington Peninsula, Tasmania and Orange among them – are opening up at the speed of an out-of-control skateboarder. It seems that the new recipe for wine down-under may be: cool climate + cool winemakers = cool wine.

*GET A HANDLE...

THE PACE OF CHANGE DOWN-UNDER IS BREATHTAKING. THE 'BIG-HAIR' WINES ARE BEING RAPIDLY REPLACED BY ALTOGETHER COOLER, MORE STYLISH WAYS OF DOING THINGS AND EVEN THE AUSSIES DRINK MORE SAUVIGNON BLANC THAN CHARDONNAY NOW.

Western Australia

The varied climates and terrains of the 350-odd-mile coast of 'WA' suit a wide range of grape varieties that make wine in a wide variety of styles, almost all of which have one thing in common: high quality. There are very few WA wines in super-markets and even the lowest-priced are well above average price. This is a good thing and reflects the fact that, refreshingly, the biggest producers (Houghton [1] – pronounced 'horton', Plantagenet [1] and Evans & Tate [2]) seem to make only good – and often good value – wines.

The southernmost region of WA is Great Southern, where Antarctic Ocean currents cool coastal areas sufficiently for succulent Pinot Noir and racy Riesling while intense Shiraz and rich Chardonnays emerge from the warmer interior. Most wineries are brand-spanking but there are established role-models in the Mount Barker sub-region (Plantagenet [1], Forest Hill [1]) to give the tyros in Denmark (Howard Park [2], West Cape [1]) and Frankland River (Alkoomi [2], Ferngrove [1], Frankland Estate [2]) something to aim for. In the latter the Westfield Vineyard (Houghton) was where winemaker Jack Mann started the modern WA industry and the remaining two easternmost regions Albany and Porongurup have yet to hit their export stride.

Heading west, the Pemberton region (Brookland Valley [1] – also in Margaret River; Fonty's Pool [1]; Picardy [2]; Seven Day Road [1]) is rapidly making a name for itself beyond its perimeters. The name of the beguiling Margaret River region is probably known to more people than that of WA itself. Cooled by the onshore Fremantle Doctor breeze, it's not just a pretty face: there are over 100 producers, many of them adept with a wide range of varietals including Cape Mentelle [2], Evans and Tate [2], Marchand & Burch [3], McHenry Hohnen [1], Palandri [1], Suckfizzle/Stella Bella [2] and Voyager [2], with rich age-worthy Cabernet Sauvignon (Vasse Felix 2), rounded Bordeaux blends (Cullen 2) and tropical Chardonnay (Leeuwin 2, Moss Wood 2, Pierro 3, Woodlands 3) at the top of the list and Shiraz, Semillon and Sauvignon Blanc not far behind.

The Swan Valley north of Perth is where things started (1834 saw the first vintage) – it once made ninety per cent of the region's wine. That's now down to ten per cent: the 100°F summer temperatures don't suit modern styles – most of the original wines were fortified. The cooler Perth Hills area to the east is seeing a lot of new investment and is one to watch.

South Australia

Even with about fifty per cent of the country's total wine production, it's stretching it to call South Australia (Red Fin 2, Tiddy Widdy Well 2) – or that south-eastern corner of it below about 33°S where the grapes are grown – Australia's California. It is the heart of it though, with most vineyards within 70–80 miles of Adelaide, and only the relatively featureless Riverland and Limestone Coast beyond the easy reach of the wine tourist.

In contrast, it's impossible to avoid calling the Barossa Valley Australia's Napa – it's the biggest quality-wine region, the tourist side is admirably well-developed and as a result the big firms all need to be here – they dominate production, albeit often through prestigious subsidiary companies that seem to operate with an enviable degree of autonomy. (Penfolds – their Grange, Australia's 'first growth', an icon for decades and traditionally a blend of wines from all over and is assembled in Barossa. The ultimate South-Eastern Australian? It may have the cult status, and a price to match, but its un-oaked sibling Saint Henri is the insider's choice and a comparative bargain; Lion Nathan's St Hallett 1, Jacob's Creek 1, Wolf Blass 1 and

Hardy's [1] all have bases here. It's the medium-sized firms, many of them independent, including Bethany [2], Charles Melton [2], Duval [2], Elderton [2], Glaetzer [2], Grant Burge [1], Greenock Creek [3], Kaesler [2], Langmeil [2] (who have Shiraz vines from 1843), Maverick [2], Peter Lehmann [1], Rockford [2], Spinifex [2], Teusner [3], Torbreck [2], Turkey Flat [1], Two Hands [2] and Yalumba [1] that make most of the wines that maintain Barossa's world-class reputation.)

There are also lots of small farmers, some of whom, if they're lucky enough to have old-vine Syrah and Grenache, are assiduously courted by bigger firms for their crop. Lucky to survive the Cabernet Sauvignon invasion, some of the vines are over 100 years old and only these old-timers have root systems deep enough to be dry-farmed, i.e., without irrigation, which is essential elsewhere due to the hot, dry summers. The old vines make the distinctive, richly concentrated, brooding style – often accented by something chocolatey – that is one of Barossa's trademarks. That Aussie knack of mixing tradition and innovation is always in evidence, though, and the shiny new things are suave, Côte-Rôtie-style blends (with a little Viognier to soothe the Shiraz's knitted brow) and, another juicy Rhône-U-like blend – GSM, that's Grenache, Syrah and Mourvèdre. Good Cabernet Sauvignon (Penfolds [1]) and sophisticated Semillon (Peter Lehmann [1]) keep the flag flying for Bordeaux varieties.

Barossa is contiguous with the Eden Valley to the east, where cooler temperatures at higher altitude are ideal for Riesling (Grosset [2], Heggies [2], Pewsey Vale [2], Hewitson [2], Yalumba [1], Thorn-Clarke [1], Torzi Matthews [2]). Eden emerged in the 1960s in the Steingarten vineyard (Jacob's Creek [1]) and now produces some of the best Riesling in the world. Leading the charge has been Jeffrey Grosset who, in the crucible of contemporary Aussie winemaking, including a joint venture with Yalumba (called Mesh [2]), has nonetheless gone full circle back to the nineteenth-century roots of it all, admitting it's taken him thirty years to fully understand his two plots of land. Roistering reds are provided from Shiraz. Eden's other claim to fame is as the home to one of the few pretenders to Grange's crown: Henschke's Hill of Grace [3] and, with a supporting role, the fine and fruit-cakey Irvine's Grand Merlot [2].

Pretty, winding Clare Valley, where winemaking also dates from the 1840s, has varied soils, even higher slopes and cooler temperatures to give its elegant Riesling, mostly teased from the limestone terra rossa soil by small independent growers (Tim Adams [2], Jim Barry [1], Grosset [2], Kilikanoon [2], Leasingham [2], Mitchell [2], Mount Horrocks [2], Neagle's Rock [2], O'Leary Walker [2], Petaluma [2], Pikes [1], Skillogalee [2], Wakefield [1], Wendouree [3]) the edge of extra acidity. The slate of Polish Hill – lots of Silesian Lutherans sought sanctuary in South Australia in the nineteenth century – makes it one of the best sites. Reds are never neglected in Australia and Shiraz and Cabernet Sauvignon, with a notably eucalyptus twang, are particularly good.

South of Adelaide, McLaren Vale is another big name in Australian wine and the wide variation of soils in its rolling countryside account for an equally wide variety of grapes and styles of wine. Full-throttle Grenache and Shiraz shine – some are from 100-plus-year-old, dry-grown vines – and Cabernet Sauvignon from here makes big chocolate, mocha-toned wines. Warm summers cooled by sea breezes – always a good combination – complete the recipe for success. John Reynell spotted the potential in 1838 and his Chateau Reynella [2] is now HQ for Hardy's. (Battle of Bosworth [1], Chapel Hill [2], Clarendon Hills [3], Geoff Merrill [1], Kangarilla Road [2], Kay Brothers [2], Leconfield [2], Lloyd [3], Mitolo [1], Noon Winery [3], SC Pannell [2], Paxton [2], Rockbare [1], Simon Hackett [1], Willunga [1], Wirra Wirra [2], Woodstock [2] and

D'Arenberg 1 – labels on their McLaren Vale wines have the red sash.) The region runs into the Southern Fleurieu peninsula where the cool maritime climate has attracted major investment in making sumptuous Pinot Noir (Tappanappa 3) and great things are already happening.

The long-established Langhorne Creek area made wines for blending into the likes of Jacob's Creek until recently, but that's changing fast for the best producers and Jacob's loss is our gain (Bleasdale 1, Bremerton 1, Brothers in Arms 2, Glaetzer 2, Matilda Plains 1).

Out of Adelaide's back door and up the Mount Lofty Ranges, the Adelaide Hills have all the variety to be expected from a region that spans fifty miles but a common thread is the coolness to be expected on sites mostly above 400m. Australia's best Sauvignon Blanc is grown here, but half is red, mainly Cabernet Sauvignon, Pinot Noir and Merlot (Ashton Hills 2, Bird in Hand 2, Geoff Weaver 2, Henschke 3, Leabrook 3, Nepenthe 1, Setanta 2, Shaw and Smith 2, Petaluma-owned Tim Knappstein 2).

Winemakers all over Australia have been running their slide-rules ('Dad? What's a slide-rule?') over the terra rossa soil of the vast Limestone Coast area (and its twenty-four sub-regions, most of which nobody outside of them has ever heard of). Of the ones some people have heard of, most of Padthaway's (Henry's Drive 3, Two Hands 2) wines were trucked out for blending until Hardy's slide-ruler in chief worked out it was cheaper to build the Stonehaven winery which put the place on the map; Mount Benson (Norfolk Rise 1) must have promise if France's Michel Chapoutier and the Hunter Valley's Ralph Fowler want to make wine there and ditto Wrattonbully (Hollick 2, Tappanappa 3, Yalumba 1).

The one that everybody *has* heard of – Coonawarra – is a featureless, flat strip of terra rossa ten miles long by one mile wide. This is where all sorts of silly fruits were originally grown before the wine thing started in the 1960s. The best Cabernet Sauvignon (it accounts for sixty per cent of the vines) in Australia comes from this cool, southernmost sector where frost and rain are a problem – it's all rather French, in fact. It's a traditional place and being so narrowly confined, there's not much space for the tyros (who wouldn't like it much anyway – not many people do – it's too isolated and too quiet, there's no 'scene' here, just a couple of dozen wineries, including Fosters brands, which predominate with Wynns [1] – much the biggest – Penfolds [1], Lindemans [1] and Jamieson's Run [1]; otherwise, there are Balnaves [2], Bowen [3], Hollick [2], Katnook [2], Leconfield [2], Majella [2], Mildara [1], Parker Estate [3], Penley [2], Petaluma [2] and Rymill [2]) with not enough labour so they carefully use machines.

Up north, Riverland is the South Australian contribution to the great irrigated winescape that stretches away along the Murray River into Victoria and New South Wales and is the 'real' South-Eastern Australia. As in California's Central Valley this is desert – as opposed to dessert – wine, although amazingly some of the latter is made too, and has been described by Australia's leading wine writer, James Halliday, as 'hydroponically grown'. It accounts for over half of SA's output (and nearly a third of the whole of Australia's) and relies completely on being able to turn on the tap to good effect – doesn't mean there aren't some good-value wines though.

Victoria

The biggest producing state until phylloxera struck, now the most varied with 600 producers spanning from the desert to the coolest, southernmost spots on the entire mainland, and heading up in to the hills. A whistle-stop tour is in order.

Those billion exported bottles? The own labels, pop-up brands, private brands, the bag-in-box wine, the tanker wine? The Murray-Darling is where it comes from (and it accounts for eighty per cent of Victoria's production). So does the bulk of the fruit for the big brands – the more quality-aware of them supplement it with some fresher cooler-climate stuff. The French have been doing it for centuries – they call it *élevage*. There is good stuff as well from some of the small(er) producers (Andrew Peace 1, Angove's 1, Broken Shackle 1, Deakin 1, Marktree 1, Sunnycliff 1, Trentham Estate 1, Willandra 1, Wombat Hill 1).

The north-east Victoria Zone includes sweltering Rutherglen, (Buller 2, Campbells 2, Chambers 2, Morris 1, Stanton and Killeen 2) and Glenrowan (Bailey's 3) where unique, fortified Liqueur Muscat and Tokay (the Muscadelle of Sauternes), toffee-and-coffee-rich stickies are aged forever in small barrels. There are big reds as well – Durif is a speciality in Rutherglen. The King Valley is dominated by family-owned Brown Brothers 1 in Milawa, where they have done more to advanced the proliferation of varieties through research in their Kindergarten winery than anyone. At around 300m in the Alpine Valleys, the wines have the freshness of cool nights about them (Castagna 3, Gapsted 1 and Giaconda 3 – one of the best Australian Chardonnays).

To the south-east the vast Gippsland area is, with a few exceptions (William Downie 3, Bass Philip 3), the untapped future, while heading west through the Strathbogie Ranges, a glass of the fizz sourced here (Green Point 2, owned by Moët et Chandon, and perhaps the best Australian sparkling wine) is a good idea on the way to Nagambie Lakes, a sub-region of Goulburn Valley, with Shiraz vines from 1860 plus extraordinary wines from the oldest Marsanne vines in the world (Tahbilk 1, Mitchelton 2).

Next door, Heathcote is, to mix a metaphor, the crucible of cool where some of Australia's brightest new winemaking stars (and a few oldies – Brown Brothers [1], Chapoutier and Laughton [3], Greenstone [2], Heathcote Winery [2], Jackson [3], Jasper Hill [3], Redbank [1], Shelmerdine [2], Two Hands [2], Tyrrell's [1], Wild Duck Creek [3]) coax rich, dry-grown Shiraz out of the 500-million-year-old Cambrian soils. Southwards, Macedon Ranges is one of the coolest climates in Australia but Chardonnay and Pinot Noir can hack it (Bindi [3], Curly Flat [3], Virgin Hills [3]). Those Cambrian soils continue west into Bendigo (Balgownie [2], Fairbank [2]) and Pyrenees (Dalwhinnie [3], Redbank [1], Taltarni [1]) before we get to the limestone Grampians where sparkling wine stars alongside spectacular Shiraz – and sometimes both in the same wine (Best's Great Western [3], Mount Langi Ghiran [2] and Seppelt [1]).

On the coast, Henty (Crawford River [2], Tarrington [3]) heads us back towards the ring of wine areas around the thirsty, discriminating city of Melbourne. The first is empty, windswept, maritime Geelong (Scotchmans Hill [2], Gary Farr [3], Shadowfax [2]), followed by Sunbury (Craiglee [3]) before we get to Victoria's indisputably world-class wine region, the Yarra Valley, which has complex topography, a cool climate, and dauntingly high standards shared by some of Australia's best winemakers (Coldstream Hills [2], De Bortoli [1], Diamond Valley [2], Giant Steps [2], Mount Mary [3], Phi [3], Mac Forbes [3], Seville Estate [3], Yarra Yering [3], Yeringberg [3], Yering Station [1]) making Australia's best Pinot Noir, some classy Chardonnay (especially made without malolactic fermentation) and all-the-rage Shiraz-Viognier blends.

To the south of the city, the Mornington Peninsula has some top-class winemakers, including some amateurs who've been making such good, acidity-charged wine from Pinot Noir, Pinot Gris and

Chardonnay in the cool, maritime conditions that they've turned pro (Main Ridge [3], Ten Minutes by Tractor [3], Stonier [2], Kooyong [2], Yabby Lake [3], Paringa [1]).

New South Wales

The Hunter Valley is where Australia's love affair with wine started in 1828 and it still dominates any discussion of New South Wales (NSW) wine. A quick sweep through the arc of winemaking areas around Sydney will take us there.

You would have to start in the small, southernmost area for the name alone: Tumbarumba (Penfolds'). Most of Canberra's vineyards are in fact in NSW – they're at very cool altitudes, ideal for Riesling (Helm [3]), and it was here that the craze for Shiraz-Viognier blends began. Good neighbours are moving in next door in Hilltops (Chalker's Crossing [2], McWilliams [2]) but most grapes still go out to do that *élevage* thing of being blended to raise the standard of wines from some of the quality-conscious volume players (Casella [1], De Bortoli [1] – including for their Noble One, probably the best Australian Sauternes-style sweet wine).

The Central Ranges Zone comprises Cowra, for some excellent Chardonnay and Verdelho (Windowrie [1]); Orange, where, attracted by the coolness at 600m, top winemakers have been all over it like a rash recently (Cumulus [2], Logan [1], Philip Shaw [2]); and Mudgee, where good reds are made by some big names such as Rosemount [1] and Tyrrell's [1] and some smaller ones such as Huntington [1] and Poet's Corner [1].

For all that the upper part of the Hunter Valley is where Australia's now rather stormy love affair with Chardonnay began (with Tyrrell and Rosemount) in the 1970s, the bit we're most interested in is, officially, called the Lower Hunter Valley and, universally, just 'the Hunter'. Its influence punches well above its puny three per cent weight of Australia's output. It's a hot, clammy, sub-tropical region with lots of rain but with Sydney only 80 miles to the south it's very switched on to wine tourism and its age-worthy, dry Semillon is what a lot of those tourists come looking for.

Grassy enough when young to be mistaken for Sauvignon, in ageing for up to twenty years these deeply distinctive wines start to take on buttery, toasty, nutty aromas – the characteristics of oak ageing – but the surprise is that generally no new oak is used. What initially seems so familiar then takes you somewhere completely different, when lanolin and a deep, hard-edged minerality take over. A naturally low alcohol level is another part of the sleight-of-hand and, for geeks, the best producers (Brokenwood 1, Lake's Folly 3, Keith Tulloch 2, Margan 2, McWilliams 2, Tyrrells 1) prevent malolactic fermentation taking place. This is what keeps its elbows sharp. The same producers do well with Chardonnay and Shiraz, often somewhat idiosyncratically – the Shiraz is leathery, the original sweaty saddle – and Verdelho is making a comeback, but it's the Semillon which, along with Rutherglen Muscat and Barossa Shiraz, is one of Australia's primary contributions to the world's distinctive wine styles.

But in case we get too fancy – which the Aussies wouldn't like – let's not forget that away to the west, in the great square, irrigated block of desert that is Riverina (attractively aka the Murrumbidgee Irrigation Area) those hydroponically produced swathes of sunshine in a bottle have changed the world's wine-drinking habits on a scale so tectonic it makes anything that ever came out of the Hunter Valley look like a ripple on a boating pond.

Tasmania

From a standing start in the 1980s, the wines of the island state have become the subject of Tas-Mania in the last few years. The industry is starting to mature as the vines themselves age and add the dimension of complexity. It is one of the most happening regions and change occurs at breakneck pace. Most activity is around Launceston in the north (Tamar Valley 2), Pipers River to the east and the Coal River and Derwent Valley around Hobart in the south. Along with the newest, East Coast, they are at around the same latitudes as New Zealand's winegrowing regions and it shows. In the south the Antarctic influence is more real than the somehow theoretical version that shapes things on the south and south-west coast of the mainland. The topography is as diverse as the climate, which can be cooler or wetter, warmer or drier than anywhere in Victoria and the result is a slow, steady ripening of the grapes, with naturally low yields – the perfect place for wine. Here at the margins, global warming may dictate exactly which grapes it's perfect for, but for now, Pinot Noir and Chardonnay are everywhere, but Pinot Gris and the other Alsace grapes are doing well. Some are also betting that rising temperatures may make the Merlot, Cabernet Sauvignon and Shiraz route the way ahead. Of the 250-plus wineries, most are tiny, but there is a show of muscle-flexing at the next, entrepreneurial (rather than corporate), level among growers who have the experience to move nimbly to exploit the next big thing. The horse-trading over the best sites is dizzying – deals come and go in the blink of an eye. (Andrew Pirie: Tamar Ridge 1, Pirie Estate 2 and Pirie South 1; Clover Hill 3, Domaine A 3, Freycinet 3, Kreglinger 3 – owners of Ninth Island 1 and Pipers Brook 3; Stoney Rise 2.)

It's a pretty place, and wine tourism comes as part of the business plan, not as an afterthought or something grafted on. Tazzie also ships to the mainland cool-climate 'base wine' with enough of the all-important acidity to lift the quality of some of the best Aussie sparkling wine (Arras [2], Bay of Fires [2] – both now owned by Hardy's; Jansz [2] – now owned by Yalumba).

Austrian beer – an Austrian brewer called Anton Dreher started the world's love affair with clear beer with his red Vienna-style in the 1830s – up to then all beer had been more or less cloudy. He has worthy successors who make mostly medium-bodied Märzen lagers, which in most cases have evaded the attentions of the big beercos. Try these: Edelweiss, Heineken-owned Gösser, Stiegl, Trumer, Zipfer, and Schloss Eggenberg, makers of Samichlaus 14% abv lager.

Austrian wine – in the twenty-five years since the Austrian wine industry splattered itself across the windscreen of the anti-freeze scandal (when unscrupulous merchants were using diethylene-glycol to artificially sweeten late-harvest wines, including some *eiswein* as I live and breathe) it has remade itself. To the vast majority for whom Austrian wine means anything at all, it means Gruner Veltliner (Angerer Felsner [1], Jurtschitsch [2], Sepp Moser [1], Loimer [1], Prager [3], Schloss Gobelsburg [2], Steininger [2], Domäne Wachau [1], Wess [2], Wieninger [2]), the classy white grape unknown there fifty years ago but now accounting for over a third of plantings. 'Groovy' has rocked its way in to UK supermarkets and consumers' affections with – when it's good – cracklingly fresh acidity and its trademark twist of white pepper. Many of the best are from the Kamptal, Kremstal and Wachau areas of Niederösterreich, north-west of Vienna (and all of the wine regions are sprinkled around the eastern edge of the country) while simple ones are served up with a bit of bread and scrape in the charmingly basic *Heurigen* (taverns) run (and open on a rota basis) by the producers themselves.

There's much more to Austria than just Grüner, though, and there are world-class Rieslings (Alzinger 2, Bründlmayer 2, Eichinger 2, Hiedler 2, Hirtzberger 3, Nigl 3, Nikolaihof 3, Pichler 3, Salomon-Undhof 2), from their rich dry style known as *Trocken* in Germany and *Smaragd* in Austria, through to sweet wines as good as any from Germany, especially around the Neusiedlersee (Kracher 3), and international varieties as well (Tement 1, Velich 2). Reds from native varieties Blaufränkisch, the best from Burgenland on the opposite side of the capital: Feiler-Artinger 2, Heinrich 2, Nittnaus 2, Pittnaeur 2, Prieler 3, Schrock 2; Zweigelt (Schreiner) 2 and St Laurent (Pfaffi 2) – when you can find them, especially in restaurants – offer the sort of value that comes in sackcloth and ashes. The number of organic, biodynamic and just plain bonkers-but-brilliant producers (such as Angerer 2 and Opitz 3) also seems evidence of a real desire to wipe that windscreen clean.

bacardi cocktail bacchus B & B baga barbera bastardo beer bellini B-52 bitters black russian black velvet blaufränkisch blending of wine blind tasting bloody mary blush booze bonarda bual bourboulenc brachetto brandy brandy alexander brazilian wine british wine bronx cocktail bual bulgarian wine buying wine bacardi cocktail

B

Bacardi cocktail – two parts white rum to one part each lemon juice and simple syrup plus a few dashes of grenadine shaken with ice and strained into a cocktail glass . . . somewhere in the Caribbean . . . at sunset . . . preferably post-coitally.

B & B – equal parts Bénédictine and brandy layered in a balloon glass (to the sound of a brass band).

Balvenie – Speyside distillery; not the largest in the ownership of William Grant, who own Glenfiddich, but arguably the best. Perhaps try the twelve-year-old before going to Singapore Airport to pick up a bottle of the 1964 for US $12,000.

Barbera – versatile black grape originally of north-western Italy's Piedmont region, now widespread in Italy and dotted around the world, making everything from serious, oak-aged and age-worthy wines (especially around Asti and Alba) to flouncy, sweet *frizzante* things.

Beer – 'is God's way of telling us that he loves us and wants us to be happy.' Benjamin Franklin is misquoted on the T-shirts that strain at the seam to contain the consequences of all that love (indeed there is often ample space for the correct version: 'Behold the rain which descends from heaven upon our vineyards; there it enters the roots of the vines, to be changed into wine; a constant proof that God loves us, and loves to see us happy') but the point is well made.

The love goes back a lot further than revolutionary America. It has been speculated that the reason humanity gave up the hunter-gatherer existence and settled for an agrarian life was because they wanted a regular supply of grain – not for the bread they made but because what they really wanted was beer.

Anybody loitering in an English town at 10 p.m. on a Friday night might be forgiven for doubting it but there is a compelling case to be made that civilisation was founded on beer – or perhaps more accurately founded *for* beer.

The earliest documentary evidence of brewing is from Sumeria approximately 6,000 years ago. There was beermaking activity before that but not much in the way of written language – possibly a cause-and-effect thing going on there – but by the time of the Egyptians there was a sophisticated beer culture with numerous styles being brewed and serious consequences for purveyors of duff beer (such as being drowned in it).

It's a stretch to think of it as such but if all booze is one great big dysfunctional family then beer is grain (or seed) wine and – this may be too much – its distillate, whisky, is therefore oak-aged grain schnapps, i.e. vodka. Beer is much more difficult to make than wine, and only for lack of anything else – or serendipity – would anybody choose hydrolysed starch as the base for a wine. Serendipity may have started it in Mesopotamia but the reason it came into its own in northern latitudes was probably as a solution to the problem of the relative scarcity of fruit. But, in the civilising stroke of genius that was the planting of grain, it overcame the infuriating seasonality of fruit. Grain keeps . . . fruit doesn't . . . beer all year!

The by-product of yeast invisibly replicating itself is our beery bounty and that fungal fecundity gives us one of our most important preservative processes. The ploughman's lunch may have originated as a cheesy bit of 1970s advertising copy but those horny-handed tillers of the sod would be eating the cheese-free version without the wonder that is fermentation. There would be no bread, pickles or beer either – so not much of a lunch at all.

The process of brewing may be longer and more complex than that of winemaking but the end-product is less complex. Don't get me wrong – there is no man alive who loves beer more than I (or if there were, he should seek therapy immediately) – but the beauty of beer is, in some way, its very simplicity and straightforwardness, its honesty. There is complexity but it is to be found in the huge range of styles and flavours: a doom-dark double-bock is beer just as the lightest, laciest of lagers is beer and their footholds are analogous to those of, say, Port and Prosecco in the wine branch of the family tree of booze.

To make any beer, the grain – invariably barley, but wheat beer is big in Germany – is first soaked in water to induce the germination process and begin the release of the complex sugars locked up in the grains; after drying it's further 'kilned', or heated, to turn it into malt and the degree to which this is done determines much of the character of the beer – the darker the roast the darker the beer; after getting rid of the tiny sprouts from that brief germination period the malt is milled into grist which then briefly becomes mash while it's soaked in hot water in a – you've got it – mash tun, before the liquid, now called wort, is separated and transferred to a brewing copper and the other magic ingredient, hops, is added. The purity of the water is critical and almost mystical qualities are attributed by some brewers to the source and type of H_2O they use.

No doubting the influence of the hops, though, these primeval frilly pine-cone-shaped green flowers are little resinous hand grenades of supercharged bitterness and provide the descant-flavour notes to malt's bass. They grow on vines called bines, smell remarkably like their cousin marijuana – or so they tell me – and have antiseptic, anti-inflammatory and preservative qualities in addition to their contribution to aroma and flavour. Discussion of the variety (the best-known English varieties are Fuggles and Goldings, while Czech Saaz and German Hersbrucher are among the most revered), their preparation – dried or fresh ('wet-hopped') and heady with resin – and the timing of incorporation ('dry-hopped' for maximum impact) are topics for almost devout nerdism.

Styles: There are myriad, a plethora, a cornucopia of ways of making – and tweaking – beer. Unfortunately, such things as myriads, plethoras and cornucopiae attract clouds of obscurantists, obfuscators, sophists . . . and wankers. 'I wanna go to an inn for some ale,' announced an incoming Yank-in-law once, prompting the whispered conflab: 'What the hell *is* ale? And what's an inn?' Of course we know in our bellies what they are but the unmemorable answer is that ales (the original beers) are top-fermented, whereby the yeast does its business on the surface of the brew. New-fangled lagers, first smokily brewed by German monks in the 1400s (but perfected only in 1842 in Plzen, Czechoslovakia, as the crystal-clear, light-coloured beer we would recognise today) before colonising the globe in double-quick time, are made with bottom-fermenting yeasts and aged ('lagered') for a period before consumption. Other styles from 'alt' to 'zwickel' are explained in the sections on their respective countries of origin.

Bottle-conditioned beers have a little unfermented sugar remaining when bottled; thus, they undergo a second fermentation – a bit like Champagne – and they need careful pouring to avoid disturbing the sediment. All sorts of other ingredients are used from time to time, not necessarily to the detriment of the brew, both in the grist – rice, oatmeal, maize, wheat, sorghum – as well as for manipulating body and alcoholic strength (sugar) and for flavouring – fruit, fruit peel, and herbs and spices such as coriander, ginger, saffron or juniper.

Belgian beer – Belgium is beer's idea of Heaven, where the globe-bestriding march of the lager brands comes to an ignominious halt in the sticky Flanders mud, where shiny-faced drinkers cherish their local, often deeply idiosyncratic styles made by thriving, dedicated small producers and beer is on the pedestal that is the exclusive preserve of wine everywhere else, especially for accompanying fine cuisine. Well, they had to get something right, didn't they?

Of course not everything is as rosy as the cheeks of those discerning drinkers, who are shipping nearly a third less of the stuff than they did forty years ago. Brewers do get bought up (Affligem by Heineken), there is more bog-standard stuff emerging (although even 'white-van' Stella, which is brewed there, is hugely superior to the UK-brewed version) and, in amongst the couple of dozen unique Belgian styles there are some only a local could like, but taken overall the good stuff is the best in the world.

Styles

abbey beers – similar to the Trappist beers but made by (avowedly) commercial companies . . . don't get me started but AB InBev's Leffe Blonde does seem to taste of saccharine, doesn't it (and the Brune doesn't);

ales – sometimes made in the style of British versions, which is encouraging;

bière brut – fine things made in the image of Champagne, and with similarly labour-intensive methods and prices (Bosteels);

lambics – 'wild beers', taste of the woods – wine-like, tart, sour even, smoky and spicy. They are a true artisan product, using a third raw wheat in the grist, just a few hops as a preservative and then are fermented over an extended period, sometimes years, by airborne yeasts that are encouraged to thrive in a hygiene regime that would give most head brewers the screaming ab-dabs. An acquired taste, the best route in is via Geuze (aka Gueuze) the semi-commercial form, which mixes young and old beers (Belle-Vue, Cantillon, De Ranke, Girardin, Timmermans). Fruit beers like Kriek (with cherries – Liefmans) and framboise (with raspberries – Chapeau) are made with lambics and are fine as long as you think of them as being something other than beer;

red and brown beers – tart enough to shock the uninitiated, the former with a vinegar twang, these are a Flemish speciality (Rodenbach);

Saison – strong, sharp, copper-coloured ales brewed for summer;

Trappist beer – unlike monastery breweries elsewhere Achel, Chimay, Orval, Rochefort, Westmalle and Westvleteren produce the traditional 'triple' and 'double' styles, unique to them and the results, respectively, of the first and second soakings of the mash. The names reflect that they are thrice and twice as strong as the third soaking, which makes the weakest beer, a 'small beer'. The triples – rich, strong and complex – are, along

with an upstart 'quadruple' style, among the finest things a brewer can do;
witbier – Hoegaarden, the brand that got the whole white-beer wave started, was set up by Pierre Celis who subsequently moved to the USA in 1991 and became something of a cult figure among brewers of cloudy ales. It's the biggest brand and now owned by AB InBev. Flavoured with bitter-orange peel and coriander seed, and perfectly OK, as long as you have some lemon to cut the soapiness;
wicked beers – the late Michael Jackson (no, not that one, but the Ur-beer writer) came up with the term to plug the gap in the nomenclature for a bunch of beers made to flatter Moortgaat's peerless Duvel (pronounced 'doov'l' and literally 'devil' after an early guinea-pig apparently pronounced it a 'devil of a beer'). From Flanders, with its light body and billowing head it looks like a lager but it's top-fermented to 8.5% abv – you'd never guess, until it's too late. Its little brother, Vedette, is a saintly 5.2% abv.
Try Abbaye des Rocs, Achouffe, Anker, De Proef, De Struise, Drei Fonteinen, Alken-Maes, Mort Subite (OK, but I'd die happy in the perfection of their Brussels bar), Lefèbvre or St Bernardus.

bellini – gently stir one part fresh peach purée with two parts chilled Prosecco in a flute glass and get naked.

B-52 – layer equal parts Kahlua, Bailey's and Grand Marnier in a liqueur glass. For US college-kids only.

bitters – loosely defined group of quasi-medicinal spirits and liqueurs of various strengths flavoured with bitter herbs, spices, roots and barks e.g. angelica, gentian, cinchona – the source of quinine –

juniper, bay, rue, citrus peel (including Seville oranges – Amer Picon), liquorice, lemon balm and celery (recently revived by new German company The Bitter Truth) and varying in strength from the relatively mild (popular in Italy and aka amaro, Campari being the most famous and popularised in the USA during Prohibition due to a loophole that exempted it), which can be drunk straight or with mixers, to those used sparingly for flavour such as Angostura, which experienced a shortage in 2009 due to limited availability of some ingredients, with subsequent stockpiling that exacerbated the situation). Stronger versions are considered stomach-settlers and digestifs (Underberg, and Fernet Branca) – which has inexplicably become so popular in Argentina, where it is mixed with cola, that they are now its biggest consumers. And then there's foul, globe-artichoke-flavoured Cynar, which is just plain weird.

Black Russian – stir two parts vodka with one part coffee liqueur and ice. Serve in a rocks glass, lower your voice by an octave and quote some Pushkin.

Black Velvet – layer equal parts chilled stout and Champagne in a flute glass. For a classy twist, try drinking them separately.

Blaufränkisch – middle-European red-wine grape (aka Lemberger in Germany and Kékfrankos in Hungary) making some of Austria's best and brightest, berry-filled wines often somewhat in the style of good Beaujolais and equally often bargains on restaurant wine lists.

blending – is used for the purposes of maximising either consistency, quality or quantity of a drink and has been practised since Roman times as far as wine is concerned. The first case involves blending numerous different whiskies, brandies, rums or wines – especially sherry and Champagne (where it is referred to as *assemblage*) – in order to maintain a house style. It is also important for branded wines made from juice from diverse sources (Portugal's Sogrape has a particularly large laboratory that conducts numerous tests to make the 20-odd million bottles of Mateus Rosé it sells annually taste the same). Where supply is limited, e.g. within a single domaine or demarcated region, blending is done between wines from different vineyards or from different blocks of vines, with different ages or aspects within a single vineyard, in order to maximise the quality of the whole. The equivalent process with spirits is usually aimed at maximising smoothness (sometimes at the risks of losing character, it seems to me). Maximising quantity at a given quality level (the process of *élevage* – 'bringing up' in wine) uses some higher-quality stuff to improve duller basic material and is practised by canny winemakers and distillers worldwide. Australia's phenomenally successful Yellow Tail is a good example. They blend fresher wines from cooler sites in with the stuff grown in the desert Big Rivers region, which otherwise often would be the lowest-level tanker supermarket wines. The same principle applies in blending spirits where judicious use of some high-quality single-malt whiskies, for example, can raise the quality of otherwise 'bog standard' blended whiskies.

blind tasting – one in which the identity of the drink is concealed. The Riedel glass company offers another stage through usage of their black glasses, which conceal the colour of the drink. I have also been to a blind tasting conducted in pitch darkness, which was a nightmare.

Bloody Mary – wine writer Jonathan Ray sagely stirs six parts tomato juice with two parts vodka, one each of orange juice and dry sherry, a dash of Tabasco and Worcestershire sauces, ice and a pinch of celery salt all poured in a highball glass. A Bull Shot substitutes beef consommé for some, or all, of the tomato juice. In the USA, Mr and Mrs T's Bloody-Mary mix is good in a pinch.

blush – California term for rosé, usefully identifies the crappiest ones.

booze – slang term both for spiritous liquors and more generally for all alcoholic drinks and the consumption thereof. The etymology is unclear but the c 1300 Middle English verb 'bouse' – to drink heavily – obviously has a strong claim; however, a Philadelphia distiller, one EG Booz, flourished in the 1860s.

Botrytis – (aka noble rot) properly *Botrytis cynerea*, a fungal disease of grapes that – while fatally destructive in most circumstances – can in otherwise healthy white grapes late-harvested in damp conditions cause a glorious intensification of sugars resulting in some of the world's great sweet wines, especially in Bordeaux's Sauternes and Barsac.

bottle sizes – wine – the standard 75cl bottle of wine shared between two at dinner is the ideal daily ration (but comes about from being the result of your average glass-blower's lung-full). In the States, that size is known as a 'fifth' – i.e. a fifth of a US gallon – and usually applies to whiskey bottles, while a 'split' is a quarter bottle. As far as large-formats go, a magnum is equivalent to two standard 75cl bottles; a double-magnum is four (and is also called a jeroboam in

Champagne and Burgundy but, confusingly, in Bordeaux, a jeroboam is the six-bottle size). Of the seriously big bottles, an imperial is eight: a salmanazar is a dozen; a Balthazar sixteen and a Nebuchadnezzar is, well, an out-of-control twenty. You could pour 300 airline-style 5cl miniatures into one – but why? Pouring from large bottles is a skill and one tiny part of a sommelier's training involves pouring twenty-four flutes to the same level (give or take a few millimetres) straight off from a magnum of Champagne without spilling a drop. It's unbelievably difficult to do.

Bowmore – Islay distillery dating from 1779 and owned since 1994 by the Japanese Suntory firm, which has exported much expertise back to Nippon, to the extent they can now match the quality of any Scottish producer dram for dram.

brandy – is a broad church these days, as least as much in terms of the drinks defined by the name itself as by its consumers, be they dyspeptic colonels in oak-panelled libraries sipping Cognac or Armagnac from a snifter bigger than Busta Rhymes's baseball cap, or the rap star himself swigging from a bottle backstage. The derivation of the word is from the Dutch 'brand' meaning burnt, and the congregation includes more than just the familiar French and Spanish versions distilled from grape wine. The Spanish industry, based around Jerez and dominated by the big sherry producers – and, indeed, often using a *solera* system for ageing – is the largest (Carlos I, Gran Duque de Alba, Lepanto, Osborne, Romate, Torres). Pomace brandies include the marc, aguardiente, pisco and grappa distilled from the fermented detritus – skins, seeds and what have you – left over from the winemaking process itself; and then there are the schnapps, slivovitz and eaux-de-vie-de-this-and-that, made from fruits other than grapes. It should be noted that, really and truly, brandy is grape schnapps.

Most brandy drinkers seem to have a preference for either Cognac or Armagnac so it's useful to summarise the differences. It's simple enough geographically: the Cognac region is north of Bordeaux in the Charentes; Armagnac is to the south, in Gascony. Different methods of distillation are used, Cognac traditionally being twice-distilled in a pot still (called a *pot Charentais*) while 'Armers' is now generally made by single distillation in a continuous (or 'column') still. It being traditionally more of a 'farmhouse' product, the various contraptions and portable stills from which Armagnac was for centuries made fell foul of reforming zeal in a law of 1970. In terms of quantity, Cognac is the daddy, making almost twenty times as much; Armagnac gets the nod on history as it was first made a couple of hundred years earlier, around 1400.

Ugni Blanc, Colombard and Folle Blanche grapes make the wines that Armagnac is distilled from, but the first (which, as Trebbiano, makes some of Italy's least inspiring whites) is nowadays the only grape of significance in Cognac. Both regions are subdivided, Grande Champagne and Petite Champagne (no relation) being the most significant bits of Cognac while the other place is principally divided into Haut-Armagnac and Bas-Armagnac.

Very Special (VS) is interchangeable with 'three star' and means that the spirit has been aged in oak for a minimum of three years and, as such, is not really very special at all. VO isn't really 'very old' – it requires only four years' ageing. As with whisky, barrel maturation is the key to everything, providing mellowness and complexity, and the longer the better. VSOP, the next significant step up (to five star) inanely changes 'Special' to 'Superior' and adds 'Old Pale' to describe the fact that it spends at least eight – but typically ten to fifteen years –

in barrel. Older yet, XO (have a guess . . .) and *hors d'age* (donkeys' years) have at least some meaning while 'Napoleon' 'Extra' and 'Vieille Reserve' appear to have none. The four biggest brands – USA Beam Global's Courvoisier, Pernod Ricard-owned Martell, Rémy Martin and LVMH's Hennessy – dominate Cognac while Hine, Frapin and Delamain shine among the smaller producers. Janneau is the nearest thing to a brand in Armagnac, where Aubade, Baron de Sigognac, Castarède, Delord, Gelas, Monbel, Nismes-Delclou and Tariquet are a handful of the many excellent small fry (the most expensive of which are termed Arm-and-a-leg-magnac).

In the glass, Cognac is generally the more austere of the two: drier, lighter and somehow more ascetic; Armagnac's charms are darker, deeper, curvier – in many people's word more rustic. The top rung of Cognacs take a lot longer – fully fifty years – to prove their superiority (while Armagnacs reach their best in around half that time) and any informed debate about which is better needs to take that, rather than just the hefty prices, into account. Vintage-dated brandies, especially those 'early-landed' in the UK and bottled here after a couple of decades of maturation, in general make far less nerve-racking year-of-birth or anniversary presents than wine.

The fact that the Chinese have stormed past the UK as the second-largest consumers of Brandy – and are fast catching up with the USA – is all the more remarkable in light of the fact that ten years ago they were not even in the top ten. Unsurprisingly, it's Cognac's image of prestige and luxury – that whole leather-armchairs-in-the-library thing – that is the main attraction in China, even if (*sacré bleu*!) much of it is consumed over ice and with cola. But, having been in a situation where its most enthusiastic consumers were distinctly more hip-op than hip-hop and where – as recently as a decade ago – their very survival looked in doubt, the big producers aren't going to let the odd faux pas worry them unduly.

Of the other European grape brandies to consider, should circumstances necessitate it, Germany's Asbach Uralt is good and Greece's Metaxa, which is blended with sweet wine, has near-monopoly status and is currently owned by Remy-Cointreau, who should know what they're doing by now.

Brandy Alexander – equal parts brandy, dark crème de cacao and fresh cream shaken with ice; cut out the middle man and strain directly into a condom (a funnel helps) – otherwise use a cocktail glass and sprinkle with ground nutmeg.

Brazilian/Brasilian wine – is in its infancy, but with large potential and one very determined individual – Adriano Miolo, with top Bordeaux-consultant Michel Rolland in tow – is showing what can be done. The Vale dos Vinhedos in the far south is where the action is, much of it sparkling until now, but every conceivable varietal is being trialled on this *tabula rasa*. In the north, the product of irrigated vineyards (closer to the equator than in any other country) threatens to play havoc with the traditional concept of vintages as they are able to produce more than one a year. Currently, lovely cachaça cane rum is making bigger strides in the export market, but give it a few years and it could be a much closer shave.

Breakfast Martini – two parts gin to one part each of lemon juice and Cointreau and a teaspoon of marmalade shaken with ice, strained in to a cocktail glass and garnished with a tiny triangle of toast. Generally consumed as – rather than as an accompaniment to – the most important meal of the day.

brewing industry – beer might be difficult for you and I to make but you may want to try your hand at mastering the art once you get a sniff of the profits to be made from a product that is ninety-five per cent water. Beer is big business – not as big as wine or fags (fags still haul in enormous profits) – but bigger than spirits. For example, in the UK the world's biggest brewer AB InBev sells almost ten-million-quids' worth of their once-excellent, market-leading, 'wife-beating' Stella Artois every week. The global industry is much-consolidated – not as consolidated as that of spirits but much more consolidated than that of wine – to the extent that as the biggest brewer and one of the handful of biggest consumer-product companies in the world, AB InBev brew almost a quarter of the world's beer. Not just because of Stella, which is not even in the top ten globally, but because the 'AB' bit is Anheuser-Busch, maker of Budweiser, the second-biggest selling beer brand in the world after . . . go on, have a guess, but it's not good news . . . Bud Light. (OK, the beers may not be up to much because they spend all the money on advertising them rather than improving them, but some of the US TV ads are so good I can almost forgive them.)

AB InBev is the result of the 2008 merger of Anheuser-Busch with InBev (which itself sprang from the loins of Belgium's InterBrew, after impregnation by Brazilian behemoth Brahma) and, more importantly (although the smell of Whitbread Pale Ale pre-dates it), is provider of my earliest beer memory, being the lady behind the counter in the grocer's in Ticehurst, East Sussex, asking if my father would 'like any Stella Artoyz today'. AB plonk quite a few other handy little brands on the table too, such as Labatt's, Rolling Rock, Bass, Beck's, Leffe, Spaten-Löwenbräu, Hoegaarden and Michelob. They are also a tasty fifty per cent of Grupo Modelo, makers of Corona and, as such, providers of more than sixty per cent of the beer that slakes thirsty

Mexican throats. No 'Bod-head' oop north ever would have thought in the 1980s that their odd brew – Boddingtons, the essence of soapy, burpy Northern-ness – could ever attract the attention of the biggest beerco in the world, but it did, and fell in to AB's maw.

In late 2009 AB InBev took the profits on most of its Eastern European operations in a deal with private-equity group CVC, which sees a new name – StarBev – in the firmament. The Czech brand Staropramen, which seemed to have only just appeared in UK boozers, was valued at £1.9bn – yes, billion – five per cent less than the capitalisation of British Airways at the time. Oh, yes indeedy – beer makes big bucks, not just big bellies (even though, pricelessly, AB reported that there was 'weakness' in the US beer market).

The other half of the US-based global beer duopoly is MillerCoors, a joint venture between Molson Coors and SAB Miller, incorporating the diverse portfolio of the former South African Breweries with the core (sorry) Coors and Miller stuff in the USA and Molson in Canada. Both Miller Lite and Coors Light are among the top-ten beer brands in the world even though the spelling is about the only noticeable difference between them. Their 'other' brands include Grolsch, Peroni, Castle, Gambrinus, the wonderful Pilsner Urquell and Velkopopovický Kozel of the Czech Republic; Tyskie and Żubr of Poland; and last, but by no means least, China's supernova Snow (the world's fourth biggest beer brand as I write this, but doubtless higher yet as you read it and tipped to become the biggest beer of all, when they can work out how much of it they're actually selling).

Of the other majors, Diageo is the world's biggest drinks company – so big that even though twenty-two per cent of their sales come from beer, it is still a relatively small part – or as small as it can be with Guinness in their stable. It's their most popular beer brand by far, with Harp,

Red Stripe, Smithwick's and Satzenbrau mere stragglers. In Europe Carlsberg holds the licence for AB InBev's Skol – the prototype of global lager brands, and still third-biggest in the world. Carlsberg also has Kronenbourg, Holsten, Hürlimann, Kanterbräu, Okocim Mocne, Mythos, Baltika, Grimbergen, Henninger, Tetley's, Tuborg and, er, Carlsberg, which is not only *not* the best lager in the world, it's not even the best lager in Carlsberg. Heineken Group distribute Amstel, Cruzcampo, Desperados (their most aptly named, tequila-flavoured lager), Hacker-Pschorr, Kulmbacher/EKU, Moretti, Murphy's, Paulaner, Pelforth, Sagres, Tiger, 33 and Zywiec (pronounced 'zuh-vee-etch').

Among the other big names, Fosters funnily enough has a much higher profile in its export markets than at home – where it has only a small fraction of the Australian beer market – but they also have the much bigger VB brand and are in any case much bigger in wine these days; Japan's thirsty salarymen propelled Asahi to position number ten in the world's top sellers in 2009; Pabst, invisible outside the USA, is the third most visible inside it. These big players shuffle their packs of brands to fit their various markets and maximise sales. Remember Castlemaine XXXX? It was massive in the UK in the 1990s but has now been quietly withdrawn because its face no longer suits our twenty-first-century demographic.

Horrified by the sheer corporate-greed hellishness of it all? It gets worse. The big beercos have a complex web of distribution deals with each other in which, for example, Heineken sells Diageo's Guinness in Spain and AB InBev's Löwenbräu in Russia; MillerCoors sells Fosters in the US, Fosters sells AB InBev's Stella in Australia, and AB InBev in turn make Skol the biggest-selling beer in Brazil (Carlsberg owns distribution rights in the rest of the world), while being proprietor of its biggest competitor there, Brahma – itself a top-ten global brand.

Nowhere is the big beer spaghetti more tangled than in the UK. A long way after the US-Belgian-Brazilian beast Stella, the next best-selling beer is Fosters, from 'our' biggest brewer, Scottish and Newcastle, which burps out Kronenbourg and Heineken and also John Smith's (which at a million pints a day is the best-selling UK bitter and the only one to scrape into the top ten). Scottish and Newcastle now – heretically – brew Newcastle Brown Ale in Yorkshire but needless to say, S&N isn't British at all – it was carved up between Heineken and Carlsberg in 2008 leaving the merged Wells and Young's (which includes Courage) as the largest remaining independent. After Fosters, the third best-seller is MillerCoors-owned Carling Black Label.

None of these big beer brands have great character but most are nonetheless decent products given the truly industrial scale on which they are made. It's usually meaningless to associate them with the country of their origin (unless that's where you are) as they are often brewed elsewhere, especially the draught versions. It makes no more sense to think of Kronenbourg as French or of Grolsch as Dutch than it does to think of Coca-Cola as American. All seem best in the versions made in their original location, famously in the case of Guinness; I can't think of one that is better brewed under licence elsewhere. I'm not sure exactly what this is telling us but it seems as if there may be some *genius loci* and thankfully the brewers seem to be picking up on this in a few cases.

It's not all gloom and doom – some fantastic brands are owned by the big boys and they seem to have worked out that it's best not to interfere too much. Craft brewing is thriving as never before although the fact that Boston Brewery (makers of Samuel Adams) is the fourth-biggest in the US says more about just how big the big two are than anything else. Things always go full circle and big beer is now sizing up craft brewers as possible acquisitional snacks. We'll see what happens to quality there.

British beer – things have changed a lot since half of England's brewers headed for Burton-upon-Trent in Staffordshire in the late eighteenth century in search of the perfect brewing water, and although some of the more familiar brewers have disappeared – Whitbread and Bass, for example, both morphed into hotels and leisure – and crap pubs are closing by the thousand, craft brewing in the UK is in the rudest health with over 700 producers – three times as many by population as in the USA.

For all the dangerously swinging big-beer business dicks (see brewing industry), the British beer drinker, like the wine drinker, has never had it so good. The phenomenal success of the Campaign for Real Ale (CAMRA), begun in 1971 and perhaps the most effective consumer-advocacy group ever, put into reverse a deplorable decline in standards and laid the foundation for a renaissance in the art of brewing that is now widespread across the Anglophone world and in to those parts of Europe where beer has traditionally been the also-ran to wine. The Red Barrel has now thankfully rolled a long way in to the tall grass.

British styles of beer, now widely replicated (and often revived) wherever microbrewers ply their trade include:

barley wine **– extra strong ale (JW Lees), up to 11% abv, and now big in the USA. 'Two valium and a barley wine . . .' more a way of life than just a quote from Lindsay Anderson's 1973 film *O Lucky Man!* but poor preparation for an interview at Balliol.**

bitter **– well-hopped English ale. Best bitter is the brewer's stronger version; ESB is 'extra special' and HSB 'Horndean Special Bitter', now brewed by Fuller's in Chiswick, London, where they still use former brewers Gale's yeast, which is 'alive and well'.**

blonde ale – (aka summer ale) the fastest-growing style, being a lighter, brighter version of bitter;
brown ale – dark-malted, sweeter, stronger bottled style of mild and just as unfashionable;
heavy – Scottish term for bitter;
India pale ale (aka IPA) – well-hopped, bottled bitter robust enough to stand the sea voyage to India (pre-Suez Canal). The best and bitterest now made in the USA where it has been embraced with enthusiasm;
light ale – bottled bitter;
mild ale – making a bit of a comeback as brewers update the unfashionable sudsy, low-alcohol, lightly hopped version of yore;
Morocco ale – spiced ginger-cakey winter warmer revived by Daleside breweries;
oatmeal stout – oats added to the mash and thought to be nourishing (Maclay's);
old ale – as in old-fashioned, rather than long-aged, and in essence a strong version of mild (Theakston's Old Peculier sets the standard);
porter – the first mass-produced beer, well-hopped and dark (using chocolate malt), ubiquitous in eighteenth-century London. Stout is its stronger, modern form although the original has been revived in US microbreweries;
stout – family of black, well-hopped ales made familiar the world over by Guinness. Milk and cream stouts use some lactose sugar (Mackeson); Imperial Russian stout is an extra strong (7–10% abv) version. The name originates from its popularity with the Russian nobility (Harvey's, Samuel Smith's). Chocolate stout is named for the dark colour and bitterness derived from heavily roasted chocolate malt, but sometimes a little chocolate is also added.

Regional differences still affect taste although the boundaries are blurring as adventurous and well-trained brewers experiment with every style and the roll-call of excellence is too long to list here for well-deserved praise but I'll list a few of my favourites. Deep breath:

Adnam's – for Broadside; ***Anglo Dutch*** – partly but not only for naming a beer Tabatha the Knackered; ***Archers*** – for making nearly 200 different beers in a year; *Arkells* for 2B – a 3.2% abv beer that tastes good; ***Arundel*** – for Sussex Mild; ***Badger*** – for Tanglefoot; ***Banks's*** – for keeping mild alive; ***Bateman's*** – for experiments like Combined Harvest multigrain ale; ***Belhaven*** – for Wee Heavy; ***Black Sheep*** – for Riggwelter; ***Brains*** – for keeping Welsh brewing alive; ***Brakspear*** – for staying alive and Special; ***Brewdog*** – for making a 41% abv beer called Sink the Bismarck; *Cains* – for brains; ***Caledonian*** – for Deuchar's IPA (don't pronounce the 'ch') and keeping the 'shilling' naming tradition; ***Camerons*** – for Strongarm; ***Crouch Vale*** – for Brewers Gold; ***Durham*** – for Evensong; ***Everard's*** – for Original; ***Exmoor*** – for Wild Cat; ***Felinfoel*** – for Double Dragon; ***Freeminer*** – for Deep Shaft; ***Fuller, Smith & Turner*** – for the complex, dark amber stuff of dried orange peel, spices and caramel that is London Pride, named for the saxifrage that colonised many of the bombsites of the Blitz, and for continuing to brew HSB after they took over Gales even though it's better than Pride; ***Greene King*** – for Old Speckled Hen, which flies the flag for good bitter, creeping in at number twenty of the bestselling beers, and proving that you can't make an omelette without breaking eggs; ***Harvey's*** – for weaning me off my mother's milk; ***Harviestoun*** – for Ola Dubh; ***Hook Norton*** – for Old Hooky; ***Hop Back*** – for Summer Lightning, what else?; ***Hydes*** – for mild; ***Itchen Valley*** – for Fagins; ***Marston's*** – for scintillating, super-dry, Seville orange marmalade

Double Drop; ***Meantime Brewery*** – for everything; ***Moorhouse's*** – for Black Cat; ***O'Hanlon's*** – for Firefly; ***Porterhouse Brewery*** – for good bars; ***Ringwood*** – for Old Thumper; ***Robinson's*** – for Old Tom; ***Roosters*** – for not compromising; *St Austell* – for austere, almost astringent dryness and for leaving some sweetness down in there too; ***St Peter's*** – for purity; ***Samuel Smith's*** – for its big, creamy northern head with a southern hoppiness, well-balanced with sweet malt (in some of the most characterful pub buildings in London); ***Shepherd Neame*** – England's oldest brewer and another formative one for me, for Spitfire a soft, amber pillow of toasty maltiness with a curacao nightcap and Whitstable Bay's peanut brittle hoppiness the bottle can barely contain; ***Thwaites*** – for Lancaster Bomber; ***Timothy Taylor*** – for celebrated Landlord, the best all-rounder: light but never 'lite', dry but never harsh, a harmonious thing of dried fruits like a fine sercial Madeira; ***Traquair House*** – for Jacobite; ***Wadworth*** – for quality in quantity; ***Williams Bros*** – for Froach Heather Ale; ***Wychwood*** – for Hobgoblin. And all of them for keeping the great tradition of cask-conditioned draught beer – Britain's dowry to the world of beer – not only alive and well but also in the rudest of health.

GET A HANDLE...

WE'VE NEVER HAD IT SO GOOD AND A WAVE OF TOP-CLASS CRAFT-BREWERS ARE MAKING A KALEIDOSCOPE OF THE BEST BEERS THAT HAVE EVER BEEN BREWED IN THIS SCEPTRED ISLE.

British wine – made from imported, concentrated grape-must that is rehydrated and fermented (i.e. 'made wine' see p.256) and every bit as appetising as it sounds. The term is the bane of English-wine producers. Still big sellers for park-bench drinkers of a certain age who favour

Mansion House, which I thought was a floor polish but then again maybe it is; QC; Tudor Rose – owned by Constellation; VP.

Bronx Cocktail – two parts gin to one part each of sweet and dry vermouths and orange juice shaken with ice and strained in to the East River (or a cocktail glass if you must).

Bual – (aka Boal) most widely planted white-grape variety on the island of Madeira to make the eponymous zesty, smoky, second-sweetest of the island's fortified wine styles.

Buck's Fizz – (aka Mimosa) build, if you must, two parts chilled fresh orange juice and one of Champagne in a flute and thereby diminish both ingredients. Revivify the zombie by simple means of the addition of one part vodka to four of the mix and you have Agua de Valencia. The disingenuousness of the name greatly enhances the frisson of naughtiness surrounding the consumption of the typical jugful of it. Anybody fortunate enough to have witnessed a traditional Valenciano firework fight will have pondered to what extent the intake of 'Agua' will have been influential upon the conduct of the 'fuegos' and vice versa.

Bulgarian wine – the tide of toothsome Bulgarian Cabernet Sauvignon that swept through the UK in the 1980s (helped along by favourable comments from wine writer Auberon Waugh) was: a) many people's first introduction to the idea of a varietally labelled wine; b) ditto to the idea of wine from anywhere other than the traditional west-European-producer countries; c) astonishingly cheap and d) short-lived, as Gorbachev's crackdown on alcohol consumption in the Soviet Bloc decimated production. Characterful reds from indigenous Mavrud and Melnik grapes and good dessert muscats such as Boyar [2], Enira [1], and Miroglio [2] are rarely exported as domestic demand is high and reflected in prices but EU membership has been the impetus for British supermarkets and brands to take the first tentative steps in sourcing wine there again.

Bunnahabhain – Islay distillery (try 'boona-harven') owned by Burn Stewart, thus by Trinidadian CL WorldBrands who own Angostura bitters. I'll bet you could make a nice Old Fashioned with it, too.

buying wine – apparently nearly ninety per cent of wine is consumed on the day it is purchased. As a result, this entry is in two sections, the first about those on-the-day bottles and the second about the other ten per cent, or less, as it's not about tomorrow's wine or really even next week's. In fact, I'll just come out with it and say it's about building up a cellar. It's a great thing to do, a bit like raising children or making a garden: it requires a lot of patience and forbearance but the rewards are uniquely satisfying.

GET A HANDLE...

AND MAKE FRIENDS WITH ONE OF THE NEW BREED OF ENTHUSIASTIC, LOCAL, INDEPENDENT MERCHANTS AND IN READING THE NATIONAL NEWSPAPER WINE WRITERS NOW AND AGAIN TO SEE WHAT'S HOT IN YOUR LOCAL SUPERMARKET.

Supermarkets

Of all those *carpe diem* bottles, three-quarters are bought in supermarkets that essentially sell four types of wine: brands, own brands, private brands and, er . . . non-branded wines. Depressed? Don't worry – the likes of Blossom Hill are not exactly in a monopoly situation.

In general wine writers enjoy bashing all the supermarkets except the one or two who are performing best at any given time. It's a very British way of keeping up the pressure on standards – it's the same process that makes the NHS so amazing – but any notional graph of improved quality over the last twenty years shows a very steep line indeed, out of all possible recognition in fact. It's because of the buying power of the supermarkets that much bulk, cheap wine is so good these days but, then again, that's what makes people think there's no point spending more than a fiver or so.

Wine doesn't always fit plans for global branding and it's small fry next to the Bacardis and Smirnoffs (go into virtually any bar in world and you'll find them). The frustration of Fosters, who bought up great swathes of Australia's wine business in the 1990s, has been palpable – the fact is that wine is variable, the better stuff is by nature limited, it's not possible to respond swiftly to demand and the whole weather thing is a nightmare.

But these chaps are smart as hell and they don't give up. Currently the top ten brands in the UK account for a little under thirty per cent of the total market, which at £5bn, means that each single per cent translates to sales of a million pounds a week. Pernod have taken the route of simplification and consolidation and Jacob's Creek comes closer to being a global wine brand than most (while being, with multiple levels of irony, the biggest 'French' wine brand). They appear to be experimenting with the possibilities of making a region – Rioja – interchangeable or confusable with a brand at certain levels with their phenomenally successful Campo Viejo. Another new approach is nomadic or supra-national brands – some Blossom Hill wines, the number-one seller in the UK, are from the USA, some from Italy and some from Chile and does anyone care?

Those top-ten UK sellers and their owners, where appropriate in

2009 were, in order: Blossom Hill (Diageo); Hardy's (Constellation); Gallo; Jacob's Creek (Pernod-Ricard); Lindemans (Fosters); Echo Falls (Constellation); First Cape (Brand Phoenix); Kumala, Stowells – yes, really! (both Constellation); Wolf Blass (Fosters). Some of them are perfectly decent, the southern hemisphere ones are better than the California-based ones and – if push comes to shove – I would drink any of them if nothing else were available.

Supermarket own brands used to be the 'grey goo' of wine. There has been significant improvement but they still are not to be bought randomly. The job of finding what I estimate to be the fifteen to twenty per cent of genuinely good ones has been made somewhat easier by the introduction of premium ranges by most chains – upping the hit rate to maybe twenty-five to thirty-three per cent. The three to five per cent of real honeys, regardless of range, are sometimes the product of leading winemakers and are not too difficult to identify as most of the national press wine writers hone in on the same few dozen wines.

Private brands are all those Castellos de This and Châteaux de That when really there aren't any such places. What happens is that the retailer does his market research and then tells the supplier – often a cooperative or a mid-size producer – that they have room for, say, five thousand cases of an up front, medium-quality reserva Rioja if they can get it on the shelf for XYZ pounds a bottle in X weeks' time. The winemaker does his sums, taps into the world's ocean of surplus wine and, bingo, Baron de Haro – or, if an Aussie Chardonnay, 'Windy Ridge' or, for all I care, 'Windy Bottom' – is born.

M&S, who don't sell branded products, were the first UK retailer to do this. They felt they had to give the wines names in order to distinguish them from their own labels and to some ears, 'Chevalier de How's-Your-Father' has more cachet than 'M&S Chablis'. Meanwhile, the Wine Society did different quality levels successfully with its 'Exhibition' range and this seems to have been the model for the tiered offerings elsewhere.

All the majors now send their own experts – not just buyers – out into the world to work with producers. Some eventually become mini-brands in themselves and get sold to other supermarkets. It's all about positioning and they are generally pitched above the own labels at around the same level as the big international brands and attract customers who want to feel they're getting a wine made by real people in a real place rather than by a bunch of machines owned by a corporation. As it happens, they often are – it's just not the people or the place they think it is.

Private brands are more profitable than real brands because there are few marketing costs involved and the best of them are among the best-value wines on supermarket shelves – reading the knowledgeable and conscientious newspaper wine writers is the best way to find out which are the ones to go for.

A Word on Discounting

Consumers know what to expect from average-priced wines – unexceptionable, reasonably well-made, easy-drinking, and – above all – consistent Wednesday-night bottles. When they spend more than a tenner, they're hoping for something to make their dinner-party guests sit up and take notice. I'm not sure that people have any idea of what to expect from wines in between those price levels because the big winemakers and the big wine sellers have muddied the waters so much with systematic discounting.

Presumably, very few people are sufficiently taken with a particular wine that has been discounted from, say, £8.99 to £4.49 to subsequently pay the higher price when there's another, similar-seeming bottle from another of the big brands parked next to it and which now has the big discount. So there seems to be no reason ever to pay more than a fiver or so. The poor bewildered punter, standing friendless and frequently clueless in the typical four-, five-, six-hundred bottle aisle could very easily be forgiven for asking themselves whether any wines are actually *worth* six or seven or eight or nine quid or – if they buy one – are they simply falling in to the elephant trap that is the zombie, un-discounted wine? The answer, of course, is that there are many but so advanced is the erosion of confidence in that price bracket that only very careful selection or – better – buying from independent merchants can offer relief.

The UK High Street

The tumbleweed rolling around the UK high street as far as off-licences are concerned proliferated anew with the collapse in 2009 of First Quench – not surprising with a name like that. The company owned the 1,200 Threshers, Wine Racks, The Local and Haddows shops. It could be fairly said that they discounted themselves to death. The wines generally weren't up to much anyway. It hardly seems possible that a whole generation can have graduated to an NVQ in binge-drinking and been rewarded with its first ASBO without ever knowing why old people have such a soft spot for Oddbins. The company is now back in private hands – those of the son of the man who started it – after having been bought and sold a few times, most recently by French giant Castel, the biggest wine company in Europe and owners of the useful Nicolas chain. In the eighties Oddbins awakened millions of Brits to the fact that wine could actually taste nice and here's hoping they can get back to doing what they did best. The steadily burning light in UK town centres – although not the high street itself – is Majestic, who are experimenting with reducing their minimum purchase from twelve to six bottles of their well-chosen wines.

Wine Merchants

The supermarkets and multiples all sell some good wines but making friends with a well-established, enthusiastic wine merchant who can advise, cajole, celebrate and commiserate should be a natural progression. I'm always banging on about it. Most people buy a couple of bottles at a time and the step of buying that first whole case seems to be a big one (and does require a little organisation – carrying a twelve-bottle case more than a few yards is something to avoid).

Some of the advantages of buying wine by the mixed case from a wine merchant are: that they do all the work of weeding out the dull stuff. Their reputations rest on the quality of the wines they choose and as a result they get more interesting wines, often from small, individual producers who care about what they're making; they usually offer pre-selected mixed cases at many price levels; they sell wine at (nearly) all price levels and for mid-range wines they can be cheaper than the supermarkets and multiples; there really isn't much snobbery involved unless you want there to be; you don't have to schlep the stuff about. Having a case on hand gives you the luxury of choice: 'Sweetie, do you think this Chilean Merlot or the Lalande de Pomerol would go better with these Wall's bangers?'

Nobody who ever started buying by the case from good merchants ever stopped without a good reason (which basically means penury, liver disease or death – and only the last of these is good enough). As confidence increases you can begin to have the fun of scouting their lists – they make mistakes and mistakes are priced better than discounts and sales, when there is often a good reason for cutting the price – good for them, that is.

I learned much of whatever I know about wine from bottles bought from the top merchants who comprise the loose alliance called 'The Bunch': Tanners of Shrewsbury, Berry Brothers & Rudd, Adnams of Southwold, Yapp Brothers, Corney and Barrow, and newbies Lea and Sandeman. They're all good, but with so much dynamic new competition none can rest on their laurels: while one has newly established itself as the best, another has become rather expensive, or has been distracted by other projects, or is a bit stuck in the mud or is quite uneven quality-wise.

Until as recently as the 1970s wine merchants imported wine in casks and bottled it themselves. The tradition lives on in the form of merchants' house wines, although thankfully they are all bottled at source these days. They're a big part of their business, their calling cards almost, and they usually offer exceptional value. There's some cachet in having the name of an illustrious wine merchant on the label I suppose but it's what's in the bottle that counts. These wines are often made by leading producers and châteaux and some of the old guard of merchants like Berry's and Justerini & Brooks (now Diageo-owned since they bought the J&B whisky brand) have relationships with individual châteaux that go back to the eighteenth century.

Some of their ranges run to as many as sixty bottles, including Ports, sherries and Madeira, and the name of a top merchant on the bottle is about as close as wine gets to coming with a guarantee – it's the consumer-end version of the handshakes on which, refreshingly, a lot of the wine trade is still run. Some object in principle to the fact that the merchants' everyday wines are often non-vintage – i.e. a blend of wines from different vintages – but that's the tradition and, in practice, such objections are seldom sustained when they actually taste these fruits of the blenders' art.

Local Heroes

The noughties saw a profoundly encouraging spate of start-ups of small, independent wine merchants devoting themselves to providing high-quality wines at every price level. Most deliver nationwide but if you're fortunate to have one nearby it adds something special to the experience if you can walk in and have a chat. In London Planet of the Grapes, Vinoteca, Highbury Vintners and The Sampler deserve particular praise as do The Secret Cellar, The Butler's Wine Cellar, Cooden Cellars, South Downs Cellars, Fareham Cellars, Noel Young and Corks Out elsewhere – and there are many more. The Association of Direct Wine Merchants brings together some up-and-coming and decidedly individualistic folk too.

Mail Order

Obviously, wine merchants and supermarkets will send wine to you – by mail or otherwise – but there are differences in what the mail-order merchants and wine clubs do. The chief difference being that in most cases the wines are pre-selected and if that sounds alarming it's because most of the time it is. The sector – with about five per cent of the UK market – is bestridden by Direct Wines, set up by Tony Laithwaite in 1969. They run *The Sunday Times* Wine Club, *Daily Telegraph* Wines, Avery's of Bristol, the Richard and Judy Wine Club, British Airways Executive Wine Club, Virgin Wines and of course Laithwaite's itself – formerly known as Bordeaux Direct. I'm relieved that their Barclaycard Wine Service appears to be defunct because even the idea of having a credit-card company choosing anybody's wine gives me the creeps.

All of the above have good wines but they're unlikely to send them if you don't ask for them – why would they? Importantly, there has been an uptick in quality generally from some of their outfits. The fact that – to the astonishment of many in the trade – in March 2010 Laithwaite's took a delivery of their own in the form of Justin Howard-Sneyd from Waitrose, where as head of wine he took their list from *primus inter pares* among the grocers to nobody-in-second-place, hopefully signals a seriousness of intent as far as wine-club quality is concerned.

The original mail-order merchant, The Wine Society, was founded as a cooperative in 1874 by a 'committee of gentlemen' at the Albert Hall with the purpose of purchasing wines in 'unadulterated condition direct from the producers and offering them to the membership at the lowest possible price'. And it still does the very same. Another of the 'Objects of the Society' was 'to introduce foreign wines hitherto unknown or but little known in this country' and to this end they were selling Californian Zinfandels and Australian wines 100 years ago, which is rather impressive. Membership is open to all and you can forget the Groucho Marx line about not wanting to join any club that would have him – the quality of the wines is very high. My own *Eureka!* moment with wine was a Sancerre from the Wine Society. It had – alongside the usual quality of being a reasonably efficient inebriant – the hitherto unknown one of being completely delicious.

Starting a Wine Cellar

An actual cellar isn't necessary except for long-term ageing, i.e. five years plus, and even then I'm not sure it's essential if you've got a good spot above ground. It needs to be cool (preferably under 20°C and never, ever over 25°C – so forget the kitchen) and just as important, reasonably consistent in temperature – say within a band of 5°–10°C over the year, which shouldn't be a problem indoors but forget the garage). Spend a few quid on a 'max-min' thermometer to monitor the situation and save hundreds on storage (except for blue-chip wines), which is typically £10–12 per case, per year. Look for dark, usually north-facing spots, free from strong smells and vibration (so forget teenagers' bedrooms as well, as if . . .).

Most wine is made for early drinking and keeping will not improve it but, now that you've made friends with that nice merchant, they'll be happy to advise on some medium-term wines (one-to-five years) so you can start to see results. In that time frame, there's a real sweet spot where it is not profitable for producers or retailers to store wines for long enough to reach their best; however, if you store them, they'll give you better wine for no more money. And that, unsurprisingly when you think about it, is what it's all about.

Buying wine *en primeur* (when it is offered for sale by merchants in advance of bottling and shipment by the producer) has been growing as fast as the hype that surrounds each new 'Vintage of the Century!' There were three Bordeaux Vintages of the Century in the noughties. The top merchants, having descended *en masse* to taste the young wines from the barrel, have a pretty shrewd idea of how they should turn out. All you have to do is sit back and watch the prices rise once the wine is shipped and then go through the roof when they're ready to drink a few years later. That's the theory anyway. In practice, there is no cheaper way to buy good wine.

Buying wine at auction is fun and there are bargains to be had for the assiduous. A few (dozen) cases of mature vintages solves the luxurious 'problem' of what to drink while your *en primeur* is quietly maturing. All the major London auction houses have regular sales, as do a number of country auctioneers. Prices range from as little as

£1–200 per case up to the stratospheric; however, there are pitfalls to be aware of, especially the ever increasing charges. Some of them (e.g. excise duty) are fixed, so they have a disproportionate effect at the lower end of the price scale. Always read the small print – a lot that sells for £200 'on the hammer' can end up costing very close to £300 if it was offered 'in bond', with the excise duty per case payable by the buyer. Add VAT on the total, auctioneers' commission (typically twenty per cent plus VAT), delivery of around £7–8 per case and you'll begin to see what I mean.

At auction, provenance is important. Wines kept in a specialist storage facility by the original merchants or sometimes in the château's own cellars will have a note to this effect in the catalogue and will fetch more. If no provenance is given it's better to ask than to run the risk that the wine has been kept year round in somebody's mum's garage. One last thing – don't buy an eleven-bottle case. Stands to reason, really.

Some good things to buy at auction:

. . . wines from great producers in less-than-great vintages. A top wine from a middling vintage might be less than half the price of the best year but it's a lot more quality than half the wine.

. . . wines with 'bin-soiled' labels. It puts off perfectionist collectors and if your friends are the sort who would care about a soiled label, get some new friends.

. . . wines from less-fashionable regions, the Loire, sweet and dry white Bordeaux, vintage Port, Rioja, Chianti, and all of Germany are undervalued and can improve amazingly.

. . . 'second wines' of the top Bordeaux châteaux – these people generally make only good wine.

cabernet franc cabernet sauvignon caipirinha calimocho calvados canadian wine canaiolo capsule carignan carmenère catarratto celebrity wines cesanese chacolí champagne cocktail chardonnay chardonnay chasselas chenin blanc chilean

Cabernet Franc – fine, widespread red-wine grape most at home in western France, especially along the Loire (one of a few places where it makes single-varietal wines) and in blends in Bordeaux. There's a lot in north-eastern Italy – though some is now known to be the chameleon Carmenère – and in California, New Zealand, Australia, South Africa, Argentina and Chile and basically dotted everywhere (especially where people want to make Bordeaux-style blends). A parent of Cabernet Sauvignon, its characteristic aromas can be herbaceous, with something like graphite (often referred to as 'lead pencil') and it's important to say that it makes excellent outdoors-y, chill-able picnic-able summer reds before mentioning that, saving your Grace, it can sometimes have something vaguely, um . . . excremental. Yes, in southern France, as I live and breathe, now and again it smells of something like poo.

Cabernet Sauvignon – my dad was never a major wine man – people weren't in the fifties, sixties and seventies, when outside of France, Spain, Italy and maybe Germany it was beer and spirits (as in 'How many fingers, George?'). But Dad would put an expensive (and probably awful) bottle of Châteauneuf or Gevrey-Chambertin on the table on high days and holidays. Even so, I'm by no means sure that he would have been able to come up with the name of a single grape variety. Things change and nowadays everyone will tell you their favourites and the first name of a red-wine grape to pass most of their lips will have been that of the king – Cabernet Sauvignon. Long maturation, first in the best oak and then in bottle, softens the green bell pepper or eucalyptus edges of young Cabernet and, in common with other age-worthy grapes, the better it gets the less it tastes of its characteristic blackcurrant fruit – it's what the fruit turns into that's the really interesting part.

The world seems to have overlooked the fact that, in its castle in Bordeaux's left bank, CabSauv is always accompanied by its court – one or more of Merlot, Cabernet Franc and Petit Verdot are the foils to set if off – but it's the single varietal wines, made everywhere from Chile to China to the Cape, that have been the pretenders to the throne, with Australia's Coonawarra and California's Napa Valley getting closest to a coup.

Old and complex, King Cab in his ermine-lined crown of oak settles on the scarlet-velvet cushion of his throne – the edges tinged with brick from long service – sets before us a dish of red fruits stewed with cassis, rich with herbs and roasted spices, liquorice and truffles, then freshens our breath with a Parma violet and proffers a cedar-lined box from which to pluck a fine cigar to enjoy with coffee and dark chocolates. All hail the King!

Caipirinha – in a rocks glass muddle half a lime cut into 1cm pieces with two teaspoons of sugar, top with ice and add 6–9cl cachaça (see p. 335) and strap on your hardest hat because you're probably going to finish the bottle.

Calimocho – (aka Kalimotxo) red wine and Coca-Cola, popular as a fast-acting inebriant among the Spanish Basque-country yoof.

Calvados – the apple brandy (aka applejack in the USA) of Normandy and as such technically a schnapps, but long ageing in oak gives it more in common with brandy (the nomenclature is also similar: 'Fine' or 'Three star' spends a minimum of two years in oak; 'Vieux' or 'Réserve' gets three; 'Vieille Reserve', 'VO' or 'VSOP' four; six or (very often) more and it's 'XO' or '*hors d'age*,' 'Napoleon' or 'Extra'. (Berneroy, Camut, Drouin, Du Breuil, Dupont, Henri de Querville, Lemorton, Morise, Victot-Pontfol).

Having seen off all competitiors since its founding in 1780 – as the first licensed distillery in the USA – the sole commercial producer of applejack (Lairds) may not be too alarmed at the arrival of a new competitor in 2009 (Hudson River Valley Winery). The success of an English version (Somerset Cider Brandy Company) has also spawned some competition. Pommeau (the cider version of *mistelle*) is cider brandy added to unfermented apple juice.

Canadian beer – overshadowed by its neighbour's craft-brew industry, Canada has reacted the way countries seem to when consolidation amongst brewers becomes a virtual monopoly – though in their case a duopoly of Molson and Labatt with only Michelob for comfort (though both Labatt and Michelob are now AB InBev brands) – they have started up breweries at a pace that brings to mind the speed of yeast reproducing itself. Now businesses include Amsterdam Brewing Co, Creemore Springs, Dieu du Ciel!, Moosehead, Niagara Falls and Russell Brewing Co. Early days, but there is real quality to be had already.

Canadian wine – best known for Niagara's German-style 'ice wine' made from individually picked grapes harvested so late in the year – and even into the new year – that they're frozen on the vines. Each grape gives up a few drops of super-concentrated nectar, which explains not only the price but also the stunning loveliness of the wine. Riesling and hard-arsed French-hybrid Vidal are the grapes and some – the essence of decadence – is sparkling. The success of labels such as Clos Jordanne, Inniskillin, and Pelee Island (among others) has paved the way for many producers to branch into confident, fresh table wines from many of the international varieties.

On the west coast the vineyards of British Columbia continue where those of Washington state leave off but the best vineyards are further east in Okanagan Valley, where the Bordeaux grapes and Chardonnay flourish in the drought and cold. Try Mission Hill or Osoyoo-Larose.

capsule – (aka foil) is the covering that protects the cork. A really flimsy, thin one still says, 'Don't open me – find something else' even though the seriously heavy ones of old that said the opposite have been banned as they contained lots of lead. Take off the whole thing when opening the bottle.

carbonic maceration – a winemaking technique of whole-grape fermentation, where the process takes place inside the uncrushed grapes; used for early drinking wines such as Beaujolais that require low tannin. Seldom mentioned on back labels but you can spot 'em a mile off once you recognise the bright pinkish colour, crunchy texture and bubblegum aromas.

Caribbean beer – Jamaica's molasses-dark stouts (Dragon and Lion Heart) frankly make Foreign Extra Guinness seem like a drink for pussies. Lighter relief is at hand from Ansa McAl of Trinidad's Carib and (Diageo-owned) Desnoes and Geddes's Red Stripe lagers.

Carignan – once ubiquitous, extremely productive red-wine grape of southern France and northern Spain, where it is aka Cariñena, after the place, and Mazuelo, when planted in Rioja. More rubbish red wine has been made of it than of everything else put together even though, like most demonised grape varieties, in the right hands, in the right place . . . you know the rest.

Carménère – robust red-wine grape, originally of Bordeaux but now most at home in Chile where thousands of hectares of it were thought to be Merlot until recently. Also in northern Italy, where – spookily – thousands of hectares of it were thought to be Cabernet Franc until recently. There is food-friendly value to be had while it makes its name (most are too chewy to drink on their own).

celebrity wines – taken as a class, should be much worse than they are. Francis Ford Coppola was the first and is still the godfather – what started as a hobby is now in the top twenty US wine companies and is estimated to be shifting over ten million bottles a year.

If you think there's a lot of bullshit around wine, try fashion, or rock and roll. The dangers of hubris are never far away: Italian designer Roberto Cavalli's Tenuta degli Dei (Domaine of the Gods), shortlisted in the competitive 'most overpriced' category, appears not to be for sale in Italy (except on eBay!); golfers Ernie Els and Greg Norman chip in some decent stuff and there really is a John Daly range (and they're not alcohol-free); cricketing B[otham]

M[errill] W[illis] wines are hilariously old-fashioned New World sloggers; thesp Gérard Depardieu puts his name to a number of good wines and Sam Neill does OK with Two Paddocks. But a lot of celebs are more reliable when they're dead: the 'star-tribute' category is blessedly small but Marilyn Wines are to die for and Graceland Cellars won't leave you feeling all shook up.

Pol Roger's Winston Churchill is heroic but in the UK, a healthy respect for *Schadenfreude* (amazing we don't have our own term) keeps a brake on these activities; Sir Cliff Richard's Onda Nova is respectable and stocked by Waitrose no less, with a premium range that would be perfectly fine if it weren't for the celebrity premium on the price, which all these wines attract. It has survived the fiasco in which Cliff was stitched up by Gordon Ramsay on telly when he failed to recognise his own wine, said that he 'wouldn't buy it', and then called it 'harsh' – probably rightly as he'd just been given a 1990 Vieux Château Certan to taste. (Ramsay also gave him 'Bob Dylan's £100 wine' to taste. All good stuff, except it's not Bob Dylan's – he merely let the excellent producer, Fattoria Le Terrazze, use the name Planet Waves – and it cost about a quarter of that before, like so many celeb wines, it slipped quietly beneath the wet sort of waves. I notice Mick Hucknall's Il Cantante doesn't seem to be available in the UK and the launch of Sting's Chianti has been 'delayed'. Anyone for a glass of Martha Stewart Merlot?

Cesanese – useful, lightweight red-wine grape of central Italy's Lazio region with its own DOCs in Cesanese del Piglio and Cesanese di Affili, south of Rome. Also blended in the local Velletri DOC, in SuperTuscan Tenuta di Trinoro and – bringing together more dodgy wine trends than I can easily handle – popped up as the tent-pole grape in US porn star Savanna Samson's Sogno Uno celebrity wine that, despite an upstanding (sorry, outstanding) score from the immensely influential American wine writer Robert Parker, appears to have wilted away.

chacolí – Spain's *vinho verde* (aka txakoli in the Basque Country, where they make it, so they can spell it how they like) made mainly from the Hondarribi Zuri grape. How this sharp (but refreshing) stuff, drunk in situ for a few pence while still cloudy and fizzing, has ended up on posh London restaurant tables for £30 a bottle is one of the true mysteries of wine.

Champagne Cocktail – build a small lump of sugar, two dashes of bitters, one part brandy and nine parts chilled Champagne in a flute glass, garnish with a maraschino cherry, a twist of orange and an unshakeable sense of superiority.

Chardonnay – was the breakthrough grape, the first of its type to have a recognisable name à la Twiggy, Angela Rippon, Linda Lovelace. Riesling is its only other serious contender as the 'great white' but it hasn't yet cut the sharp elbows needed to compete. The fact is that Chardonnay makes more great wine, in more styles, in more places and, encouragingly, the list is growing, than any other white grape. There's not much in common between a toasty, buttery brioche of a *blanc de blancs* Champagne, a tungsten-edged *grand cru* Chablis and the tropical sunset in a frame of glowing oak that might describe some of the best New World offerings – except for class.

The whole 'ABC' thing – that's 'anything but chardonnay' – is daft but has had its effect. You can tie me kangaroo down sport, but in 2008 Sauvignon Blanc (seventy per cent of it from New Zealand) *outsold Chardonnay in Australia*. It's an ill-wind, though, and a lot of the blowsy over-oaked stuff has been superseded the world over by cleaner, fresher styles and the *ennui* has given so many once-neglected white grapes their chance to sparkle in the sun.

Chardonnay is one of the malleable, blank-canvas type of grapes, like Semillon and Pinot Grigio, and how it turns out depends on where it's grown (and it's grown in every conceivable *terroir*, from Uruguay to the UK), on how it's grown and on what the winemaker wants to do with it. Nonetheless, it can be characterised as making heavier, broader, rounder wines than most white grapes and, as such, it perhaps expresses itself better in the mouth than in the nose. It attracts a bewildering range of comparative terms which, again, often reflect what's been done with it: the creamy, butterscotch side of things has much to do with malolactic fermentation; the toasty, smoky aspects are often to do with oak-ageing and whether the aromas and flavours are talked about in terms of melons, pineapple and peaches or wet stones, citrus fruits and hazenuts depends as much on location and temperature as on anything else.

Chenin Blanc – unsung white grape, originally of France's Loire region (where it is aka Pineau), now widespread in South Africa, California's Central Valley and the Antipodes where it makes high volumes of rather neutral, reasonably crisp stuff. But, in the right place, in the right hands when the yield is low and the acidity is high, Chenin makes some of the great white wines of the world. Dry and beeswaxy from Savennières, but still with a lick of honey on the end: full-on sweet from Coteaux du Layon, Quarts de Chaume and Bonnezeaux; jamming with different variations on the theme of appley sweetness in Vouvray, and with bubbles in Saumur, these wines combine richness with freshness, are among the longest-lived of all and share a mineral-laden complexity in their DNA. If it sounds like a buying opportunity, it is, but word is getting out and some New World producers are shaping up as well.

Chilean wine – is a reminder (to me) that harbouring prejudices in today's world of wine is not a good idea. So fast is the pace of change that, if you look away for a couple of years, you may not recognise anything when you look back. I had the Chileños pegged as disarmingly eager-to-please purveyors of ridiculously cheap, overly hot Merlots and Cabernets (it didn't really matter which as they were so sunburnt as to be unrecognisable) and feral Sauvignon Blancs that would pee on your gooseberries the moment your back was turned. And as for the so-called fine wines – I once had a Chilean Cab that was such a ridiculous caricature of what it was trying to be that I actually laughed out loud when I took a sniff (thankfully the anxious – and illustrious – producer didn't hear).

Chilean wine had its biggest moment at a blind tasting in Berlin in 2004 where Viñedo Chadwick 2000 and Seña 2001 took the top spots over Lafite 2000, Margaux 2001 and a bevy of Super-Tuscans. No matter that the Chileans are early drinkers and the European wines were decades from maturity: it gave the industry a shock of excitement.

The passage of a handful of vintages has seen them set their bar as high as any in the southern hemisphere – and in a country where the biggest producers are some of the best you have to ask 'Where did it all go right?' A growing number of the showboating wines have a finesse and a lightness of touch that is unrecognisable compared to the heavy-handed 'more is more' wines of a few years ago. Winemakers the length of the nearly 900-mile vine-growing zone have spread their wings adding Syrah and Pinot Noir to the well-established Cabernet Sauvignon and Merlot (much of which is now known to be Carmenère) and there are aromatic whites – Viognier, Riesling and Gewürz along with the other expected international varieties.

With no phylloxera to worry about it's relatively easy for Chile's inquiring spirits to experiment with planting in cooler sites that are better exposed to the cold air descending from the Andes as well as the breezes coming in over the cool coastal waters brought up from the Antarctic by the Humboldt current. Winemakers here are at the cutting edge of everything techno, from clonal selection to the drip-or-drench irrigation debate.

DRINK LIKE A KING
With ...

Anakena
Calbuco
Chocalán
Elki
Emiliana
Indómita
Los Espinos
Sierra Grande
Tabali
Sieto Soles

... FOR THE PRICE OF JUST DRINKING

Even though the number of exporting wineries has grown from the dozen of the early 1990s to something closer to a hundred, the Chilean industry is still one of the most heavily consolidated. The big producers have multiple subsidiaries and brands, often in different regions and often quite autonomous, which in itself explains much about the high-quality levels such as from Concha y Toro [1], the world's second-biggest wine brand that includes Casillero del Diablo [1], Cono Sur [1], Emiliana [1], Cánepa [1], Maycas de Limarí [2] and, with Bordeaux's Rothschild, Almaviva [3]; family-owned Errázuriz includes Arboleda [2], Caliterra [1] and Viñedo Chadwick [3] – the family name of the owners; San Pedro has 35 South [1], Altaïr [2], Tabalí [2], Casa Rivas [2] and Viña Leyda [1].

The second tier of producers, size-wise, is a rich seam of quality and value with Anakena [1]; Casa Lapostolle [1] – French-owned, with top Bordeaux consultant Michel Rolland on board; Casa Silva [1],

Montes [1], whose founder, Aurelio, is a pivotal figure in the industry; Santa Carolina [1]; Santa Rita [1]; Undurraga [1]; Veramonte [1]; Valdivieso [1]; and Ventisquero [1]. The earthquake of 2010 resulted in the loss of over twelve per cent of Chile's cellared wine but as there was oversupply at the time it was not a disaster for the industry.

Foreign dough hasn't poured in as it has over the Andes in Argentina but there has been a steady supply. Spain's Miguel Torres was the first flying winemaker, Bordeaux's Rothschilds' Los Vascos [1] and Lurtons' Araucano [2] now also fly the tricolore and the UK is represented by *négociants* Paul Boutinot with his Sierra Grande [1] and Alliance Wines' Los Espinos [1]. Many come with their own experts but a few have sought out leading oenologist (and now biodynamist) Alvaro Espinoza (Antiyal [3]) or soil-boffin Pedro Parra to get things moving in the right direction.

Oop north in the Coquimbo region, better known by the names of the valleys of the Limarí (Maycas de Limarí [2], Sutil [2], Tabali [1], Tamaya – part of Tierra Antica [1]), Choapa (DeMartino) [2] and Elqui (Elki [1], Falernia [1]) rivers, the belt-and-braces of cooling sea breezes and vineyards planted at up to 2000m are proving the point that good things can be done even within 800km of the Tropic of Capricorn and with a diverse range of grapes.

Northernmost of the established regions, Aconcagua includes cool, dry Casablanca where the whole white-wine ball started rolling (Indómita [1], Viña Casablanca [1] and William Cole [1]); in sea-breezy San Antonio you'll find Garcés Silva [2], Marín [2] and Matetic [3]. It includes the Leyda micro-zone, as well as the Aconcagua Valley itself, dominated for a century by Errázuriz in Panquehue, but now also Von Siebenthal [2] shines.

The Central Valley (Calbuco [1], Las Montañas [1]), by far the most important of the winegrowing areas, is divided into four river-valley areas: Maipo, encircling Santiago, was the first Chilean appellation to gain an international reputation and was planted with red Bordeaux varieties before phylloxera struck Europe and they returned for replacement vines. Many top wines are still made here: Carmen [1]; Chocalán [1]; Cousiño Macul [1]; De Martino [2]; Domus [2]; Haras de Pirque [1]; Odfjell [1]; Perez Cruz [2]; Santa Alicia [1]; Santa Rita [1], Siete Soles [1]; Valdevista [1]; and William Fèvre of Chablis [1]. The Rapel (Château Los Boldos [1]) which is on a roll and is itself divided between two areas whose names are more likely to be seen on labels, namely Colchagua to the south, with some fine Carmenère – try Apaltagua [1], Casa Silva [1], Estampa [1], La Joya [1], Luis Felipe Edwards [1], MontGras [1], Neyen [3] or Viu Manent [1] – and lesser-known Cachapoal to the north, try Anakena [1], Altaïr [3], Cornellana [1], Quinta las Cabras [1], la Rosa [1] or Torreón de Paredes [1]. South again to Curicó Valley, where Miguel Torres pitched camp in 1979 and where you can find Botalcura [1], Los Almendros Fair-trade [1] and Echeverría [1]. The up-and-coming Maule Valley is the fourth (Carta Vieja [1], Donoso [1], O Fournier [1], Gillmore [2], Kintu [1] and Villarrica [1]).

Vines flourish only in a fairly small central section of Chile's near-6,000km length and the most southerly are in the Valleys of the Bío Bío (Agustinos [1], Gracia [1] and Porta [1]), Itata and Malleco rivers, where Bordeaux's Pontallier and Prats families make excellent Chardonnay at Aquitania [3].

GET A HANDLE

> CHILEAN WINE HAS GROWN UP AND STOPPED TRYING TOO HARD – IT'S PROBABLY THE BEST-VALUE WINE COUNTRY OF ALL AND, HAVING LEFT MOST OF THOSE OVERLY INTENSE 'HOT' REDS BEHIND, WILL GO FROM STRENGTH TO STRENGTH.

Chinese wine – believe it or not, China is the world's sixth-biggest producer of wine. You wouldn't want to drink much of it (yet) but the ones beginning to appear on UK supermarket shelves are okay and you may find a perfectly decent bottle from the three dominant producers, Changyu [1], Dynasty [1] and Great Wall [1]. Foreign investment is coming in, domestic consumption is exploding and if their enthusiasm for wines from their own nascent quality producers matches their thirst for Bordeaux's first growths, especially Lafite for some reason, the sky's the limit.

cider – is apple wine. I seldom drink it and it's difficult for me to write about it. Due to some bizarre legal knot-hole, cider was on sale in sweet shops when I was growing up. I dare say you can guess the rest and, yes, aversion therapy does work, or at least it does if you're twelve. The UK is the biggest consumer, and it's not just besmocked carrot-crunchers guzzling it these days. The phenomenal success of Magners, an Irish brand served over ice, provided the impetus for the whole industry to reinvigorate itself.

Cider is made wherever apples are grown and historically consumed mainly in situ but these days the traditional (some would say 'industrial') British producers such as Bulmers (owned by Scottish & Newcastle, hence by Heineken) and Gaymers (also owned by Magners people C&C) have been innovating. S&N's Jacques brand specialises in flavoured ciders, for example. The jostle for space is not just with the quality producers such as Aspall's, Weston's and Thatchers but with the upstarts such as Frosty Jack's, which attempts to reposition white cider somewhere, anywhere, other than the park bench. The WKD alcopopsicle firm also owns Merrydown. There are now imports as well with Sweden's Kopparberg,

South Africa's Savannah, Normandy's Dupont and Bayeux and Brittany's Kerisac (if you can find them). The Spanish give us El Gaiterro and are very keen. In Asturias and the Basque Country barmen make a big thing of pouring their *sidra* from a great height to get some bubbles into it. And in the USA you'd do well to remember that you need to ask for 'hard cider' to avoid getting a nasty, non-alcoholic shock.

The fragile reputation of lacy perry from the likes of family-owned Bufford Farm and Dunkerton is at risk of being drowned in a tide of industrially produced pear cider. Most cider makers now have one on their books but at least it has remedied the rather sad situation in which a drink celebrated by the diarist John Evelyn in his 1664 essay 'Pomona' should for so long have been synonymous with something as mired in seventies naffness as Babycham. Perry's long and proud history was something the original makers of 'The Happiest Drink in the World' – the Showering family, now makers of Brothers Cider – went to great lengths to distance themselves from in their astonishingly successful campaigns of the 1960s and 1970s to present Babycham as an economical English alternative to Champagne, even though Babycham lacks any flavour other than a dull sweetness. Some drinks brands appear to have a cockroach-like indestructibility and the prancing fawn doesn't need your sympathy – enough people apparently still 'Love a Babycham' to have spent nearly four million quid on it in 2008.

cocktails – there is no coherent etymology for the word, indeed there is very little that *is* coherent in the world of the 'mixologist'. What is one to make of such a species, some of whom think a Corpse Reviver is brandy mixed with the juice of lemons and oranges, a little grenadine and topped up with Champagne and yet others believe it to be a mix of brandy, Calvados and sweet vermouth? These people exhibit a total lack of concern for even the most basic tenets of methodological rigour – they're an absolute shower. Nonetheless, there is a deeply symbiotic thing that happens across the bar: for the seller, the cocktail is a means of extracting more money from the buyer than the sum of the parts would suggest might be reasonable; for the customer, the price provides a promise of solace, of sophistication, even of seduction.

One reason there are so many cocktails is that people are needy: they like to feel they belong, that they are on the inside whilst you – schmuck that you are – don't even know what's *in* a Lonsdale let alone where to go for the best one. (I, of course, know that it's basically a basil-mojito-type thing, but made with gin and topped up with apple juice, so not very mojito-like, and the only place that serves it is Beretta in San Francisco, which is one of those embarrassing places that call themselves speakeasies and have no sign to indicate where they are and of course this in turn makes you feel a complete prat because alcohol has been legal since, ooh, 1933. (Anyway, a cocktail is generally either two or more alcoholic ingredients mixed together or one or more of them mixed with one or more of the following: fruit or fruit juice, bitters, sugar, or herbs (for flavour); and/or ice, carbonated drinks, wine or Champagne, milk, cream, or egg (for texture, temperature or dilution). There are five methods of putting these ingredients together (in ascending order of violence: layering; building; stirring; shaking and blending. Stirring with ice doesn't dilute the alcohol as much as shaking, by the way, so there *is* a difference.

Colombard – unexceptionable white-grape variety of south-western France, in particular Gascony, where much was blended and distilled for the local Armagnac. How it got from there to being California's most widely planted grape is a bit of a mystery but the easy-drinking (i.e. bland), but crisp, wines it makes in the Central Valley have been much replicated, often blended with Chardonnay in Australia, South Africa and south-western France, in particular Gascony (repeat until fade).

cooling devices – cool air sinks, so keep it in contact with a cold bottle for longer with one of those things you stand the bottle in. Bubble-wrap works better but is not exactly stylish.

congeners – compounds, including those contributing to flavour, formed during the process of fermentation. Current research appears to have proved that dark-coloured drinks do indeed have more congeners, thus more flavour, but as many of them are toxic they make for a worse hangover. (Though not if you drink them sparingly while your chum necks a bottle of voddy.)

corks and other closures – anything other than a screwtop (aka Stelvin) for everyday, early-drinking wine is a bit irritating these days, although some countries such as Portugal, the home of cork, may never use screwtops. It's estimated (very variously) that the bark of the cork-oak tree messes with about one in twenty of the bottles it's used to seal, though that's from the barely noticeable to the infrequent, undrinkable 'corked' scenario. Cork has served us well for hundreds of years and is preferable to the agglomerated cork jobs made from bits of cork glued together or those horrid plastic ones.

The jury is still out, but as the science catches up and wines with artificial closures are aged side-by-side with those with corks, the myths (i.e. that tiny, beneficial quantities of oxygen sneak in and out through the cork – presumably wearing a false moustache – and make it irreplaceable for venerable wines) are falling away one by one.

Cosmopolitan – three parts citrus vodka, two parts cranberry juice and one part each of lime juice and Cointreau shaken with ice, strained into a cocktail glass and garnished with a man-bag.

Croatia – makes some good wine (Badel 1862 [3], Coronica [2]) from good grapes (Plavac Mali and Babić) in good places (Dalmatian Coast, Istria). Try finding any.

cru – (literally 'growth') designating both a particularly favoured site (Premier Cru) in a particular village, or the best site(s) (Grand Cru) and the wine made from grapes grown there. In Bordeaux there are five numbered levels, translating as 'first' to 'fifth' growths, with cru Bourgeois a consolation level beneath for the rest of us.

Cuba Libre – (literally, 'free cuba') rum and coke. Ice necessary but wedge of lime optional. ¡Viva!

cuvée – fugitive French term referring to a particular batch of wine and which can vary from meaningless ('Cuvée du Patron') to semi-specific ('Tête de Cuvée' – in theory, the best bottling of a particular wine) to the gamble-worthy (those with a proper name, i.e. 'Cuvée Joséphine Bloggs' often done in *hommage*, perhaps to a former winemaker, so at least the producer thinks it's good).

Cyprus – strangely chose to chuck nearly 3,000 years of documented wine-producing history (and a lot before that) out of the window in favour of producing tankers full of rubbish fortified wine called 'Cyprus sherry' – a park-bench classic of the 1960s and 1970s. Even that market has a bottom, and it was exposed when the EEC, or whatever it was then, told them they couldn't call it sherry any more. So they flogged it in concentrated form to us for the making of even more debased, so-called 'British Wine'. Emva Cream?

It's a long way back from oblivion but why haven't they come up with more decent, solid, bistro reds like Othello, which has been around for the thirty years since I first enjoyed it? But efforts *are* being made, winemakers are flying, and Commandaria, the ancient, oxidised, dried-grape sweet wine, made from Xynisteri and enjoyed by Richard the Lionheart on his way to (or from, I forget) the Crusades, is the flagship.

Czech Republic beer – in 1842, when the citizenry of Plzeň in Bohemia had a whip-round to pay Bavarian Josef Groll to come up with a style of beer to compete with the clear 'Vienna style' that was going down such a treat everywhere else, they had no idea what was about to kick off. The tidal wave of clear, golden pilsener (aka pilsner, pils and, of course, lager) runs unabated around the world, although Star Bev-owned Ostravar and Staropramen prove that quantity and quality are not always at odds. If all of it were as good as Pilsner Urquell (the Ur – original – pilsener, still brewed at the Plzeňský Prazdroj brewery) and Budvar (from neighbouring town České Budějovice – formerly known as Budweis – hence the Budweiser name and the protracted legal dispute with the other Budweiser) I'd be a happy man. These – not that Danish nonsense – are 'probably the best lagers in the world' although Gambrinus, Herold, Krušovice, Radegast, U Fleků (the oldest brewery in Prague, from 1499, and only sold there – how about that for an excuse?) and Žatec would dispute that . . . if only beers could talk.

demi-sec distillation dolcetto dornfelder drunkenness dubonnet cocktail durella durif daïquiri demi-sec distillation dolcetto dornfelder drunkenness dubonnet cocktail durella durif daïquiri demi-sec distillation dolcetto

daïquiri demi-sec distillation dolcetto dornfelder drunkenness dubonnet cocktail durella durif

D

Daïquiri – five parts light rum to two parts lime juice and simple syrup to taste shaken with ice and slipped into something more comfortable (or strained into a cocktail glass).

Dalmore, The – Highland distillery (north of Inverness) owned by India's United Breweries via their Whyte & Mackay subsidiary – I nearly fell off my chair when I spelled it Daalmore by mistake. In 2005 one of a dozen bottles of a blend of five vintages from 1868 to 1939 sold at auction for £32,000.

demi-sec – dodgy term meaning literally 'half dry' but covering wide-ranging degrees of sweetness in wine, though the one thing it won't be is dry.

deterioration of wine – the problem of the half-finished bottle is one that exercises many people and although the simple solution is never to countenance such a thing as a half-finished bottle, there are some strategies.

The age of the wine is the key to the speed of the decline and although ancient Madeiras seem to be indestructible (and fortified wines in general last well once opened – a few days, weeks even for younger wines, but not for old vintage ports, which can die overnight), that doesn't get us very far in the real world.

Dry white wines – especially if more than a couple of years old – tend to deteriorate quite rapidly and should be drunk within a day or two while sweeter wines are much slower to go off – most fully sweet ones are happy for up to a week. A lot of big New World-style reds can keep improving for 24 hours or more (even if left entirely unstopped) and keeping for two or three days is usually no problem. Frailer elderly reds are the most vulnerable (although most posh bottles will be polished off on the night in the natural order of things).

The same oxygen which lets a wine 'breathe' will ultimately overwhelm it and there are various ways to protect wine from it. I did an experiment to preserve some venerable (in fact, declining but still delicious) claret (a wag christened it 'Helen Mirren') overnight using, respectively, a Vacuvin (which pumps most of the air out); an inert gas preserver (which you spray in to displace the oxygen on the surface of the wine) and the 'put-it-in-a-smaller-bottle' method. The remainder I simply re-corked and left for nature to take its course. It did, while the others were fine.

distillation – for our purposes, the separation of the alcohol from some of the water in a previously fermented liquid by means of heating to the point of evaporation, and collection by inducing condensation through cooling. Discovered by the Babylonians, the Chinese or – for all I care – the Bay City Rollers but perfected in eighth-century Araby with the invention of the *al-ambiq* (alembic, or long-necked pot still) and subsequently raised to the form of art in the cold, Celtic and Nordic fringes of Europe.

Essentially the same method – often referred to as small-batch distillation and requiring great skill and judgement on the part of the still master – remains in use for producing many premium spirits. Large-scale distillation became possible thanks to Irishman Aeneas Coffey's invention of the column, or continuous, still. The names explain the process.

D

Dolcetto – joyful red-wine grape, the low-acidity 'little sweetie' produces the lighter (although not always in colour), young-drinking wines, often with bitter-cherry and almond notes, of north-western Italy's Piedmont region, most notably in the Dolcetto d'Alba DOC.

drunkenness – the physical and mental state resulting from intoxication through alcohol – i.e. consumption of ethanol at a faster rate than the individual is able to metabolise (approximately one 10ml unit per hour). Symptoms may include slurred speech, blurred or beer-goggled vision, impaired balance and coordination, confusion and disinhibition.

dry martini – whole books have been written on the subject (when surely the monograph is the appropriate form?) but all that really needs to be said is that a dash of vermouth (even Cinzano in a pinch) is stirred with 6cl of good gin and some ice, strained into a chilled cocktail glass and garnished with a plain green olive or a twist of lemon peel. The 'dirty' version disgustingly adds a teaspoon of the brine from the olives. All the variants should be treated with scorn (except the ones listed in this book).

Dubonnet Cocktail – two parts gin to one part Dubonnet (see vermouth p. 397) stirred with ice and strained in to a tacky plastic cocktail glass.

Doesn't sound like much, but caused havoc in the 1970s. One of the Queen's favourites.

Dutch beer – as well you might be with Heineken (who also own Amstel) and Grolsch on your doorstep, Holland is hooked on the pilsener style, but microbrew action abounds there, albeit very micro indeed. Try beers from: Arcense Stoombierbouwerij/Jan Hertog, Budels, Browerij de Bekeerde Suster, de 3 Horne, de Hemel, de Molen, de Prael, de Schans, Jopen, de Koningshoeven, Lindeboom, Mommeriete, Sint Christoffel, and SNAB, an acronym that stands for the North Holland Alternative Beer Brewers' Foundation.

erbaluce espresso martini eau-de-vie egg nog eighteenth

eau-de-vie egg nog eighteenth amendment English wine espresso martinieau-de-vie egg nog

erbaluce espresso martini eau-de-vie egg nog

English wine erbaluce espresso martini eau-de-vie egg nog

Eastern European beer – across Europe and out into the wide world, most of the best-known names have been swallowed by Big Beercos – people are thirsty and profits are high – but these Big Beercos still produce a few good beers: Starbev own Croatia's Zagrebačka Pivovara and Serbia's Apatinska Pivara – the biggest brewer in the Balkans; Carlsberg are big-swinging in the Baltic with Russia's Baltika, Estonia's Saku Õlletehase, Latvia's Aldaris – and in Lithuania (where the names sound like STDs, with Švyturys-Utenos Alus – though thankfully the only nasty thing about a case of their Stipriausias is the 8% abv). MillerCoors have Hungary's Dreher and Slovakia's Topvar; Heineken have Romania's Brau-Union and Slovakia's Zlatý Bažant.

Of the squillions more independents a few notable ones (either for having eluded the clutches of Big Beer or for making good beer are Turkey's Efes, Ukraine's Obolon (who ought to change the name of their witbier, now called Bile), Bosnia and Herzegovina's Banjaluka Nektar; Cyprus's Keo; Estonia's A Le Coq. And has anyone tried Korca? It's from Albania.

eau de vie – (aka schnapps, slivovitz) a spiritous liquor, typically 40% abv, characterised by its distillation from fermented fruit pulp rather than as a neutral spirit flavoured with the fruit and sweetened, as with liqueurs, and, counter-intuitively, tasting less of their origins than liqueurs. Most are not oak-aged and are therefore colourless and those made from grapes are by convention usually excluded from the category, except for Pomace brandies (aka marc or grappa). Some particular eaux de vie have generic names such as Kirsch for cherries, Framboise for raspberries, Mirabelle for plums, Poire William(s) for pears. Alsace specialises in them.

An old friend bet the landlord of our local that he could find a bottle of Eau de Vie de Viper, in which a live adder is introduced to the bottle of spirit with the idea that the venom it spits as it struggles to avoid its fate will add an extra dimension. He did (in Brasparts, in the wild west of Brittany) but it didn't.

Eggnog – one egg to two parts each of light rum and brandy, three of single cream and simple syrup to taste, shaken with ice, strained into a highball glass and finished with a sprinkle of nutmeg. Omitting the cream makes it an Egg Flip. Just say 'nog' to eggnog.

18th amendment – on 16 January 1919, Amendment XVIII to the Constitution of the United States of America established Prohibition (and its by-product, the speakeasy).

English wine – English winemakers have worked it out: fizz is what they can compete with on the world stage and plantings of the Champagne grapes Pinot Noir, Pinot Meunier and Chardonnay now account for half of the total acreage under vine. The Kimmeridge limestone basin – the other end of which pops up in Chablis – is the key to it all, apparently, but reports that land-hungry Champagne growers have been eyeing up south-coast sites are unsubstantiated. The best producers such as Breaky Bottom [3], Camel Valley [2], Chapel Down [1], Denbies [1], Nyetimber [3] (the breakthrough Champagne-style wine and still one of the best), Ridge View [3] and Three Choirs [1] have all turned their hands to sparkling wines, often with first-class results.

For still whites, Madeleine Angevine and Bacchus are establishing themselves as the varieties best suited for making crisp, aromatic wines, although Seyval Blanc is still the most widely planted variety and early ripening Huxelrebe shows promise (Frome Valley [1]). 'Mad Angy' is grown as far north as Yorkshire (it ripens early . . . very early – Leventhorpe [1]), has a flouncy, floral character and will need sharp elbows not to be upstaged by the increasingly popular Bacchus, which is all about Sauvignon Blanc-style green things: nettles, gooseberries, newly mown grass and a chalky minerality that conjures Dover's white cliffs (cue the Elgar).

Reds will probably never catch up, given the climate, but people struggle on with Pinot Noir (Bolney [2]), such is its allure although promise has also been shown by Dornfelder and the new (1989) 'interspecific hybrid' (whatever that means) called Regent. If growers can pull their socks up on the business side of things (and somehow squeeze prices down for a bit) the future looks promising.

espresso martini – equal parts cold espresso coffee, Kahlua, white crème de cacao and vodka shaken with ice and strained into a cocktail glass. Not all new cocktails are tricksy rubbish.

fair trade wine falanghina faults in wine fer fermentation fernão pires fiano fino flying wine makers folle blanche food and wine matching fortified

french wine frappato freisa friulano fruit wine

F

Fairtrade wine – was something of a laggard compared to coffee, bananas and chocolate but is catching up fast. It may seem ironic that most is sold by big business – the supermarkets and the high-street multiples – and the whole thing might seem a form of tokenism, another ethical-ecological box for the corporations to tick. BUT what most of these grass-roots projects need in order to thrive is high-volume sales and economies of scale in a ruthlessly competitive wine market. Only the big retailers can guarantee the kind of numbers they need; meanwhile, those retailers are very well aware that fair trade has been, after rosé, one of a small number of growth areas.

In the UK, the Co-op has taken the lead giving double the usual forty to fifty pence per case that typically goes to local initiatives. It may not seem much, but their quid goes a lot further in rural Chile or South Africa than it does at home. On the whole, fair-trade wines compare favourably to 'conventional' wines in similar price brackets and those made from the traditional grape varieties – Torrontés, Malbec and Bonarda from Argentina, Carmeñere from Chile, and Cinsault from South Africa – can be an excellent opportunity to try a glass or two of something new. Try these for starters: Du Toitskloof, Fairhills, Ormer Bay, La Riojana, Los Robles, Stellar, Thandi.

It's important that mainstream producers recognise the power they themselves have to improve the lives of thousands of people by direct means. One South African winemaker gave me the example of being at a vineyard and seeing that the only toilet in the men's dormitory was blocked. He told the foreman to get it fixed by the time he came back the next day or he wouldn't buy their grapes. Guess what? It was fixed.

faults in wine – the archetypal, cut-and-dried, 'Waiter, this bottle is corked!' situation arises quite infrequently. What does arise frequently – very frequently according to estimates that between two and five per cent of cork-sealed bottles are affected – is, in variable degrees, cork taint. It can vary from the minor, what I call 'bottle fart', which is banished by the pouring of a glass or two and the circulation of a little fresh air, to the major – a nagging, dull, dusty bitterness that, halfway through the bottle, has you wishing you'd done that HM Bateman thing in the first place and been done with it.

Most faults are to do with mould of one kind or another, be it in the cork or in the wine and that's the type of smell to be on the alert for – and faults reveal themselves to the nose far more readily than to the tongue. Corks are responsible for more bad bottles than everything else put together times a squillion – assuming, obviously, that the stuff was going to be any good in the first place. To an extent, the point is that if your nose tells you it ain't right then send, or take, it back. (Probably not a good moment to mention that the first ever time I tried a really oaky Rioja, I sent two bottles back before they told me that was what it was supposed to be like. But, hey, I was young.)

fermentation – the sort we're interested in involves the digestion of carbohydrates (sugars) by certain yeasts, which then belch carbon dioxide and, crucially, pee out ethanol. God bless 'em entirely.

flying winemakers – when hyperactive Penedès winemaker Miguel Torres first realised in 1978 that buying a vineyard in Chile would solve his problem of what to do in the winter, he unwittingly started a revolution. British merchant Tony Laithwaite – the first and still biggest mail-order merchant – took up the baton (and coined the phrase) in the late 1980s by zapping seasonally under-employed Aussie grape-jockeys all over the place a few years later. Surely the migration of winemakers around the world would have happened anyway, but it had to start somewhere.

food and wine matching – people get nervous on the subject, but there's really no cause for alarm. There are clangers to be dropped, sure, but you weren't about to pour a big red wine with those oysters, were you? Or a spritzy little flibbertigibbet of a Moscato d'Asti with the venison, cooked rare?

It is useful to get to grips with the idea of a wine's 'body' or 'weight', which seems to be the way ahead. And we are talking about, literally, the weight here – how 'big' or heavy a wine is depends on the amount of solid matter held in suspension and it's the key to working out the kind of food it'll go best with or what might overwhelm it. You can see it readily enough – a viscous, full-bodied wine swirls more slowly round the glass and clings to the sides. The 'legs' that run down the inside are thicker and slower-moving in a big wine. And where there is body, in general, there is flavour.

The principle is that the 'bigger' the food – a lot of which comes down to sauces and how rich they are – the bigger the wine, and for my money this is more important even than colour. Full-bodied whites from the Rhône or Alsace can be bigger than light reds from Beaujolais or the Loire and they can hold their own with stronger flavours and richer textures. A huge improvement in the quality of rosé wines – perhaps the first truly global winemaking trend – puts a welcome new card on the table and it's no longer only wines from Tavel and Bandol that have the body to go with serious food instead of just salads and picnics.

Sometimes, unlikely matches are made in heaven – fortified wines, especially those that have been allowed to oxidise as well, like dry Marsala and Madeira, have an amazing affinity with 'umami' flavours, not just soy, but all sorts of stock-based sauces as well as prosciutto and bacon, Parmesan cheese and pretty much anything that's been caramelised.

Pudding wines are a fairly straightforward business but I'm prepared to die in the attempt to find one of those perfect matches. The neglect of the sweeter styles of Champagne is a crime and the problem of what to drink with chocolate puddings has been a hard nut to crack – but has met its match, for my taste anyway, in sweet black Muscat.

Acidity and sweetness are almost as important as body. The good burghers of Alsace, who started experimenting with late harvesting some of their grapes in the Middle Ages, presumably didn't cook much with galangal and lemon grass, coconut milk and fish sauce but their winemaking had similarities with Thai cooking: the burghers, by letting their grapes ripen to maximum sweetness, set up a beguiling balancing act between the sweetness and the natural acidity of the fruit, between sugars and sharpness. The same process is at work when a chef mixes opposing flavours by adding both palm sugar and rice wine, say, or coconut milk and fish sauce to a dish. A wine that also has both elements would be an ideal complement and Gewürztraminer, with its additional spicy aspect, has the greatest affinity with oriental food.

I've never been sure how anybody's tastebuds survived those early food-and-wine matching blind alleys – the wine'n'cheese parties of the seventies. All those soft cheeses – Bries and Camemberts – with their ammoniac flavours clashing horribly with all that red Château Chunder? Now I know that on the rare occasions when the cheese actually tasted of anything, the flavour was immediately swamped by the rasping 'flavours' of the rot-gut. There *are* cheese matches made in heaven – Sauvignon Blanc and soft goat's cheese; sweet wines and blue cheese – but we didn't know about things like that back then.

fortified wines – are wines in which the fermentation process is stopped at some point by the addition of grape spirit which, at around ninety per cent alcohol, would stop pretty much anything in its tracks. This arrested development usually preserves some of the sweetness of the fruit. Port, Australia's liqueur Muscats and the *vins doux naturels* of southern France (*naturel* in quite what sense I've never been sure, given the foregoing) are all fortified with this in mind. The various types of mistelle and *vins de liqueur* are fortified before fermentation begins in order to preserve all the sweetness of the grape must; in sherry and Madeira the process takes place near the end of fermentation. Where sweetness is present in some styles of these, it is the result of adding a mistelle-like wine during blending so it comes full circle. Alcohol content of fortified wines is generally between 16–20% abv.

French beer – the major brewers of anonymous but refreshing *bière blonde* (Fischer, Kanterbräu, Kronenbourg, Pelforth, '33' and the like) all long ago surrendered to Big Beer (mainly to Heineken and Carlsberg) but some regional specialities are hanging in there, notably around Lille for *bière de garde* – ales to be 'kept' (until the summer when it is more difficult to brew) often in cork-sealed bottles in damp, mouldy cellars that transmit something of their mushroomy character to the beer. Try: Jenlain; Ch'ti; La Choulette; Gavroche. Brittany is where the microbrewers are mushrooming. Look for Deux Rivières or Lancelot.

French wine – we barbarous Anglo-Saxons are fortunate to share the richest language – we have 'scuttle' and 'scutter' and 'scurry' in case 'skitter' isn't quite 'scattery' enough. We've got 'glimmer' and 'glisten' (as well as 'glister') in case 'glitter' is just a bit too 'glitzy'. But when it comes to booze you've just got to hand it to the frogs – they've got Bouzy and Bouzeron as well as Buzet and Buxy and there's every bit as much nuance in their wines as in our words. In Gaillac, Pauillac, Marcillac and Cadillac, France has more of its acres (not to mention in Monbazillac) under vines than anywhere except Spain and is the world's biggest producer.

One of the reasons for my confirmed Francophilia is that there's no style of wine they don't make. The fact that France is so 'provincial' – in a positive sense – means that the same benefit is often to be had in microcosm within individual regions. Your average Frenchman expects to be locally provided for from the fizz and apéritifs through whites, rosés and reds of all kinds to the stickies (and with something spiritous at the end, just to aid the digestion) and, in general he gets it, be he steaming in a Strasbourg Weinstube or roasting on an Irouléguy terrace. This is obviously to his very great advantage (not least in terms of price), but not necessarily to ours. He knows what to expect and where it comes from and that's what he calls it. Most often he doesn't know (and doesn't care) what grapes it is made from.

France devised the first comprehensive appellation contrôlée (AC) system for his benefit – so that what he got was what he thought he was going to get – and not for telling us what's what. Here's the rub: *the way into understanding French wine is through places first and grapes second.*

Their exports were a thumping twenty per cent down in 2009 but there is upside too – the quality being offered by enterprising brands (La Différence) and the best of the big regional producers – be they private (Gérard Bertrand, Paul Mas, Laurent Miquel, Skalli) or cooperative (Blason de Bourgogne, Mont Tauch, Plaimont) – is at an all-time high.

Bordeaux

If France is home, Bordeaux is the hearth. Let other wine-producing places have their claims to this and that but let there be no doubt that Bordeaux is the world's foremost wine region. A glance at any fine wine-broker's list will confirm that this region produces as many of the most valued wines as everywhere else combined – and then some.

It's not surprising that the British have always had a fondness for claret – the whole region was under English rule from 1152 when Eleanor of Aquitaine took up with the soon-to-be Henry II. The deals that were done then to the advantage of *rosbif* importers kept us in the driving seat long after 300 years of English rule ended and to this day there are Brits involved in all aspects of the Bordeaux trade.

Bordeaux is vast: 300,000 acres farmed by 18,000 individual growers making, in a big year, almost a billion bottles in fully '57 varieties' (57 different appellations, anyway). Only Languedoc-Roussillon makes more. The basic appellation, AC Bordeaux (Berry's Good Ordinary claret [1], Calvet [1], Fontenille [1], Fougère La Noble [1], Gontrie [1], Grand Bateau [1], Grand Jean [1], Nicot [1], Terre Burdigala [1]) covers every drop in every bottle of supermarket claret and most of the 5,000 (or is it 10,000 – nobody seems to know) '*petits châteaux*', some of which can be excellent value. Bordeaux Supérieur (des Antonins [1], d'Argadens [1], Beau Rivage [1], Cabos Lauduc [1], Mahon Laville [2], Saint-Jacques [2], Méaume [1], Majureau-Sercillan [1] is generally a notch up and if the label mentions the district of production (Médoc or Saint Émilion, for example) it's on the next rung. Mention of a village (especially Pauillac, Saint Julien, Saint Estèphe and Margaux in the Médoc) takes us up another step. Above this level, things diverge between the different classifications of the left and right banks of the Gironde river, which divides the region.

On the left, the 250 *Cru Bourgeois* châteaux are being re-jigged and now are assessed annually for their fitness to use the term. The top-two tiers of '*exceptionnel*' and '*supérieur*' have been done away with. The very top rung of the five dozen, five-tier *cru classé* (classed-growth) properties, although established in 1855 – and based on the value of their land – is still a broadly accurate guide to quality and price. The five first-growth châteaux are: Latour [3], Lafite-Rothschild [3], Mouton-Rothschild [3], Margaux [3] and Haut-Brion [3]. Unofficially, the right-bank châteaux Cheval Blanc [3], Ausone [3], Pétrus [3] and d'Yquem [3], in Sauternes, are in the same bracket. Prices have rocketed recently, too, partly due to demand from China.

Below this tier, and within the fourteen second-growths (not to be confused with 'second wines' – see p. 343), the informal grouping of 'super seconds' comprises: Cos d'Estournel, Ducru-Beaucaillon: Léoville Barton; Léoville Las Cases; Montrose; the two Pichon-Longuevilles – Baron and Comtesse de Lalande – and, although neither is in fact a second growth, Palmer (a third growth) and La Mission Haut-Brion can sometimes be of comparable quality to the firsts and offer relatively (and I mean relatively) good value.

There are other outperformers such as Calon Ségur, Giscours and Langoa Barton among the fourteen third growths, as among the ten fourth growths (such as Beychevelle, Branaire-Ducru, Duhart-Milon and Talbot) and, especially encouraging value-wise, almost all of the eighteen fifth growths, but in particular Batailley, Clerc Milon, Grand-Puy-Lacoste, Haut-Bages-Libéral, Haut Batailley, Lynch-Bages, Pédesclaux, Pontet-Canet and du Tertre.

On the Right Bank of the Gironde the classification is a) more straightforward; b) largely free of meaning below the top levels; and c) in chaos, since an attempt to reorganise it in 2006 has been declared illegal and they've more or less gone back to the old version. Basically, there's a top rank of just two *premiers grands crus classés* 'A' (Ausone and Cheval Blanc), a second tier of eleven class 'B', fifty-five *grands crus classés* of variable quality and finally hundreds and hundreds of *grand crus* that include some excellent wines but many more real stinkers.

Nearby, on the relatively flat and less regulated playing field of Pomerol a small group of *microcuvée* winemakers (aka *garagistes* – that's all the space they need) have chosen to go their own way and hope to sell their intense, New World styles as a result of demand rather than denomination. The top few are among the most expensive wines of all (Lafleur, Le Pin).

Thankfully, as far as grapes are concerned it's all rather more simple. All wines are blends but Cabernet Sauvignon is king in the Médoc, usually blended with Merlot, which rules on the Right Bank where it is itself usually blended with Cabernet Franc. On both sides of the river supporting roles are played by Malbec and Petit Verdot, which are used in the final blend to add complexity – and it's the complexity of its wines that makes Bordeaux what it is.

In terms of styles, claret straightforwardly is any red wine produced anywhere in the Bordeaux region although, as an English term, you don't very often see it on labels. It seems we pinched the word from the Spanish, whose own red wines, called *tinto* (meaning ink), were *so* inky-dark that they used their name for rosé – *clarete* – to describe their French neighbours' lighter style of reds. That's one story, the other is that today's *clairet* style – little-exported wines that are a bit too red to be rosé and a bit too rosé to be red – is thought to be much like the original wines that those Plantagenets took such a shine to.

Whites made from Semillon and Sauvignon Blanc run the full range of styles from austere, elegant, full-bodied dry wines, of which the best are world-class and the neglected treasures of the region, to the world's finest sweet wines from Sauternes and Barsac.

There is a rather dynastic feel (let's not use the word 'feudal', – it seems to have such negative connotations nowadays) to the Bordeaux trade. The châteaux-owning classes – including high-profile names like those of the Lurton, Rothschild, Thienpont, Barton, Cazes and Moueix families – are, as one might expect, rather grand. Some of them, the latter two, for example, started out as merchants or *négociants* like the Cordier [2], Dourthe [1], and Sichel [1] families. The merchant trade is still important – there are still over 500 and newer ones like Yvon Mau and Millésima can still make an impact. Some of the older names are concentrating on building brands – traditionally (as it were) an area of weakness in Bordeaux and France generally, even though Mouton Cadet (probably the first wine I sipped – the Réserve wines are good) and Piat d'Or (which the French, in fact, abhor) were ground-breakers.

***GET A HANDLE**

> BORDEAUX REMAINS THE MOST PRESTIGIOUS NAME IN WINE AND CONTINUING IMPROVEMENTS AT ALL LEVELS FOR GRAND, COMPLEX, CABERNET SAUVIGNON- AND MERLOT-BASED REDS (AND NOT FORGETTING SOME OF THE BEST – SWEET, DRY AND UNDERVALUED – WHITES) WILL KEEP IT THAT WAY.

Left Bank

Northern Médoc: The flat, northernmost area of the Left Bank – formerly the 'Bas Médoc' – has no great names but makes up for it with great value which, as elsewhere in Bordeaux, is often to be found in the margins and among the *Crus Bourgeois* and *petits châteaux* such as Charmail 3, Goulée 3, Le Grand Sigognac 2, Greysac 2, Labadie 2, Loudenne 2, Les Ormes Sorbet 2, Potensac 3, Patache d'Aux 2, Rousseau de Sipian 2, Soudars 3, La Tour de By 3, La Tour Haut Caussan 3, La Tour Saint-Bonnet 2, Verdignan 3.

Saint Estèphe: A few miles south, the Haut-Médoc – the Sunset Strip, the Golden Mile (or thirty) – begins in the commune of Saint Estèphe, considered the weakest of the area's four great villages but not for the nature of the wines, which are tough, tannic and inky and take ages to soften (or, often, even be drinkable). Nonetheless, Saint Estèphe is home to two of the 'super seconds' mentioned earlier: Cos 3, as it's known – and 'coss' as it's pronounced – and

Montrose [3]; other outperformers include Calon Ségur [3], Lafon Rochet [3] and the improving Cos Labory among the *cru classés*. The bourgeois drinker is especially well catered for here with Haut-Marbuzet [3], Les Ormes de Pez [3], Phélan Ségur [3], le Boscq [3], Cissac [2], Clauzet [3], le Crock [3], de Pez [3], Lilian Ladouys [3], Meyney [3] and Tronquoy-Lalande [3]. Andron Blanquet [3] and Haut Beauséjour [3] step liveliest of the NCOs and Serilhan [3] and Sociando-Mallet [3] are 'other wines' to seek out.

Pauillac: Pauillac is the centre of the wine universe. It looks more like Lee-on-Solent and it's rather top-heavy, what with the three first growths and two Pichon super seconds mentioned above. Frankly, there's not much else except Duhart-Milon [3] until you start slumming it with those outperforming fifth growths. The others – all good – are d'Armailhac [3], Croizet Bages [3], Grand-Puy-Ducasse [3] and Lynch-Moussas [3]. What are the wines like? Well, there might be some of that toasty, cedar cigar-box nonsense, and lots of sweetly simmered black fruits (maybe garlanded round with playful violets) and possibly some deeper, spicily decaying things. Should you be interested, the relatively few local bourgeois efforts of the likes of Fontesteau [3], Liversan [2], Peyrabon [2], Pibran [3] or Ramage La Batisse [2] shine a light for we mere mortals while Bernadotte [2] and Fonbadet [3] are beacons amongst the petits châteaux.

Saint Julien: In Saint Julien, if you see any of the words 'Léoville', 'Ducru' or 'Barton' on a label it will be a) fabulous, and b) expensive, but thankfully not *always* fabulously expensive. Other conjurable names are our outperforming fourths (Beychevelle [3], Talbot [3]) as well as Gruaud-Larose [3], Lagrange [3] and St-Pierre [3]. There's little room left for the bourgeoisie – Devise d'Ardilley [2], Glana [3], Larose

Trintaudon 2, Moulin de la Rose 3 and among the ACs Gloria 3, Hortevie 3 and Lalande-Borie 3 make the typically rich, balanced style.

Inland are a few classed growths (Belgrave 3, Camensac 3, La Tour Carnet 3) then a cluster of bourgeois values on the way (Caronne Sainte Gemme 3, de Lamarque 3, Lamothe Bergeron 3, Lanessan 3, Malescasse 3, Tour du Haut Moulin 3) to Moulis-en-Médoc (Chasse Spleen 3, Citran 3, Gressier-Grand-Poujeaux 3, Poujeaux 3, Maucaillou 3) and Listrac-Médoc (Clarke 3, Fonréaud 2, Fourcas-Dupré 2, Fourcas-Hosten 2, Peyre-Lebade 3, Saransot-Dupré 2). Other wines to find: D'Avensan 2, Beaumont 2, Semonlon 2.

Margaux: Before the Médoc hits the buffers at Bordeaux we must recite the roll of honour of the poised-and-perfumed plethora of Margaux-classed growths, which account for over a third of the total: second growths Rauzan-Ségla 3, Durfort-Vivens 3, Lascombes 3, Brane-Cantenac 3; thirds Palmer 3, Kirwan 3, d'Issan 3, Giscours 3, Malescot St-Exupéry 3, Boyd-Cantenac 3, Cantenac-Brown 3, Desmirail 3, Ferrière 3, outlying La Lagune 3, obscure, improving Marquis d'Alesme Becker 3 and laggardly Rauzan-Gassies 3; fourths Prieuré Lichine 3, Marquis-de-Terme 3 and Pouget 3; fifths du Tertre 3, Dauzac 3 and neighbouring Cantemerle 3. Labégorce-Zédé 3 and Siran 3 are exceptional among the *crus bourgeois*, which is to take nothing away from d'Agassac 3, d'Angludet 3, d'Arsac 3, Cambon La Pelouse 2, La Galiane 3, La Gurgue 3, Martinens 3, Monbrison 3, Paveil de Luze 3, Sénéjac 2, Tour de Mons 3 and AC Margaux Canuet 3.

Other weapons in the struggle for value: the 'second wines' of some of the best châteaux are made from the younger vines and vats that are not quite up to scratch for the *grand vin*, some of which are very good and sometimes – in lesser vintages when maybe smaller quantities of the big 'un are made – very good value. Some consistent performers (with the name of the Château in brackets where it's not obvious) are (all 3): Forts de Latour, Carruades de Lafite, Alter Ego de Palmer, Reserve de Léoville Barton, Pagodes de Cos, Dame de Montrose, Connétable (Talbot), Sarget Larose (Gruaud Larose), Lacoste-Borie (Grand Puy Lacoste), Blason de l'Evangile, Les Fiefs de Lagrange, Moulin Richie (Léoville Poyferré), Haut Bages Averous (Lynch Bages), Moulin de la Lagune, Moulin d'Angludet, Clos du Marquis (Léoville-las-Cases). Meanwhile, the *grand vins* themselves can be great value in lesser years; these people don't make dull wine. In the Médoc, as in Bordeaux as a whole, merchants' regional and village bottlings are often made by leading producers and are a good introduction.

Graves: Graves, the cradle of claret, is named for the gravel that permeates not only its soil but also the flavours of its self-possessed, Cabernet-based reds and oak-aged Sauvignon Blanc/Semillon-blended whites, which, though scarcer, are often even better. Luckily, the wines of both colours from the better producers, including those in the surrounding Cérons AC (Archambeau 2, Chantegrive 2, Clos Floridène 2, Du Seuil 2, La Garde 3, Gaubert 3, des Gravières 2, Mayne d'Imbert 2, Mouras 2, Respide 2, Trebiac 2, Villa Bel Air 2) have much in common with their very posh neighbours in the Pessac-Léognan appellation that emerges from the southern suburbs of Bordeaux and which declared independence in 1987 within the rather wishy-washy appellation system (Bouscaut 3 – in the care of Sophie Lurton, whose uncle André is the biggest mover and shaker in the area; Brown 3; Carbonnieux 3; Cardaillan 2; Les Carmes Haut-Brion 3; Couhins-Lurton 2 (half the 2007 red was the first-ever classed-growth to be bottled under screwtop, but that wasn't the half that was for sale in France); Dom de Chevalier 3; de Cruzeau 3; de Fieuzal 3; Haut Bailly 3; Haut-Brion 3; Lafont-Menaut 3; Larrivet-Haut-Brion 3; Latour Martillac 3; La Louvière 3; Malartic Lagravière 3; La Mission-Haut-Brion 3 and sister white Laville-Haut-Brion 3; Pape-Clément 3; Pique-Caillou 2; Pontac Monplaisir 2; and Smith-Haut-Lafitte 3).

Quite a few of the formerly potless neighbours in the vast Entre-Deux-Mers region (literally 'between two seas' but in this case between two rivers, the Garonne and the Dordogne) have looked over the fence and got their acts together for their whites, the reds being AC Bordeaux or supérieur (Bonnet 1, Fontenille 1, Marjosse 2, Reignac 2, Reynier 1, Sainte Marie 1, Thieuley 2, Tour de Mirambeau 2, Turcaud 2). At the far eastern end, little Sainte-Foy quietly goes about its business of making solid reds. Try Capelle 1 or Parenchère 2.

In the best Sauternes (including the next-door village of Barsac), shrivelled, noble rot-, or botrytis-affected grapes are picked a few at a time over several weeks from vines so heavily pruned that each produces only a couple of glasses of wine and, if the weather doesn't cooperate, none at all. And people think the unctuous, honey-gold nectar that results is *expensive*? Pish-tosh. Pay up and look big – these are the greatest sweet wines in the world and fantastic value (prices indicated are for half bottles). Start sampling some of these: d'Arche 3; Bastor Lamontagne 3; Cantegril 2; Climens 3; Coutet 3; Doisy Daene 3; Doisy-Dubroca 3; Doisy-Vedrines 2; de Fargues 3; Filhot 2; Gilette 3; Guiraud 3; Lafaurie-Peyraguey 3; Laville 2; Liot 2; de Malle 2; Nairac 3; de La Peyre 2; Raymond-Lafon 3; Rabaud-Promis 3; Rayne-Vigneau 3; Rieusse 3; Sigalas-Rabaud 3; Suduiraut 3; Tour Blanche 3; and d'Yquem 3, greatest of them all.

Right Bank

Across the river to the Right Bank and the Premières Côtes de Bordeaux (Bertrande [2], Haut Gaudin [2], Haut Rian [1], Lezongars [2], Reynon [2]), which includes Cadillac (Fayau [1]). Côtes de Castillon (Domaine de l'A [3], Belcier [2], Brisson [2], la Gasparde [2], Lideyre [2], Manoir du Gravoux [2], Pitray [1], Sainte Colombe [2]), Premières Côtes de Blaye (Peyredoulle [2], Segonzac [1]) and Côtes de Francs (de Francs [2], Marsau [2], Puygueraud [2]) have joined up to form a new, and not very confusing, appellation of Côtes de Bordeaux with effect from the 2008 vintage.

Hereabouts Loupiac (Loupiac-Gaudiet [2], Dom du Noble [2], Ricaud [1]) and Sainte-Croix-du-Mont (Loubens [2], la Rame [2]) are good value for sumptuous, but straightforward, sweet whites. The Côtes de Bourg (Civrac [2], Le Monastère [1], and especially Roc de Cambes [3]), bucolic Fronsac (Dalem [3], de la Dauphine [3], Haut Lariveau [3], Mayne Vieil [2], Moulin-Haut-Laroque [2], de la Rivière [2], La Vieille Cure [2]) and its fancier sub-division Canon-Fronsac (Cassagne Haut-Canon [3], Gaby [3], Gazin [3], du Pavillon [2]) have, like so many of the 'lesser' Bordeaux regions, seen a major upturn in quality – the results are not *raffiné* but they're satisfyingly good value.

Pomerol is the New World, the Napa of the Old World. It even looks like it – the wineries maybe called châteaux but they're not and it's hard to tell them apart – some say the same of the wines, young-drinking merlots that taste like the New World and go for ripeness and richness and opulence over finesse. Be careful with the lovely names, too, they also seem to blend into one another and there's no fuddy-duddy classification here – confounding Lafleur with La Fleur-Pétrus will cost dear. These are the big names (look in vain for less than a three-bottle rating): Beauregard; Bonalgue; Le

Bon Pasteur; Bourgneuf-Vayron; Certan de May; Clinet; Clos l'Eglise; La Conseillante; Croix du Casse; Croix de Gay; Dom de l'Eglise; L'Eglise-Clinet; L'Enclos; l'Evangile; Feytit Clinet; La Fleur-de-Gay; La Fleur-Pétrus; Le Gay; Gombaude Guillot; La Grave à Pomerol; Hosanna; Lafleur; Lafleur Gazin; Latour-à-Pomerol; Mazeyres; Mouline; Nenin; Petit Village; Pétrus; Le Pin; Plince; La Pointe; Rouget; Taillefer; Trotanoy; and Vieux Chateau Certan.

Lalande-de-Pomerol sits satisfyingly between Pomerol and Saint Émilion in style and is becoming a haven for refugees from Pomerol requiring sticker-shock therapy at least for now. Venture here with: L'Ancien 3; des Annereaux 2; Croix des Moines 2; Garraud 3; Perron 3; Pierrefitte 2; Rosalcy 3; and Tournefeuille 3.

The same can't always be said for the adjoining Saint Émilion satellite villages that append their names to its, but careful selection satisfies (Lussac Saint Émilion for Courlat 2; La Croix de Rambeau 2; Lucas 2; Montagne Saint Émilion for La Fleur 2; Montaiguillon 2; Roudier 2; Treytins 2; Tricot 2; Puisseguin-Saint Émilion for Durand-Laplagne 2; Hauts Sainte Claire 2; Laurets 2; La Mauriane 2; Saint-Georges Saint Émilion for Tour-du-Pas-Saint-Georges 2).

Saint Émilion exists for wine and only for wine (and maybe the odd macaroon). The beautiful village itself is stuffed with wineries and wine shops and the countryside around it is one big vineyard – there's nothing else. The wines, of Merlot and Cabernet Franc, are fruitier, more generous and approachable than the ones from across the river, but not as much as the ones next door, and are subject to a very thorough and refreshingly democratic classification, carried out every ten years and which divides them solemnly into, firstly, the two immovable *premiers grand crus classés* 'A' (as above), followed by the 'Bs' (all 3): Angélus, Beau-Séjour Bécot, Beauséjour-Duffaux Lagarrosse, Belair-Monange, Canon, Clos Fourtet, Figeac, laGaffelière, Magdelaine, Pavie, Trottevieille. Beneath them are the straightforward *grand cru classé* properties (all 3): L'Arrosée, Balestard-la-Tonnelle, Berliquet, Canon La Gaffelière, Clos des Jacobins, Clos de l'Oratoire, Clos Saint Martin, La Dominique, Larmande, Pavie-Decesse, Pavie-Macquin, Soutard, Troplong-Mondot, Yon Figeac.

The word 'classé' is of the utmost importance – come on, it's France – because there are then hundreds of plain old *grand cru*, which can be terrible or terrific. Among them are some of the most sought-after *garagistes* as well as traditionalists (all 3) (Bellefont-Belcier, Caze Bellevue, Clos de la Cure, La Croix Chantecaille, de Ferrand, Fleur Cardinale, Fombrauge, Monbousquet, La Mondotte, Moulin-Saint-Georges, Puy Blanquet, Rol Valentin, La Tour Figeac, Tertre Rôteboeuf, Teyssier, Trianon, Valandraud).

Bergerac

The wine lands continue out of Bordeaux along the Dordogne and those of the river's eponymous *département* take the baton. Rather as Bordeaux is shorthand for all the region's wines (nobody ever refers to a sumptuous or silky Gironde), Bergerac is the catch-all here – unless the name of one of its many enthusiastic acolytes is specified. Most of the best Bergeracs (des Eyssards 1, Le Fagé 1, Jonc Blanc 2, Les Miaudoux 1, La Tour des Gendres 2) are clustered a little south of the town itself.

As everywhere, the long journey to excellence starts with the first footsteps of a few choice souls who refuse to settle for mediocrity. Luc de Ponti, proprietor of the last-named establishment and flag-bearer for the region, is one such – another in tiny Saussignac is a Sassenach called Patricia Atkinson, who has done more to get it on the map than anyone. Like every winemaker in Bergerac she covers a lot of bases – with the different wines being labelled under a variety of appellations – and with the lush, but fresh, sweet wines being the star turns (her base is Clos d'Yvigne [2]; Les Miaudoux [1] and de Richard [2] also twinkle).

Next door, equally tiny Monbazillac gives Muscadelle – so often the handmaiden to the Semillon and Sauvignon Blanc it's blended with – a chance to shine in these golden, botrytised sweeties: Bélingard [1]; Pech la Calevie [2]; Poulvère [3]; Septy [2]; Theulet [2]; and Tirecul la Gravière [3]. Eastwards, whites bottled as Montravel are dry, Haut-Montravel are sweet and Côtes de Montravel are in between – the best of each are worth tracking down: Laulerie [1]; Moulin Caresse [1]; and Perreau [1]. Southwards, the Côtes du Duras is making reds as well as Sauvignon Blancs that are attracting attention: Dom de Laulan [1] and Dom les Méritz. On the other side of town, and tiniest of all, Pécharmant makes arguably the best local reds, powerful and age- and oak-worthy: Dom de l'Ancienne Cure [2] and Tiregand [2].

The South-West

A giant's step (by Bergerac standards) east to Cahors where the Côt may look at a king – the burly, beefy reds seem to snap into focus when you know them as the more familiar Argentinian Malbec. Like a lot of south-western reds a quick double-decant will do as many wonders for your tango as it will for a juicy piece of barbecued red meat. Try: du Cayrou [2], du Cedre [1], de Chambert [2], Clos Triguedina [2], Lagrézette [2], Paillas [2], or Pineraie [2].

Gaillac is a world on its own with a long story and Fer Savadou, Duras, Len de L'El and Mauzac grapes making wines of every type and hue that are all candidates for the Next Big Thing if recent improvements are any indication (Causse Marines [3], d'Escausses [2], Gineste [2], Plageoles [3], Rotier [2]). Not to be outdone, Fronton to the west has its own red-wine grape – Négrette – which makes a light Loire-like contrast to the nearby machismo (Baudare [1], Plaisance [2], du Roc [2]).

A side trip north-east to Marcillac, the middle of nowhere, is called for to sample its crunchy, spicy Fer Servadou reds (Dom Laurens [1], Dom du Cros [2], Le Vieux Porche [2]) and, while we're at it – a candidate for 'most obscure' – neighbouring category *Vins Delimité de Qualité Supérieure* (VDQS) Vins d'Entraygues et du Fel's Mousset [2].

To begin the return, a long way away, nestling under the Pyrenees in France's Basque Country (that's the people, not the lingerie) is Irouléguy where the titanic reds that the tannic Tannat makes are a tonic for the winter chill: Arretxea [3]; Illaria [2]; Mignaberry [2] – the local co-op is the Cave de Saint Etienne de Baigorry [2] and by gorry – sorry – it's good. Irouléguy also make classy whites like those of Jurançon, twenty-five miles north-east, where the lucky locals consume the majority of the tangy, grapefruity dry wines made from Gros Manseng, and the luscious, late-harvested sweet moëlleux lovelies made from its sibling, Petit Manseng, which keep a streak of acidity to stop them cloying. Try: Bellegarde [2]; Dom Cauhape [2]; Charles Hours [2]; Clos Lapeyre [2]; and Larrédya [2].

Yet another twenty-five miles north-east is Madiran, and neighbouring VDQS Saint Mont, making more dense, chewy Tannat (some with local Fer Servadou), with the highest levels of any grape of the antioxidant resveratrol, which is thought to protect against cancer. Excellent quality abounds from Berthoumieu [2] and Lafitte-Teston [2], as well as in the hands of two more of those inspirational types – Gascon heroes Alain Brumont (Montus [3]; Bouscassé [2]) and André Dubosc (Producteurs Plaimont [1]). Dubosc began a renaissance in fascinating Pacherenc du Vic-Bilh whites from 'rescued' varieties like Arrufiac and Petit Courbu (as well as the two Manseng varieties) – he tested the new wines on the old folk by seeing if their eyes lit up.

A long hop north to Buzet (De Gueyze [3], Dom du Pech [2]) then a short step to Marmande (Clos Bacquey [3], de Beaulieu [2]) – formerly Côtes du Marmandais – where you'll find some excellent Cabernet/Merlot blends to remind you that it's just a hop and you're back in Bordeaux.

Loire

It's too easy to say that the term 'Loire wines' only has any meaning because that indolent river randomly winds between them. True, the stony, lip-smacking Sauvignons of Sancerre are made well to the east of Paris – as far from their maritime Muscadet counterparts as they are from Lille or, for that matter, l'Italie. Equally, is it fanciful to say that some lineage, some common source – the river? – seems to connect them one to the other, even if the family resemblance is only caught out of the corner of the eye? The best way to ponder these and many other questions is on a stately cruise downriver past pleasure domes and caverns measureless to man.

#GET A HANDLE

> AND ENJOY THE LOIRE'S WILD DIVERSITY OF CRUNCHY, SUMMER REDS, VIVACIOUS FIZZ, ARISTOCRATIC CHENIN BLANC IN EVERY HUE FROM BONE DRY TO SWOONING SWEET AND OH, YES, THERE'S SOME PRETTY DECENT SAUVIGNON BLANC, TOO.

It all starts with Sauvignon Blanc around the twin towns of Pouilly-sur-Loire (Bardin [2], Bel Air [2], Masson-Blondelet [2], Bouchie-Chatellier [2], Cailbourdin [2], Chatelain [2], Didier Dagueneau [3], Favray [3], de Ladoucette [3], Maltaverne [2], Marchand [2], Pabiot [2], Seguin [2], de Tracy [3]) and Sancerre (Bailly-Reverdy [2], Balland [3], Brosses [2], Carrou [2], Cotat [3], Crochet [2], Dezat [2], Jolivet [2], Mellot [2],

Merisiére [2], Morin [3], Pinard [2], Riffault [3], Sautereau [2], Vacheron [3]) a-straddle the river. Pouilly is rounder but often you couldn't put a fag-paper between their grassy, gooseberryish wines, the best of which (and only the best) have a flash of gun-smoke minerality to them – that's the 'fumé' bit.

If it seemed at times recently that the whole world had stolen their wines, folk hereabouts could comfort themselves with the fact that at least they kept coming back to the source for more. The local vineyard area has trebled in size to meet demand and the flattery is now so sincere that all those untamed New World Sauvignons have been refined and refined again so that the best now seem very much like these (and could probably even do business with the local goat cheese). Some vibrant reds and rosés are passionately wrought from Pinot Noir but careful selection is necessary.

A little to the west Menetou-Salon (Bourgeois [2], Chatenoy [2], Girard [2], Pellé [2], Roger [2]) is still an economical source of Sauvignons to rival its illustrious neighbours although prices are catching up. Still further west, I'm yet to find a Reuilly that I really, really want although some (Lafond [2], de Reuilly [2], Sorbe [2]) and, equally, from Quincy (Ballandors [2], Chevilly [2], Commanderie [2], Lecomte [2]) do service if you're happy to lower your sights a notch.

The river's vast bend takes us through the Coteaux du Giennois (de Montbenoit [2], Villargeau [1]) and the new AC of Valençay (Vaillant [2], Vignerons de Valençay [1]) almost to Orléans for our first taste of the great white-wine grape of the Loire – Chenin Blanc. Calm down, dear, wine is all about opinions, and I love its Apple-Charlotte-in-a-glass completeness. The name of Vouvray could probably use help from an image consultant but, whatever, it keeps it cheap for the converted. They come *sec* – seriously *sec* – but always with a lick of the honey and plenty of the acidity and minerality that allow the classic *demi-sec* and fully sweet *moëlleux* wines to age for decades in the endless caves scraped easily out of the soft tuffeau. Some Touraine wines sparkle too – the proud winemakers (Bourillon Dorléans [2], Brédif [2], Champalou [2], Clos Baudoin [3], Clos de Nouys [2], Coteaux Tufiers [1], Gaudrelle [2], Huet [3], Vigneau-Chevreau [2]) make them in off years. Similar things occur across the river in up-and-coming Montlouis (Chidaine [2], Cossais [3], Frantz Saumon [2], Taille-aux-Loups [3]) further north in Jasnières and the Coteaux de Loir (le Briseau [3], de Bellivière [3]) and next door in the Coteaux du Vendômois (de Montrieux [2]) where they also make pale pink *vin gris* and light, peppery reds from the local Pineau d'Aunis.

A few miles further west begins serious red country in Chinon (Baudry [2], Beauséjour [2] – also rosé, Couly-Duthiel [2] – also white, Joguet [3], Lorieux [2]), Bourgueil – a name the saying of which, by the way, should take two seconds, and Saint-Nicolas-de-Bourgueil, longer (Amirault [2], Blot [3], Chevalerie [2], Lorieux [2], Mabileau [2]). Made from lead-scented, strawberry-flavoured Cabernet Franc, which here throws off the handmaiden status it has in Bordeaux and shakes its booty. Good young, purple and chilled – they can be overpoweringly mineral at room temperature – but they age gracefully too.

A little further to Saumur-Champigny, which makes exclusively crunchy reds (Cave de Saumur [1], Hureau [2], Roches Neuves [2], Rougeard [3]), much adored, like the others, in Paris, where, after all, they are the local choice. Saumur itself (Bouvet [1], Langlois-Château [1], Roches Neuves [2], de Villeneuve [2]) is best known abroad for fizz but the diversity here points up that the Loire is a joyous jumble of styles and grapes and colours (and appellations) – the most varied palette in France and perhaps anywhere except north-east Italy's Tre Venezie.

Gamay adds variety to the reds, as does Cabernet Sauvignon, which crops up in Anjou Villages (Ogereau [2], Mosse les Rochelles [2]) and in some rosé Cabernet d'Anjou along with the Franc (Mauny [1]) – these are an unrecognisable improvement on the bad old Rosé d'Anjou days. Crémant de Loire also includes some rosé, and adds the bubbles, the best of which are made by Aureus [2]. Good everyday dry Anjou Blanc supplements the better Cheverny (try Salvard [1]), and the best, Savennières (try Chamboureau [3], du Closel [3], Fournier [3], Pierre-Bise [2] and the pioneering, polarising biodynamist Nicolas Joly [3]) with its two *grands crus* of Coulée de Serrant and La Roche aux Moines, which were once pricier than Montrachet and remain a revelation of mineral and beeswax profundity.

As for lush, appley, late-harvested Chenin Blanc, the names Coteaux de l'Aubance (Richou [2], Montgilet [3]) or Coteaux du Layon (des Baumard [2], Cady [3], des Forges [2], Ogereau [2]), especially with the *lieu-dit* Chaume on the label pretty much guarantee a good time. Better yet, the sub-regions (effectively *grands crus*) of Quarts de Chaume and Bonnezeaux guarantee a mineral-laden symphony in sweetness (try Fesles [3], Petite Croix [3], Petit Val [3]). No need for fancy puds or foie gras – just an ice-bucket and a sunset.

The river can hardly wait to get to the seaside for a piled-up *fruits de mer* washed down by a fresh, dry Muscadet – definitely from one of the sub-regions de Sèvre-et-Maine (du Coing [1], de l'Ecu [1], Goulaine [1], des Hauts Pemoins [1], Poiron [2]), Coteaux de la Loire (Guindon [1]) or Côtes de Grand Lieu (Bâtard [1], des Hautes Noëlles [2]) – a slightly yeasty *sur lie* (see p. 369) one, needless to say. It's nothing to do with Muscat – it's made of Melon de Bourgogne and is as refreshing as cold fino and clicks like the liquid incarnation of all those salty shells. If the terrible frost of 2008 meant that they had none I might look for a VDQS Vins du Thouarsais (Gigon [1]), and if I had to settle for Gros Plant Nantais, made from Folle Blanche, I'd cross my fingers and hope against hope for a good producer.

Sipping it, I might conclude that there does seem to be a thread running through all the wild variety – no Loire wine could ever be from Bordeaux or Burgundy or the Rhône. They have a shared DNA and I think it's the minerals – maybe carried downriver and down the valley through the aeons – that binds them all together.

Chablis

Ever wondered why Chablis and oysters go together like . . . Chablis and oysters? It's because when the roots of the local vines delve down through the soil they hit a layer of, guess what? Oysters! Fossilised oyster shells, in fact – billions of the buggers – laid down about 180 million years ago, and now forming the edge of the Kimmeridgean limestone basin (so-called, because the far end of it emerges at Kimmeridge in Dorset).

Chablis is about subtlety, about less being more. Attempting to identify which wine was the Chablis in a blind tasting, a shrewd chum declared: 'This one – cheap wines never smell of as little as this.' He was right. At their best these cool-climate Chardonnays (exclusively), green-tinged and flinty when young later develop a taut minerality and are the Greta Garbos of wine, oozing class and every bit as sexy. Anybody expecting the buxom, buttery embonpoint of their favourite, heavily oaked Australian, Californian or, closer to home, Côtes de Beaune chardo risks confusion and will require re-education.

There's a refreshingly straightforward and accurate system of grading, with the lowest level of chabbers being the wines from the outlying areas called Petit Chablis, which, unless made by a top grower or the big co-ops, are best avoided, albeit with a few other exceptions such as Pommier 2 and Val de Mercy 2. Now I think about it, the same caveats apply to bog-standard Chablis (something like a third of which is made by the biggest co-op, the excellent La Chablisienne, although the Union des Viticulteurs 2 and the Caves des Vignerons 2 can be good too: try also Bouchard 2, Boudin 2, La Colombe 2, J Dauvissat 3, Goulley 2, Martin 2, Picq 2, Race 2, Seguinot-Bordet 2, Simonnet Febvre 2). The best stuff is grown in the wrinkles and rumples of slopes around the town of Chablis itself and, maddeningly, there are now almost eighty *premiers crus* sites and sub-zones (supermarket wines labelled just *premier cru* without a specific name are a blend of all sorts and can be good if from one of the growers listed here, but can also be dire). Some of the names to remember – and you will remember, won't you, my darlings? – are Côte de Léchet, Fourchaume (within which it is hard to forget the slope of L'Homme Mort), Mont de Milieu, Montée de Tonnerre, Montmains, Vaillons and Vaucoupin.

The seven *grands crus* vineyards (Blanchot, Bougros, Les Clos, Grenouilles, Les Preuses, Valmur and Vaudésir), comprise two per cent of the total and are clustered together – not by coincidence – on the south-west facing slopes above the town and make intense, long-lived wines that only make sense if you've already got to grips with, and fallen for, *les premières*.

There are lots of good producers, most of whom cover all the bases (including Bersan 3, Bessin 2, Billaud-Simon 2, Brocard 3, R & V Dauvissat 3, the various Defaixs 2, Droin 3, Duplessis 3, Durup 3, Fevre 2, Michel 2, Mothe 2, Ravenneau 3, Tremblay 2, Vauroux 2 and Vrignaud 2).

Similar-style whites and some good, light Pinot Noirs are made in the outlying appellations of Irancy (Les Cailles 3, Cantin 3, Colinot 3), Bourgogne Cotes d'Auxerre (Simonnet Febvre 2) while, uniquely, Sauvignon is grown around Saint-Bris to relieve Chardonnay fatigue (Felix [2], Goisot [2], Sorin Defrance [2]).

Champagne

'Come quickly . . . I am tasting stars!' was Dom Pérignon's apocryphal reaction to the first sip of his little winemaking experiment of adding some sugar to an already fermented wine, sealing it up again and leaving it for a while. Well done that monk. He's still at it – the first time I realised that the first duty of Champagne is to be great wine was on my fortieth birthday, halfway through a magnum of 'DP' 1990.

The 80,000 (and rising) demarcated acres of the region are Europe's northernmost (except for England, where similar wine is now made – honest!) and the cool temperatures are vital for retaining the tingling acidity without which no good Champagne is made. They are planted with Pinot Noir and Pinot Meunier, the black grapes that make the Champagnes called *blanc de noirs* when they are not blended with Chardonnay, the white grape, which, when unblended itself, makes the *blanc de blancs* Champagne. Increasingly popular rosé can be made either by skin contact with the black varieties or by blending in a little red wine.

It's a shame that the brut (dry) and ultra brut or 'zero dosage' (no added sugar) styles often shade the limelight from the softer, semi-sweet *sec* (I know . . .), *demi-sec* and sweetly decadent *doux* and 'rich', wedding-cake-friendly styles, but that's the way of it. Brits spent an average of around £18 on each of the 36 million bottles imported in 2009 (we're the biggest market by miles – be proud, be very proud) but the big question is: is it really worth it? It's certainly more expensive to produce than other wines. The endless blending process, all that *remuage* (riddling – the regular turning of the bottles to move and settle the sediment from that secondary fermentation into the bottleneck; the pellet of gunk is then quick-frozen and expelled before the final cork and cage are applied), the long storage time, the expensive and frequently fatuous advertising, the private jets – it all adds up.

Selling the *cuvées de luxe* presumably helps. After DP, Roederer's Cristal – first made for Tsar Alexander II of whom there is a large bust in the firm's Reims HQ and which family members give a grateful pat as they pass: 'We owe him a lot' – is probably the best known. Sufficiently so among rap aficionados that there is a market among hotel concierges for *empty* bottles, especially magnums, for wannabes to scatter around their suites before the after-party arrives. Are these wines worth the even more ruinous cost? That depends on how you feel about diminishing marginal utility. Are they better? Oh, yes . . . More of the finest *cuvées de luxe* are named in inverted commas below.

The fact is that the best of the world's other sparkling wines can only ever scale the foothills of Champagne and only occasionally look some of the lesser non-vintage (NV) wines in the eye. NV accounts for the ninety per cent of wines that are blends from more than one year's wines. The summit is out of sight and the reality is that if Champagne weren't expensive it wouldn't be extravagant and we open a bottle of it because we want to be extravagant, and our celebrations to be special. The extent of the extravagance can be controlled to some extent by shopping around – the movements in prices through discounting can be dizzying – and also through the consistently lower-priced producers, co-ops and brands such as (all 3): Bara, Beaumont de Crayères, Boizel, Devaux, Feuillatte, Jacquart, Lanson, Mailly and Thiénot, including Canard-Duchêne.

LVMH was the first company to see the full global potential of

Champagne as a brand and now owns a gaggle of the *grandes marques* and twenty per cent of the market with Moët – the 't' is pronounced – et Chandon, by far the biggest, but also DP, Veuve Clicquot; 'Grande Dame', Ruinart; 'Dom Ruinart', Mercier and . . . Krug, expensive enough, but cheap compared to its big brother Clos de Mesnil, and that was before the first vintage of Clos d'Ambonnay was released in 2007 at around US $3,000. What was I saying about value? With so much money at stake – total production is around a third of a billion bottles – a number of other top houses have changed hands (Charles Heidsieck, Gosset and Piper-Heidsieck to Rémy Cointreau; Gratien, Heidsieck Monopole and Pommery to Vranken; Mumm and Perrier-Jouët to Pernod Ricard). None of the big players has bought vineyards in England yet, but rumours abound.

There are still many proud independent houses making some of the best wines (all 3). Try Billecart-Salmon, 'Nicolas François', Bollinger, 'RD' and also Ayala, Cattier's 'Armand de Brignac', and then Delamotte, Drappier, Duval-Leroy, Henriot, Jacquesson, Joseph Perrier, Laurent-Perrier; 'Grand Siècle', and Salon, Louis Roederer, Bruno Paillard Philipponnat; 'Clos des Goisses', Pol Roger; 'Winston Churchill', and Taittinger; 'Comtes de Champagne'.

The most important recent development (apart from the expansion of the area to reclaim some nineteenth-century sites) has been the rise in the number of individual producers making their own 'growers' Champagnes instead of selling their grapes to the co-ops – 2,000 or more of them, making any attempt at selection partial, to say the least: Barnier, Brison, Brun, Beaufort, Clouet, Comte de Robart, Deville, Diebolt-Vallois, Gallimard, Geoffroy, Gimonnet, P Gonet, Gremillet, La Haut-Lemblé, Jolly, Lallier, Larmandier-Bernier, Legras, P Mignon, Montaudon, Moutard, Peters, J-P Robert, Théophile Roederer, Vilmart.

Of the satellite ACs, Coteaux Champenois has a tiny production of rather expensive, mainly still reds including pleasingly named Bouzy Rouge, some from the Champagne houses, and Rosé de Riceys is tinier yet, with only three producers.

Burgundy

Burgundy speaks to the heart, and, the heart being connected to the loins, its wines are about the commerce between those two realms and the gratification (and sometimes the denial) of the desires that stir them. At one extreme that Jezebel, Beaujolais, is a wine for getting drunk with and its smudged, ruby-red lips are as profane as Chablis' pale, anchoritic lips are chaste and pure and made only for sipping. While Bordeaux is best mapped by its places – the chateaux – Burgundy is best navigated by following the people. The system of Napoleonic law, specifically of equal inheritance, has had a bewildering effect here in terms of endless division and sub-division, especially of some of the best, most valuable sites – many fine growers have a few rows of vines here and another few there. All of these people are farmers, albeit some of them very posh ones. When it does come to places the most important thing to get to grips with is the villages where these farmers have those scraps of land and how they differ from each other, and the ranks of quality within them – the *crus*.

The grapes, at least, are straightforward – Chardonnay, Pinot Noir and that, for present purposes, is it. But the names . . . aah, the names . . . the names, they are not straightforward. They start off small – Bourgogne, say, for the bottom-line wine from the whole damn lot – then, as the place gets a bit more specific, they get bigger – Haut Côtes de Beaune – and bigger yet as they become very specific – Bienvenues-Bâtard-Montrachet – but then – *attention!* –

at the very top, they suddenly become small again – Corton, say, or Chambertin – like a very fancy 'Doctor' suddenly becomes a 'Mister' again.

It's the division thing of course, with the great sites being sliced up into, first, the very greatest bit itself, then the next greatest bits, which prefix their names to that of the greatest bit, and so on. A major thing is to be able to distinguish from the, pish-tosh, 100-odd different appellations between the cases where a specific, often adjacent, vineyard – Bienvenues-Bâtard in the case above – hitches its name to the greatest bit (Montrachet). It is also good to understand another practice, lower down the scale, where whole villages (Puligny and Chassagne in our case) come along for the ride. There are many good, and some great, wines with just the village name but the uninitiated can be in for some serious sticker-shock. Family names are a shocker as well as they, in turn, sub-divide along with the land. The profusion of some of them is dizzying but, thankfully, the good ones tend all to be good.

Côte d'Or: Geographically, the heart of it all is the Côte d'Or, a name not to be found on labels. The narrow, thirty-mile 'golden slope', the northern half of which is named the Côte de Nuits (for the village of Nuits-Saint-Georges) and the southerly Côte de Beaune, which is roughly centred on the town of that name. Despite all its sensuality, a wine from here is always called a 'Beaune wine', and never a 'Beauner' (see also Abona).

The dedicated locals are often among the best producers and are cited in their local villages although they may also have holdings in one or two others and operate as *négociants* in several. A number of growers now straddle most of the Côte d'Or, some new (Laurent [2]; Nicolas Potel [2] – now trading in his own right as Roche de Bellène [2], his name having been expropriated by his erstwhile backers – ouch!; Verget) and some well-established (Bichot [2], Giroud [3], Méo-Camuzet [3], de Montille [3]).

The sub-division of the whole Burgundy region has frustrated many an expansion plan and meant that the only route was through *negociant* status although now some of the most prestigious firms such as Comtes Lafon [3], Leroy [3] and Leflaive [3] and some of the largest-scale *négociants* such as Bouchard [2], Latour [2] (other good and long-established ones are Joseph Drouhin [2], Faiveley [2], Louis Jadot [2] and Boisset [2], including de la Vougeraie [3]) are expanding out of region. These *negociants* make wine across the region and have become fairly reliable. It must be borne in mind that the concept of good, cheap(ish) Burgundy is a very new one and that basic Bourgogne made not just by the stars mentioned here, but also by lower-key merchants such as Ente [3] or Heresztyn [3], as well as the co-ops such as Caves des Hautes-Côtes is improving rapidly.

The great *crus* are silky, sexy wines that often hide their power behind a light, pale appearance: 'an iron hand in a velvet glove' is an old saw and most are best after a minimum of ten years in the cellar (and more for the grandest). They are expensive, some very. The average bottle of wine sold in the UK in 2010 cost about £4.45; in contrast, a medium-priced *premier cru* costs the equivalent of, say, six-to-nine times that and the *grands crus* can easily knock over a baker's dozen or two of that (at the bottom end of the scale). Good village-level wines, some of which can be drunk early ('young and jammy or old and gamey' is another old saw with plenty of truth in it) can get you through the door from as little as four of five bottles-worth.

The most important single thing to remember about Burgundy is this: great winemaking people make great wine, so you're better off buying their basic wine, which will be better than Monsieur Ordinaire's fancy wine, which will cost twice as much.

Côte de Nuits: It all starts slowly enough on the southern outskirts of Dijon in Marsannay with good, light reds and lovely rosés (Charlopin [3], Pataille [3]) – sadly, and literally, undervalued throughout Burgundy – and next door to the south in Fixin for our first *premiers crus* (Gambal [3], Humbert [3], Nadeff [3]) and a serious taste of the densely concentrated silky essences to come. Another mile sees the first household name, Gevrey-Chambertin – home to one of those single-word, kingpin *grand cru* vineyards, Chambertin itself, surrounded by its court of nine or ten other grandees and, standing respectfully to one side, the retinue of *premiers crus* and the attendant village-level vineyards that comprise almost all of the rest (all [3]): Bart; Beaumont; Bouvier; Burguet: Damoy; Dugat; Dugat-Py; F Esmonin; S Esmonin; Géantet-Pansiot; Harmand-Geoffroy; Maume; Mortet; Rossignol-Trapet; Roty; Rousseau; Sérafin; Trapet; Vallet; Varoilles.

Low-profile Morey Saint Denis (Lambrays [3], H Lignier [3]), an insider's choice, has four *grands crus*, of which Clos de la Roche and the single-owner Close de Tart are best. Blink, and it gives way to Chambolle-Musigny, home of pale, perfumed wines, often said to be feminine but with a womanly strength underpinning the best from the *grands crus* of Bonnes Mares and Le Musigny itself and more than just the two irresistible, self-explanatory *premiers* of Les Amoureuses and Les Charmes. Try Amiot-Servelle, Barthod, Clerget, Comte de Vogüé, Digioia-Royer, Groffier, Hudelot-Baillet, Hudelot-Noëllat, Mugnier and Roumier.

These give on to the Clos de Vougeot, a 125-acre, walled, once-monastic patch divided amongst nearly 100 growers – good, bad and ugly. It's the ultimate Burgundian carve-up and many of the best names cited have their patch here but there are other good people, too, such as Ardhuy, d'Eugénie, Frantin, Gambal, Lamarche, Raphet and de la Tour (all 3). Inching south-west, the village of Vosne-Romanée does make wine for ordinary folk, but not much. It has the highest entry-point prices probably because it is home to the most prestigious producer in Burgundy, and maker of the world's most expensive wines – Domaine de la Romanée-Conti 3, or DRC as it's known, and stuff rubs off. Other *grands crus* include La Tâche, Grands Échézeaux and the appropriate Richebourg (all 3). Tap in to the piggybank for Cacheux, Cathiard, Clavelier, Engel, Gros family, Lamarche, Vicomte Liger-Belair, Mugneret family or Rouget (all 3).

There are no *grands crus* next door in Nuits-Saint-Georges but it makes up for it with a huge area producing solid, structured, age-worthy *premier cru* and village wines to console the upper-middle and middle classes with Ambroise, l'Arlot, Chauvenet, Chevillon, Gouges, Lechénaut, T Ligier-Belair and Rion (all 3).

Mopping up the good stuff from around the edges of the best communes, Côtes de Nuits-Villages wines from the likes of Gachot-Monot 3, Loichet 3 and Millot 3 give a satisfying inkling of what all the fuss is about, sometimes at half the price of medium-level village wines. At the next level (down, despite appearances) the Haut-Côtes de Nuits such as Gavignet 2 and Thevenot-Le Brun 2 and below that plain old Côtes de Nuits are more of a crapshoot (although generally more crap than shoot, they are immeasurably improved, often to the point of drinkability).

Of those growers who spread their wings, some fly only as far as the adjacent villages in the north (Arlaud, Drouhin-Laroze, Fourrier, Ponsot, Tortochot, Virgile-Lignier) or the south (Engel, Girardin, Jayer-Gilles), while others, some of whom have been at it for a while, cover the whole of the Côtes de Nuits (all 3: Arnoux, Bertagna, L Boillot, Clair, Clavelier, Confuron, Dujac, Grivot, Perrot-Minot, Taupenot-Merme).

Côte de Beaune: It's been almost completely red up to this point but that all changes when the hill of Corton comes into view at the northern end of the Côte de Beaune. To let you know where you are, the hill has not one but two *grands crus* – Le Corton on the south-eastern flank for burly reds and Corton-Charlemagne on the south-western for burly whites. Many of the best growers (all 3: Bonneau du Martray, Capitain Gagnerot, Chandon de Briailles, Clavelier, Corton-André, Follin-Arbelet, Tollot-Beaut) make both and much else besides including the village reds from the bottom of the hill, labelled Aloxe-Corton, where you'll catch a satisfying glimpse back up.

Similar circumstances pertain to the bottom of the Charlemagne slope, in Pernand-Vergelesses (Clos de la Croix de Pierre 3, Dubreuil-Fontaine 3, Rapet 3, Rollin 3, Vallet 3), around the corner at the base of Corton in Ladoix (Chevalier 3, Durand 3, Loichet 3) and, a little further afield in Savigny-lès-Beaune (Bize 3, Féry 3, Gambal 3, Girard 3, Guiton 3, Jacob 3, Rémy 3) and Chorey-lès-Beaune (de Chorey 3, Cornu 3, Maillard 3), where growers also make wine for we mortals.

Like Nuits-Saint-Georges, Beaune has no *grands crus* but keeps the bourgeosie afloat with a myriad *premiers* on the slopes overlooking the town, among which Clos des Mouches (some of which is white), Grèves and Bressandes are stars. Much of the vineyard belongs to the great *négociant* houses listed above, most of whom are based here. The annual November charity auction of wines – the Hospices de Beaune – is the point around which the Burgundy year revolves.

Beaune gives way to Pommard, which fits much the same description, although the best growers (Comte Armand [3], Courcel [3], Potinet-Ampeau [3]) in the best vineyards of Epenots and Rugiens would probably kill me for saying so, and Pommard in turn segues into Volnay, where the reds are pale and fragrant and those from the best plots – Clos des Chènes and Cailleret – are among the finest of the southern half of the Côte d'Or (Hospices de Beaune [3], Lafarge [3], Marquis d'Angerville [3], Prieur [3]).

The central part of the Côte de Beaune is very much red country and continues on a long spur to the west from Monthelie (Coche-Bizouard [3], Garaudet [3], Suremain [3]) through Auxey-Duresses (Fichet [3], Prunier [3]) to Saint-Romain (Gras [3], Guillemard [3]) and good value is to be had throughout – with the usual caveats carved in stone. Good whites in the last of them prepare us for the big change as we head back south to Meursault and Puligny-Montrachet – jointly the Valhalla of the world's finest dry white wines. Meursault may lack a *grand cru*, but its glittering golden wines (all [3]: Ballot-Millot, Bouzereau, Boyer-Martenot, Coche-Dury, Comtes Lafon, Fichet, Genot-Boulanger, Grivault, Javillier, Jobard, Latour-Giraud, Michelot, Mikulski, Morey-Blanc, Roulot), not just from the best *premiers crus* of Les Genevrières, Les Charmes and Les Perrières, have inspired Chardonnay growers across the globe to make fatter, richer, butterier wines (though sometimes they've gone too far in their flattery).

Puligny (all [3]: Bachelet-Monnot, J-M Boillot, Bzikot, Carillon, Chavy family, Dom Leflaive, Maroslavac-Leger, Pernot, Chateau de Puligny, Sauzet) is often restrained by comparison, the minerals more to the fore, perhaps, although wines from its *grand cru* – Le Montrachet – and its cardinals – Bâtard (shared with Chassagne), Bienvenues-Bâtard, and Chevalier, who prefix their own noble monikers to its name – have so many flavours and in such depth that any attempt to list them is invidious. As ever, the best growers give glimpses in their lesser wines, which, though never cheap, seldom disappoint these days. Between Puligny and Meursault, Blagny (Martelet de Cherisey [3], Matrot [3]) has some good value and the odd red.

The reds start again in adjoining Chassagne-Montrachet but they can be rather chewy and the deeply dry whites are better (all [3]: Coffinet-Duvernay, B Colin, Colin-Deléger, Gagnard, Jouard, Maltroye, Morey, Niellon, Pillot, Ramonet). After all, it has its share of Le Montrachet, and all of tiny Criots-Bâtard-Montrachet. Another good value bit-on-the-side is the valley to Saint-Aubin (Lamy [3], Miolane [3], Prudhon [2], Thomas [3]) and – although more variable – to the south, Santenay (D Clair [3], Lequin-Colin [3]) and finally Maranges which can also come up with the goods.

A number of merchants cover the whole – or most – of the Côtes de Beaune (d'Ardhuy [2], Champy [2], Devevey [2], Germain [3], O. Leflaive [2], J-M Morey [3], Remy [3]) and there do seem to be fewer small producers south of Aloxe. Of the catch-all appellations, Côte de Beaune-Villages is for reds only (Billard [2], Chanson [3], Charrière [2], Patriarche [3]) while Hautes-Côtes de Beaune does both (Mazilly [3], Rodet [2]), sometimes rather well.

Côte Chalonnaise: Starting immediately when the Côte d'Or ends, if not before, in most parts of the world this area would be a treasured complex of terroirs and subtle variations but, after the inexhaustible intricacies to the north, it seems as straightforward as Australia. Frankly, this can be a bit of a relief – at least they make wine we can afford to drink, some of it is excellent and it's improving very rapidly.

Bouzeron is the home of Aligoté, which is the specified grape of the AC (Jacqueson 2, de Villaine 3) – too good for the kir for which it is the favourite – but Chardonnay soon reasserts itself in style in Rully (Briday 2, D'Allaines 2, Delorme 2, Dureuil-Janthial 2, Dury 2, Meix-Foulot 2, Tupinier-Bautista 3). Reds predominate in Mercurey (Chamirey 3, Faiveley's Juillot 2, Lorenzon 3, Raquillet 3) and Givry (Chofflet-Valdenaire 2, Danjean-Berthoux 2, Joblot 3, Lumpp 3, Parize 2, Salomon 3, Sounit 2), which can rival the lower-key villages of the Côte d'Or.

Montagny (Aladame 3, Michel-Andreotti 3, Cognard 3, de la Saule 2) includes next-door Buxy and its excellent co-op and makes exclusively increasingly substantial and satisfying whites, all of which until recently were allowed to call themselves *premiers crus* (which was a bit daft) until they demoted about a third of them (which was a bit cruel, but that's local politics for you).

The Mâconnais: The southernmost part of Burgundy is one of the most rapidly improving for Chardonnay, which is almost in a monopoly, and Mâcon-Villages whites can give more than a glimpse of the pleasures to be had further north (at prices more familiar much further south, especially those made by stellar producers Lafon and Leflaive, who have expanded here). Specifically, excellent value can be had from the best producers (Cuvée à l'Ancienne 1, Bret 3, Chêne 2, Les Clochettes 2, Guffens-Heynen 3, Guillemot-Michel 3, Guillot-Broux 2, Merlin 2, Perraud 2, Rijckaert 3, Talmard 1, Tripoz 1, Verchères 1) in the couple of dozen named villages among which are Lugny, Uchizy, Prissé, Chaintré, Davayé, Solutré, Viré-Clessé. In the latter, the much-abused Jean Thevenet of Domaine de le Bongran 3 is a star. Saint-Véran (Barraud 1, Chavet 2, Deux Roches 2, Lassarat 2, Maillettes 2, Maison 2, Nembrets 2) is another AC with bits dotted here and there.

The jewel in Mâcon's crown, Pouilly-Fuissé – never, on pain of death, to be confused with the other Pouilly on the Loire – offers a final flash of Burgundian exuberance and complexity (and not just in the wines). Extravagantly rich whites from Pouilly and its insanely tiny sub-zones of Pouilly-Vinzelles and Pouilly-Loché (which can also provide fine value for junior wines labelled with the Mâcon prefix – see what I mean?) are the most ripely opulent of Burgundy, and often risk being excessively so, but I think that's probably the point. These are the most expensive wines down here and, even though quality is improving across the board, buying at random is unwise. For now, try Barraud [1], Clos des Rocs [3], Ferret [3], Chateau Fuissé [3], Gerbeaux [2], Robert-Denogent [3], Saumaize-Michelin [2], la Soufrandise [3], Tripoz [2] or Valette [3]. With a few exceptions such as Larochette-Manciat [2], reds are best avoided until Gamay has ceded more ground to Pinot Noir. Merchants such as Jaffelin [2] are less important here than the co-operatives and Lugny [1], Prissé [1] and Viré [1] are very good.

Of Burgundy's also-ran grapes, an amazing amount of everyday slurping Bourgogne Passetoutgrains – a minimum of one-third Pinot Noir blended with Gamay – is made, and drunk, locally from bottles with labels such as Lafarge [2], Lejeune [2] or Lignier [2]; Aligoté from Felix [2] or Goisot [2] quenches the thirst for something sharp and white and, should local fizz be required, *crémant* de Bourgogne is on hand, especially from Bailly Lapierre [2] or Louis Boillot [2].

*GET A HANDLE...

FINALLY, A CAT MAY LOOK AT A KING AND ORDINARY MORTALS CAN GET A GLIMPSE OF THE PINOT NOIR AND CHARDONNAY GLORY WITHOUT BREAKING THE BANK AS GREAT GROWERS EXPAND INTO THE OUTLYING AREAS, TAKING THEIR HIGH STANDARDS WITH THEM.

Beaujolais

The clammy chill of horror felt by anybody born before 1960 on hearing the phrase '*Le Beaujolais Nouveau est arrivée*!' cannot easily be understood by anybody born much after 1975. Even in the much-storied midden of marketing madness, it cannot have been common for a large, 100-odd-million-bottle industry to advertise itself by sending some of its worst products out into the world in a blaze of tacky publicity. I can't go into detail – it's still too raw – but, even though it's taken a generation to recover from the slow-mo, Ratner-esque train wreck that was *Le Nouveau*, Beaujolais is back. And it's *not* bad.

Gamay is the Beaujolais grape – think jammy Gammy, not *jamais* Gamay – and it's about headily perfumed cherries and a certain brisk crunchiness that you get nowhere else (stick with me on this). Selection is vital: if the label just says 'Beaujolais' with a few exceptions (Brun [1], Fessy [1]) or, mendaciously, 'Beaujolais Supérieure' it's probably best avoided; 'Beaujolais Villages' from thirty specified communes in the northern half of the region, which itself occupies the southernmost part of greater Burgundy, should be OK if you know who you're buying from. Here are a few: Benier [2]; Burrier [2]; Colonge [2]; Piron [2]; La Plaigne [2] and Tour de Montmelas [1].

Georges Duboeuf, the 'King of Beaujolais', has done more to rehabilitate the region than anyone (perhaps partly as penance for being a key figure in the *Nouveau* campaign) and everybody surely recognises his distinctive, flowery labels. The wines are pretty good too, as are those from some of the local (Loron [1], Potel-Aviron [2]) as well as the major Burgundy *négociants* (Jadot [1], Latour [1]), the better co-ops (Bel Air [1], Bully [1]) and the two high-quality satellite ACs Côte Roannaise to the west (Sérol [1], Fontenay [1]) and the Côteaux du Lyonnais (Chasselay [1]) to the south.

Simplest (OK, it's not that simple) is to buy bottles that specify one of the named village *crus*. The girliest and most gluggable (and gluggability is their essence) are from Brouilly (Lapalu 3, Michaud 2, Pierreux 2, des Tours 2), Chiroubles (Cheysson 2, Demont 2, Raôusset 2), the newest *cru*, Régnié (Bulliats, Rochette) and – the quintessential Beauj – Fleurie (Berrod, Chapelle des Bois, Chignard, Després, Grand Coeur, de Fleurie, Gry Sablon, Hospices de Belleville, Metrat, La Reine de l'Arenite, Vissoux).

Of the more substantial, age-worthy all-rounders, Juliénas (Capitans, Clos du Chapitre, Descombes, Perrachon, Tête) and Saint-Amour (Billards, Loron, des Pins) are practised seducers – and with those names, who could resist? Tiny Chénas (Champagnon) and Côte-de-Brouilly (Roches Bleues, Thivin, Voûtes des Crozes) have rather broader shoulders than one might expect to see on a flibbertigibbet in a tutu, while the long-lived wines of Morgon, especially the Côte de Py area (Burgaud, la Chaponne, Desvignes, Duboeuf's Jean Descombes, Foillard, Gaget, Lapierre) and Moulin-à-Vent (Janodet's Fines Graves, Jadot's des Jacques, Clos de Rochegrès, Clos des Thorins, and Champ de Cour, Manoir du Carra, Merlin, Tremblay) have in youth a darkly brooding tannic structure that is a serious shock to any wayward purchaser expecting merely a higher class of flapper to reveal itself.

Anybody doubtful about the concept of terroir has only to taste a few of these different *crus* to see just how multifarious the wines made from a single grape can be when grown in different situations, albeit sometimes only a stone's throw apart. There are some decent whites and rosés – and don't forget to chill the reds too – down to the low teens centigrade for the lightest, which puts a real spring in their step and somehow tightens up the flavours.

Rhône

Wine has been made along the Rhône since Roman times and a passion for it – especially for the reds that I suspect some of the local winemakers may have running through their veins – is one of the very few elements that are common along its course.

The austere north devotes itself to fine wines, produces only a tenth of the region's total and, frankly, couldn't care less. Its reds, made exclusively from Syrah, demand patience, sometimes the patience of a saint, and it makes just enough white – dry and sweet, from Marsanne, Rousanne and Viognier – to ensure that banquets will be well-balanced. These red/white proportions pertain throughout the Rhône and the whites – perhaps because they are perforce paid a high level of attention relative to their quantity – are always worth investigating as some of the most substantial, characterful and food-friendly anywhere.

Things down south, after the decent interval of thirty-odd more-or-less vine-less miles between Valence and Montélimar, could hardly be more different. The wines here are for carousing and clinking glasses with and even the poshest – Châteauneuf-du-Pape – would be more at home in the chubby hand of a well-placed and red-faced prêtre than in the long fingers of a cardinal attending the Papal palace in fourteenth-century Avignon.

The biggest of the best producers make wine throughout the region. Marcel Guigal [2] has been called the best winemaker in the world more than once (also look for his Vidal-Fleury [1] subsidiary). Search out also: dynamic (and biodynamic) Michel Chapoutier [2]; Delas [1]; Jaboulet Aîné [1]; and Tardieu Laurent [2], both on their own properties and working as *négociants* (and consequently only cited selectively); others work with smaller remits and some others of the best stick with what they know best in their own backyards.

Crozes-Hermitage, though seldom cheap, is the entry-level wine of the north and needs careful selection to avoid the sour variety of its otherwise pale, peppery cherries. Try: Cave de Tain 2 – the northern Rhône co-op, reliable across the board; Belle 2; Yann Chave 2; Combier 3; du Colombier 2; Darde et Ribo 3; des Entre-faux 2; Fayolle 2; Graillot 2; Pochon 2; des Remizières 2; Robin 2.

Given its ten-fold expansion in forty years to encompass almost the whole of the northern Rhône, standards in Saint Joseph have remained refreshingly high for relatively early-drinking, juicy, still substantial reds and savoury whites. Buying at random is not advised; instead, look out for Cuilleron 3, Faury 3, Gaillard 3, Paret 3, Perret 3, Villard 3 and the 'other' co-ops of Saint Pierre 2 and Saint Désirat 2, who generally do a decent job.

Cornas makes only inky-dark reds (Allemand 3, Clape 3 – choose your words carefully when ordering a 'case' of it, Colombo 3) that are traditionally as tough as old boots and almost undrinkable when young but some of the newer stars such as Dumien-Serette 3, Durand 3, Juge 3, Paris 3 and Le Tunnel 3 are making softer, more forward styles that need only a few years' gestation. Saint Péray provides the local whites, including some distinctive golden *méthode traditionelle* from Marsanne and Roussanne (Cuilleron 3, Gripa 3, Vins de Vienne 3, Voge 3). Lighter *Crémant de Die* and Muscat-based *Clairette de Die Tradition* – is bussed in from east of Valence.

Whichever genius first worked out that adding a dash of perfumed white Viognier rounded off the tannic edges and lifted the reds of Côte-Rôtie to a different level has my gratitude. The presiding genius of the appellation – again, Marcel Guigal – makes heavy use of new oak in his most expensive wines La Turque, La Moulin and La Landonne known collectively as the 'La-Las'. Wines from other of the best producers who labour on the 'roasted' slopes of up to 60° incline (in fact, I think they get other people to do that bit) include Barge, Burgaud, Clusel-Roch, Cuilleron, Duclaux, Gérin, Jamet, Jasmin, Niéro, Ogier, Rostaing, Saint Cosme, Vernay, and ally softness to amaze most Shiraz fans with power in a combination that is equalled only in fine Burgundy.

On its own the Viognier makes tiny quantities of bone-dry but bewitchingly perfumed whites in the once-endangered appellation of Condrieu. Try Cuilleron, Faury, Gaillard, Monteillet, Paret, Vernay, Villard and the returning-to-form, one-château appellation of Château-Grillet.

The granite hill of Hermitage (Chave, Faurie, Ferraton, Sorrel) has been singled out for the quality of its burly, masculine red wines since the Roman era and they've pretty much got the drop on it by now. These great walls of concentrated, perfumed fruit take a long time to soften and evolve their deeply savoury aromas of black olives and *lardons* although new-fangled earlier-drinking styles such as those from the Cave de Tain are now made and can be an excellent and more affordable introduction. The complex, enigmatic dry whites also reward patience: the tiny quantities of exquisite, sweet white *vin de paille* (see p. 398), such as Chapoutier's and Chave's – teased from grapes left to dry out on straw mats – appear to be ageless.

In the south, things look complicated as far as grape varieties go. Châteauneuf winemakers can use up to thirteen, but the reality is that fruity, jammy Grenache is the mainstay in blends where Syrah and Mourvèdre are important in stiffening it and spicing it up. Cinsaut and Counoise also play useful roles. They wouldn't give much shrift up north to the likes of Muscardin, Vaccarèse, Picpoul and Terret Noir – the remaining reds. Of the whites – Grenache

Blanc, Clairette, Bouboulenc and Marsanne – as we know, only the last is blessed.

Most of the vast output of Côtes du Rhône is from the south, and careful selection can unearth some great-value wines evoking the crackle of herb-scrub *garrigue* underfoot. Many of the better ones (Darriaud [1], Gramenon [3], Grand Moulas [1], Perrin [1], Réméjeanne [2], Vignerons d'Estézargues) are designated Côtes du Rhône Villages – with the mention of a specific village such as Cairanne (Alary [1], Brusset [1], Caves de Cairanne [1], le Goeuil [2]), Visan [1] (Roche-Audran), Laudun [1] (Courac), Massif d'Uchaux (Saint-Estève [1]), Chusclan (Seigneuries de Gicon [1]), Rasteau (Cave des Vignerons [1], Charavin [2], des Escaravailles [1], La Soumade [1], Saint Gayan [1]), Sablet (Boissan [1]), Plan de Dieu (de L'Espigouette [1]), Séguret (la Courançonne [2], les Coteaux [2], Mourchon [2]), Saint-Gervais (Saint Anne [2]) being the next step up.

Worth remembering is that some growers in the more prestigious appellations, especially Châteauneuf, also often bottle some wine as Côtes du Rhône for reasons of demarcation, declassification of second-best vats or for the wine from newer plantings. The best (Coudoulet de Beaucastel [3], Charvin [2], de Ferrand [2], Fonsalette [3], Grand Veneur [2], de la Janasse [2], Mas de Boislauzon [2], Mont Redon [2], Rocalière [2], du Trignon [2], de la Vieille Julienne [3]) are mini-Châteauneufs and better than some growers' 'real' Châteauneufs.

Good value is still to be had in sun-baked southern Rhône appellations like Côteaux du Tricastin (Chapoutier [2], de Montine [1]), Costières de Nîmes (Amphoux [2], Paul Blanc [1], de Campuget [1], Grande Cassagne [1], Mas de Bressades [1], Mourgues du Grès [1], Roubaud [1], La Tour de Beraud [1]), Côtes du Vivarais (Gallety [3], Mas de Bagnols [2]), Vinsobres (Chaume-Arnaud [2], Meffre [2]) and up-and-coming Ventoux (la Ciboise [1], Fondrèche [1], La Martinelle [1],

Perrin [1], Pesquié [2], Valcombe [2]) although prices have been creeping up in the last few years (albeit from a low base).

Moving upscale, Vacqueyras (la Charbonnière [2], Clos des Cazaux [2], Couroulu [2], la Garrigue [2], la Monardière [3], Montirius [3], de Montmirail [2]) seems to be where Gigondas (des Bosquets [3], Bouïssière [3], Brusset [2], du Cayron [3], Clos du Joncuas [3], Haut Marone [2], les Pallières [3], Raspail-Ay [3], Saint Cosme [3], Santa Duc [3]) was for price and quality for rambunctious, thigh-slapping, age-worthy, food-friendly reds and it, in turn, is perhaps where Châteauneuf was.

Man cannot live by red alone and and his need for white is well met in Lirac (with some good red and rosé as well from Charmasson [2], Corne Loup [1], Chapelle de Maillac [2] and la Fermade [1]) and, occasionally, Clairette de Bellegarde (Boutée [2]) and for big-boned, pinks pre-eminently in Tavel (d'Aqueria [2], de la Mordorée [2], Prieuré des Montézargues [2], la Rocalière [2], Trinquevedel [2]). For sweet whites, he goes to Beaumes de Venise for its famous peachy Muscat *vins doux naturels* (des Bernardins [2], Coyeux [2], Durban [2], de la Pigeade [1]) as well as some good reds (Cassan, Redortier).

For all the madness of at one extreme, one-year-old supermarket own-brands for a tenner and at the other *vieilles vignes* (see p. 397) super-cuvées costing hundreds and for all that far too many of the dozen-or-so-million embossed bottles of Châteauneuf-du-Pape produced on average each year are not worth the money, the deep, rich, complex, soupy, warming ones that are (all [3]: de Beaucastel, Beaurenard, Bonneau, Les Cailloux, Chante Cigale, de la Charbonnière, Charvin, Clos du Caillou, Clos des Papes, Clos Saint-Jean, Font de Michelle, Fortia, Grand Tinel, Grand Veneur, Marcoux, Mont-Olivet, La Nerthe, Pégaü, Rayas, Sabon, P Usseglio, R Usseglio, Vaudieu, Vieux Donjon, Vieux Télégraphe) mean its reputation is secure. And please don't – as it is so often necessary to remind oneself hereabouts – neglect the whites from these same producers.

***GET A HANDLE...**

> SUN-DRENCHED SPICE AND SAVOURINESS OF REDS FROM SYRAH (IN THE NORTH) AND GRENACHE-BASED BLENDS (IN THE SOUTH) AND THE QUALITY (INCLUDING IN FINE WHITES AND ROSÉS) IS SPILLING OUT INTO THE ADJOINING VIN DE PAYS AREAS.

Alsace

Region of mists and mellow fruitfulness, Alsace has been fought over by France and Germany down the centuries but has only ever been occupied by the latter in wartime. Nonetheless, there is much that is Germanic in the wines themselves, in terms of grape varieties used (especially Riesling), the diversity of styles (which are all about ripeness and the sugar content of the grapes), the tall, *flute* bottles and the fact that they are bizarrely underrated.

Whether as a side-effect of their homeland's precarious sovereignty or not, Alsace's winemakers (Hugel [2], Trimbach [2], Weinbach [3], Zind-Humbrecht [3], Josmeyer [2], Bott-Geyl [2], Albert Mann [2], Mittnacht Frères [2], Bruno Sorg [2], Dirler-Cadé [3], Rieffel [2], Ostertag [2], Pfister [2]) are a fiercely independent bunch and many a family firm has been going about its business behind the absurdly pretty mediaeval facades of villages and towns such as Riquewihr and Ribeauvillé for three or four hundred years. Amazingly, none has fallen into the hands of any of the large drinks corporations. In order to keep themselves busy between invasions winemakers have developed a complex approach to the subject – most make at least a dozen different wines and some two or three times that.

The asset shared by all Alsace vignerons is the climate, which is dictated by the Vosges mountains to the west. They take the force of the prevailing westerly weather, especially the rain, and shelter this part of the Rhine valley, making it, surprisingly, one of the driest and sunniest parts of France. The asset enjoyed by the owners of the most favoured sites is again owed to the mountains in that the dizzyingly steep slopes of the foothills ensure that every vine gets the benefit of direct exposure to all that sun.

In Alsace there are four grape varieties that are deemed to make the best wine; thus, they have earned the epithet 'noble grapes'. They are all white grapes and are: austere, minerally, often bone-dry Riesling; sultry, lychee-laden Gewürztraminer; grapey, fragrant Muscat and luscious, rounded Pinot Gris (still referred to as Tokay d'Alsace and Tokay Pinot Gris but not on labels).

Other important varieties are Pinot Blanc, Auxerrois (much used in *crémant*) and Sylvaner and Pinot Noir, which produces some crisp, light reds. Blends of two or more grapes are known as *Edelzwicker*, noble mix – although Hugel have revived the alternative French name *Gentil* for a blend that contains at least fifty per cent noble varieties. Not wanting to miss out on anything, the Alsaciens also make some rather delicate, sparkling *crémant*, mainly from Pinot Blanc.

For the top wines, since 1983 there has been a *grand cru* system that accounts for around four per cent of production but tradition dies hard in Alsace and many of these feisty farmers choose to ignore it and stick with the old system of using the names of the vineyards and their sub-divisions. Alsace is the only French appellation in which it is a requirement to name the grape variety on the label. The consequence is that the names of some wines can tend to do your head in but, if approached methodically, the great Zind-Humbrecht's Clos Saint Urbain, Rangen de Thann Gewürztraminer

Selection de Grains Nobles (SGN) does exactly what it says on the tin. The 'Clos' is a small section of the top-class Rangen de Thann slope, at the southernmost tip of the region; the 'Grains Nobles' refers to noble rot and is the term used to describe the upper of the two sweet-wine echelons. The extra ripening gives the high sugar levels that are important to get the right balance between sweetness and acidity. Indeed, for the finest *vendange tardive* (VT) – late-harvest – and those SGN wines, the poor blighters can shiver out on the slopes until November or even December. If there is one weakness in the Alsace system it is that the level of sweetness of a VT is impossible to even guess at from the label and wines can be as surprisingly dry as they sometimes are sumptuously sweet.

Alsace Pinot Gris – especially at the VT level – is one of the most versatile grapes in terms of food matching and in that part of France I've happily drunk a *grand cru* from a top producer throughout a five-course dinner. Going great guns with a seafood starter, followed by the foie gras for which it is a natural partner, it held its own against a steak in a cream-based sauce, and its marriages with both a rich pudding and the final sliver of blue cheese were a rather wonderful ménage à trois.

It's unusual to come across a bad Alsace wine. Don't call them Alsatian, by the way, although there must be a few dogs out there somewhere. Much can be revealed about standards in any wine region by the quality of wine produced by the growers' cooperatives and in Alsace, where the first wine cooperative in France was established in the 1920s, the bar is set very high by Caves de Turckheim, Hunewihr, Riquewihr, Bebblenheim and Pfaffenheim for entry-level varietals and the occasional VT wine.

*GET A HANDLE...

THE KEY TO IT ALL IS THE BALANCE OF TRADITION, INDIVIDUALISM AND DIVERSITY. THAT, AND THE SUN ENSURING THE RIESLING, GEWÜRZTRAMINER AND PINOT GRIS GRAPES FULLY RIPEN – AFTER THAT IT'S UP TO THE WINEMAKER TO DECIDE WHERE ON THE SCALE OF STEELY DRY TO SUMPTUOUSLY SWEET HE WANTS TO PLACE EACH WINE.

In the middle of nowhere between Alsace and Champagne, the tiny Côtes de Toul in northerly Lorraine is extraordinarily self-reliant and caters to its citizens' every vinous need with light Gamay and Pinot Noir reds, Auxerrois whites including some fizz and most importantly (if that's the right word) lots of pale rosé *vin gris* (see p. 398) and an eau de vie, a marc or a bergamot liqueur to finish – all from Laroppe 2 or Lelièvre 2 for preference. There's more chance of ripening a snowball in hell than getting any late-harvest action up here so they probably pretend they don't like sweet wines anyway.

Jura (yes, we're still in France, not Scotland)

East of Burgundy and little thought of within France, let alone abroad, when it comes to wine, Jura is a prime example of that provincial French promise to provide all wines to all men (and women). Worth tracking down, its whites centre on the local Savagnin grape, which works overtime to provide the Mistelle-style aperitif Macvin de Jura as well as very good 'conventional' dry whites; superlative semi-dried grape sweet *vin de paille*; a little *crémant* and, most distinctively, the fino-like speciality *vin jaune* (see p. 398). These oxidised, intensely nutty, *rancio* (see p. 321) wines from the Arbois (d'Arlay 2, Aviet 2, Dugois 3, Puffeney 3, Rijckaert 2, Tissot 3) and, better yet, Château-Chalon (Berthet-Bondet) ACs are an acquired taste. Not knowing what to expect from the first, distinctive 62cl *clavelin* bottle I ever opened (they are designed to contain the typical amount remaining from a litre after the minimum of six years' ageing), I have to admit that I poured the contents down the sink, thinking it corked. Apparently, I should have tried it with a roasted *poulet de Bresse*, like the locals. Light, but fragrant, succulent reds are had from Poulsard – aka Ploussard – (Houillon 3) to complete the traditional picture, while the Burgundy grapes are gaining ground for mainstream styles in the Côtes du Jura AC.

Savoie

Sporadic vineyards cling where they can to the slopes in the large Savoie region and, though the wines that emanate from them may be diverse, they have one thing in common: the Alps, which give them a bracing freshness as pure and clean as the air itself. Most Savoie wine is white, much is made from Altesse, also known here under the appellation of Roussette de Savoie (Boniface 2, Lupin 2), with some Jacquère in Apremont, and the more distinguished Rhône grape Roussanne – again under another alias here, flagship whites Chignin-Bergeron (Berlioz 2, Quenard 2). Given the solid and savoury nature of the Savoyard diet – it seems that any daily consumption of less than a pound of cheese and lardons is viewed with suspicion – their wines' pert acidity is the perfect foil. Fizz from Ayze (Belluard), rosé from Bugey (Trichon), light reds from Gamay (Vullien 2) and lusty ones from Mondeuse in Arbin (Cave du Prieuré 2, Magnin 2) complete a satisfactory picture.

The South

Out in the wilds of the Languedoc you'd want your winemaker to be somewhat wild of hair, with features sunburned to copper and a handshake firm as a blacksmith's. All those I once met with to celebrate the perfect marriage of their rambunctious reds to a robust cassoulet answered satisfyingly to this description even if they were – to a man, as it were – women. There's a tradition of strong women hereabouts and another of strong wine; it's a traditional place all round but it's also France's 'new world' – a level playing field across which range influences (and winemakers) from all over, unfettered by over-regulation. Needless to say, there are no *grands crus* here (yet) so, as in the New World, to get to the outperformers you've got to know (or know somebody who knows).

It all works (and sometimes doesn't work) on a New-World scale as well, with almost three-quarters of a million acres under vine. Not all traditions are good ones and the one in which indifferent co-ops reward growers for producing as many indifferent grapes as possible in order to make a vast quantity of indifferent wine that nobody wants, sadly, continues. Perhaps the new, catch-all Languedoc AC (d'Angles 1, Alain Chabanon 3, de Montcalmès 3, Poujol 1, and Saumarez 2), intended to simplify the entry-level wines in a complex and confusing region, will help to put that process into reverse. With encouragement, growers can emulate the many successful individual winemakers across the south and, with organisation, whole appellations like Saint Chinian (Borie Vitarèle 2, Canet Valette 2, Clos Bagatelle 2, Gabelas 1, des Jougla 2, Mas Champart 1) and Faugères (Alquier 2, Barral 2, Estanilles 2, Saint Antonin 1, du Météore 1), where high standards for rich, ripe reds, often grown at altitude, have been rewarded with their own AC status (the former now even has *crus*, godammit) and, equally importantly, with high prices.

Roussillon: The following whistle-stop tour of a region that is Catalan first and French as a formality is no substitute for a nice chat with a friendly, knowledgeable merchant, but it's a start. By the sea, on the Spanish border, small, high-quality Collioure provides big reds and whites (Cave de l'Abbé Rous 3, La Barque Catalan 3, Coume del Mas 3, de Jau 2, Mas Cornet 2, de la Rectorie 2, La Tour Vieille 3) while next door in Banyuls, a lot of the same producers make immortal, chocolate-friendly, tawny port-like *vins doux naturels* from Grenache and the best are spectacular (Mas Blanc 3, Pietri-Géraud 2). Further north, similar but more maderized wines (they leave them out in the sun in big glass bottles called *bonbonnes*) are made in Maury (Mas Amiel 2, Poudéroux 2).

All manner of grapes are grown in Roussillon but the Grenache family and Carignan predominate in the wider region (des Demoiselles 2, Lafage 2), centred around Perpignan, where the best wines are often labelled Roussillon-Villages (Gérard Gauby 2, Mas Amiel 2, Pithon 3, Roc des Anges 2, Des Schistes 1, and Bila-Haut 1, owned by Chapoutier of Rhône fame), sometimes again with the name of the particular village, i.e. Tautavel 2 (Fontanel), Caramany (Clot de l'Oum 3) or, in the southern part, under the new, quality Côtes du Roussillon Les Aspres moniker. Some ambitious estates opt for the vin de pays system, e.g. des Côtes Catalanes (Mas Jullien 2, Matassa 3, Le Soula 3), happy to let their wine do the talking. They know that the whole appellation system is wretched and long overdue for reform and that, for example, while the area's often excellent *vins doux naturels*, mostly from Muscat, are nitpickingly divided between Rivesaltes (which also covers red and dry whites) and some, usually better, Muscat de Rivesaltes (Brial 1, Cazes 2, Mas Cristine 2, de Nouvelles 2, Sarda-Malet 2), while their own, world-class wines are virtually nameless.

Languedoc: The twin prongs of Fitou sticking into the flanks of Corbières cover much the same area as Rivesaltes, and its reputation for strapping red wines, from Carignan blended with all sorts, is well-established – it was the south-west's earliest AC, demarcated in 1948. Recommendations include Bertrand-Bergé [1], Mont Tauch [1] co-op, and Roudène [1]. The best part of mountainous Corbières (Castelmaure co-op, Les Clos Perdus [3], de Lastours [1], Sainte Croix [2]) home to suntanned wines that have a streak of wildness in them, is the Corbières -Boutenac *cru*: La Bastide [1], Fontarèche [1], du Grand Crès [1], Ollieux Romanis [1], de Villemajou [1], de la Voulte [3] Gasparet. A stone's throw inland from the Med, the La Clape sub-region of Languedoc will be an AC before long, especially for whites made from Bourboulenc with a lick of sea salt to them: d'Anglès [2], de la Négly [1], Pech Céléyran [2], Ricardelle [1].

To the north, Minervois (Abbotts [1], Clos de l'Azerolle [1], Khalkhal-Pamies [2], d'Oupia [1], La Rèze [2], Tour Boisée [1], Villerambert-Julien [1]), similarly has an out-performing area for wines with a little more polish, Minervois-La Livinière (Baptiste Boutes [1], Borie de Maurel [1], Cesseras [2], Clos Centeilles [2], Faîteau [1], Laville-Bertou [1], Maris [1], Ste Eulalie [1]) which is now a separate AC in its own right. The *vin doux* thing is done with some style in the north-easternmost corner's Saint-Jean-de-Minervois AC (de Barroubio, Septimanie). Next door in the Cabardès (Jouclary [1], Pennautier [1]), Malepère (Guilhem [1]) and Limoux (de l'Aigle [1], Aimery [1], Antech [2]) ACs the relative proximity of Bordeaux makes itself felt with caberent sauvignon, merlot and malbec (aka Côt here) popping up in blends. Limoux also has some excellent chardonnay and good fizz – Blanquette de Limoux or, better yet, Crémant de Limoux (Sieur d'Arques).

The eastern Languedoc still vastly overproduces bottom-line *vin de table* – it's intractable because so many people's livelihoods depend on their few acres of Carignan (that are often outside even the basic Languedoc AC). But let them eat cake while we think about the fine stuff made at cool altitudes in the sub-regional appellations: Terrasses du Larzac (Mas Cal Demoura [2], Mas de l'Ecriture [2], La Pèira en Damaisèla [2], La Sauvageonne [1]) and, within it, the named terroirs of Montpeyroux (d'Aiguelière [3], d'Aupilhac [2], Grécaux [2]) and Saint Saturnin (d'Archimbaud [1]); rising star Pic Saint Loup (Cazeneuve [2], Clos Marie [3], de l'Hortus [1], de Lancyre [2], Mas Bruguière [2], St Daumary [2]) and one-to-watch Pézenas (les Aurelles [2], Conte des Floris [3], Mas de Mas Pézenas [1], Paul Mas [2], Montrose [1], Prieuré Saint-Jean de Bébian [3]). The Picpoul de Pinet (Picpoul is the grape and it makes tangy, seafood-ready whites such as La Croix Gratiot [1], Félines-Jourdan [1], Saint Martin de la Garrigue [1]) and Grès de Montpellier (Peyre Rose [3], Puech Haut [2]) zones are cooled by the sea rather than altitude and the latter also has named terroirs in St Georges d'Orques (de L'Engarran [1]) and La Méjanelle (Flaugergues [1], Clavel [1]). The *vins doux* – there's always *vin doux* – from the tiny enclaves of Muscat de Frontignan (Peyrade [1]), Muscat de Lunel (Grès Saint Paul [2]) and Muscat de Mireval (d'Exindre [1]) are worth finding.

***GET A HANDLE...**

> THE RULE BOOK HAS BEEN TORN UP IN THE BRAVE NEW WORLD OF INDICATION GÉOGRAPHIQUE PROTEGÉE (IGP) WINES, FORMERLY VIN DE PAYS, AND QUALITY PRODUCERS OF A MYRIAD OF GRAPE VARIETIES AND STYLES OF WINE ARE RUFFLING FEATHERS IN THE TRADITIONAL REGIONS.

Provence: The Côtes de Provence (de l'Aumerade [2], Coussin [2], Ferrages [2], Gavoty [2], Grand Cros [1], Houchart [1], Jas d'Esclans [2], Montaud [1], La Moutète [1], Ott [3], Léoube [2], Mireille [3], de Selle [3];

Richeaume [2], Rimauresq [2], Roquefort [1], Saint-André de Figuière [2], La Vieille Tour [1]) stretches east of the Rhône – up to 100 miles east for the furthest outpost and is well-placed for the irresistible rise of rosé and, although standards are also rising fast for reds and whites, it's often best practice to look for one of the smaller ACs for quality. The western-most, windy hilltop Les Baux-en-Provence (Mas de Gourgonnier [2], Hauvette [3]) shows the AC system is a mess here too with Trévallon, its best producer, labelling its fifty-quid wine as *vin de pays* because it doesn't use the 'correct' mix of grapes.

DRINK LIKE A KING
with ...

Bellefontaine
Bergerie de La Bastide
Pellehaut,
La Revolution
Vignes de l'Eglise

... FOR THE PRICE OF JUST DRINKING

Less dramatic, Coteaux d'Aix-en-Provence (Béates [3], Fonscolombe [1], Vignelaure [2]) covers all the bases with a large variety of grapes as does its tiny, high-quality offshoot Palette (Cremade [3], Simone [3]). The large Luberon area is half-and-half Provence and Rhône geographically and stylistically, with some top producers from the latter spreading their wings over the wide open spaces. Try Perrin [1], La Ferme Julien [1], Tardieu-Laurent [2], Verget du Sud [1], La Canorgue [2], Marrenon [1], Val-Joanis [2] and des Tourettes [1] – a nice wine but doesn't half make you eff-and-blind.

Other classy neighbourhoods are the central Coteaux Varois where cooler temperatures make for fresher reds (Miraval [2], d'Ollières [1], Routas [2], Triennes [2]) and, for crackly, fishy-friendly whites from Rolle (Sardinia's Vermentino), the titchy coastal enclaves of Cassis – no relation to the blackcurrant cordial – (Barbanau [2], Ste-Magdeleine [3]) and Bellet (de Bellet [3], Crémat [3], de la Source [3]). Best of all, and saved for last, Bandol (Gros Noré [3], Lafran-Veyrolles [2], Mas de la Rouvière [2], Pibarnon [3], Pradeaux [3], Roch Redonne [2], La Suffrène [2], Tempier [3]) has been Provence's flagship for generations with meaty, mineral, herb-stuffed, age-worthy reds and man-size rosés mainly from Mourvèdre and Cinsaut respectively and with crisp whites not to be overlooked either.

Corsica

Corsica, or *L'Ile de Beauté*, as all its *vins de pays* immodestly refer to their birthplace, is all about ruggedness and rusticity and there remains a certain amout of it in the wines, which are rapidly improving. It's France, so all the necessaries are catered for by the best producers such as Antoine Arena 3, Clos Culombu 2, Fiumicicoli 2, Maestracci 2, Saparale 2, Torraccia 3. They use Sardinia's Vermentino grape to make zesty, aromatic whites; come-hitherish rosés and lighter, luncheon reds are from the indigenous Sciaccarello; silkier substance for dinner comes from Sangiovese (aka here Nielluccio, and often blended with Sciaccarello); and some excellent Muscat *vins doux* from the best region, Patrimonio, and from Cap Corse, the finger at the northern tip of the island that points emphatically to Italy. Could it possibly be trying to tell us something?

Best of the Rest

The irritating, anomalous category of *Vins Delimité de Qualité Supérieure* (VDQS) has at long last been wound down and replaced with a category (of my own devising – quite an honour, I can tell you!) called *Neither Your Arse Nor Your Elbow* (NYANYE). VDQS was intended to to be a sort of probationary AC status but too seldom did what it said on the tin – so good riddance to it. The last few VDQS areas have either made AC status, like Saint-Pourçain – for decent Pinot Noir and whites from the local Tressallier (Grosbot-Barbara 2, and the co-op – especially their Nuages 1) – and, presumably by now Saint-Mont (see Gascony), or they have become raindrops in the ocean of *vin de pays*.

Vin de pays (country wine), now renamed Indication Géographique Protegée (IGP), was begun in 1973 to reward the more conscientious producers of *vin de table* and to encourage others to emulate them. It is as robust and successful as VDQS was half-arsed and moribund and has been copied in many European countries and beyond. Admirably democratic, with fairly relaxed rules regarding the vine varieties allowed to be grown, the permitted yields from them and so on, VdP wines are almost always vintage-dated, which *vins de table* may not be, and, *sacré bleu*, they almost always show the grape variety on the label. We are in France, though, so the system is organised into three categories, which are, however, no guide to quality. The six big regional *vins de pays* are 1) Pays d'Oc, the biggest producer, for Languedoc and Roussillon's near-500-million-bottle output, Bellefontaine, Bergerie de la Bastide [1], Camplazens [1], de Clovallon [2], Denois [1], Gayda [1], Pasquiers [1], Paul Mas-Claude Val rosé [1], Terres Falmet [1], Vedilhan [1], Vignes de l'Eglise [1], Boutinot's La Revolution [1]; 2) Val de Loire 3) Atlantique (north and east of Bordeaux); 4) Comté-Tolosan (the south-west); 5) Comtés-Rhodaniens (east-central) and 6) Portes de Mediterranée (the south-east and Corsica). Within them, there are fifty-four *départements* each of which has their own, such as *vin de pays* d'Hérault – the daddy for outperformers doing a mini-SuperTuscan thing (Bourguet [3], Grange des Pères [3], Mas de Daumas Gassac [3]) and then around 100 zonal districts that vary from unused obscurity through platforms for exceptional individuals such as Vaucluse (Champs du Moulin [1]), Bouche du Rhône (Trévallon [3]), Gard (Bahourat [1]), Aude (Le Fou [1]), Alpes de Haut Provence (Régusse [1]), Haut Vallée de l'Aude (Baron d'Arques [3]), Coteaux de Peyriac (Massamier la Mignarde [1]) to powerhouses like Côtes de Gascogne

(Grassa [1], Laplace [1], Maubet Pellehaut [1], Sédouprat [1]), Collines Rhodaniennes (Cuilleron [2], Gerin [2], Ogier [2], Perrin [2], Rostaing [2]), Coteaux de l'Ardèche (Ardechois co-op Terrasses [1], Chapoutier [2], Latour [1], Vigneaux [1], Romaneaux-Destezet [3], Souhaut [3]), Principauté d'Orange (Janasse [2], Romero [1], Villedieu-Buisson Co-op [1]) and Côtes Catalanes (Calvet-Thunevin [2], Mas Jullien [3], Matassa [2], Le Soula [3], Pertuisane [3]) with more quality producers than in many in an AC.

fruit wine – if there is sugar to be fermented, then there is wine to be made, but having over time worked out which ones (apart from grapes) are good and having given them generic names like cider and perry, it has been established that unless you distil the results into schnapps, it's best to leave the rest to the WI and the school fête. Surprisingly, Cherry B is still available – it's 11.5% abv and tastes OK, very cherryful, like Dr Pepper, I suppose. An exception can be made for elderflower wine, which isn't made from fruit in any case.

Fuzzy Navel – one part peach schnapps, two parts vodka (or rum) and six parts orange juice shaken with ice and strained into a highball glass. These modern names are every bit as witty and sophisticated as the drinks themselves.

gaglioppo gamay garganega georgia german wine gewürztraminer gimlet gin gin fizz glassware godello goldkapsel graciano grand cru grand vin gran reserva grappa grasă grasshopper grecanico dorato grechetto greco greece green issues grenache grenache blanc grignolino grillo grog grolleau

Garganega – white-grape variety (pronounced with the emphasis on the second syllable) of north-eastern Italy's Veneto region, notably as the principal component of Soave. At its best, it is lovely almondy stuff and a contrast to the oceans of dull stuff at ankle level on supermarket shelves. When late-harvested, semi-dried grapes are turned into Recioto di Soave, one of the great sweet wines of the world.

Georgian wine – former Soviet republic and a candidate for the birthplace of wine as early as 5,000 BC. Still at it, with some decent quality from the best of the numerous indigenous varieties: wines from Red Saperavi and white Mtsvane and Rkatsiteli grapes are making tentative steps out to the world (Old Tbilisi [1], Orovela [1], Tamada [1]).

German beer – Germany shades it over Belgium and the Czech Republic as the home of beer by virtue of the sheer scale of things. A summer-Sunday visit to the biergarten in Munich's Hirschgarten makes the point: it seats over 8,000 people and looks, after a couple of steins of Augustiner's Edelstoff, a bit like Renoir's *Le Moulin de la Galette* stretching in every direction. Staff trundle around collecting the empties on forklift trucks. There's definitely something about it that says much about what it is to be Bavarian but, sadly, such a heavy toll was exacted on my critical faculties that I left the premises in no position to provide any information as to what it could be.

The fact that Germany hasn't experienced the growth seen elsewhere in the number of new breweries dedicating themselves to quality is simply because they never stopped making quality beer in the first place. Rather, as with the rest of its industries, Germany has sensibly restricted consolidation – a lot of cross-ownership prevents people from getting too big for their boots – and the effect is to keep standards, at every level, very high. Nonetheless, the beer map is changing tectonically from the situation at the beginning of this century when big beer had steered clear; 1,400 brewers made so many different beers that Germany's beermaking industry became too fragmented, and AB InBev has bought Beck's, Diebels, Hasseröder and Spaten-Löwenbräu (the latter's Oktoberfestbier, full of crackling hops lifted by the 6.1% abv, was one of the best beers I had on my last trip to Germany, so it ain't all gone to the dogs) and Carlsberg has Holsten. Germans have kept control of jewel-rich Brau Holdings International (Kulmbacher, EKU, Paulaner, Hacker-Pschorr, Thurn und Taxis), having sold Heineken a minority 49.9 per cent in it. Oettinger, Krombacher and Dr Oetker (including the brewing bits of Radeberger, Sternburg and Tucher) remain German-owned. Other top brewers include Bitburger, Dortmunder Actien Brauerei, Dortmunder Union, Eichbaum, Einbecker, Engel Bräu, Ettaler, Hoepfner, Hofbräuhaus München, Hofbräuhaus Traunstein, Kaltenberg/König Ludwig, Rothaus, Veltins, Warsteiner, Weltenburger (a Benedictine abbey dating from 1050), Weihenstephaner (from Bavaria's oldest brewery dating from 1040 and now home to the world's leading beer-research institution – nice work if you can get it), Zehendner.

German styles

When Duke Wilhelm IV of Bavaria framed the Reinheitsgebot beer-purity law in 1516 (I can sense rather a big party coming up) he ruled that only water, malted barley and hops be permitted ingredients in beer, not to preserve its purity but to proscribe the popular use of wheat that was causing food shortages. He exempted his own brewery, of course – beer barons have been bastards for a long time.

A lot of these terms are best thought of as descriptive building-blocks for naming styles – anyone for a Dunkles Weizenbock? (Yes, please, I'll have a Schneider Aventinus.)

Altbier – German version of bitter (Schlosser, Uerige);
bock – strong, seasonally brewed German beer, literally 'billy-goat'. Maibock celebrates the arrival of summer; Doppelbocks, meaning double-bocks, are extra-strong, dark, malty, (Andechser – which unusually doesn't have a name ending in the traditional 'ator', like Ayinger's Celebrator, Augustiner's Maximator, Paulaner's Salvator, etc, and now, in the US, Procrastinator, Terminator); Weizenbock is the white/wheat version; Eisbock is frozen to remove some of the water and increase the abv. In 2010, UK's Brewdog produced a beer of 41% abv in this way to break the record for the world's strongest beer;
Dunkel/Dunkles – means dark and is applied to such styles of lager and wheat beer;
Gose – salty style of Weissbier from Leipzig;
Hefe – means yeast and indicates a bottle-conditioned beer or a cloudy draught version; Hefeweizen

applies in the case of wheat beers;
Hell(es) – means light or pale and indicates a bog-standard lager;
Kellerbier – unfiltered, well-hopped, low-carbonation lager, treated like cask-conditioned ale, and in the Zwickelbier version drawn from the lagering tank;
Kölsch – looks and tastes like a delicate lager, but made like an ale – in Cologne (or Köln) hence the name (Früh, Mühlen);
Märzen – meaning March, when beer is brewed to be fabulously ready for the Oktoberfest;
Radler – shandy, called Russen with white/wheat beer, which is what that stuff is for and what shandy is meant to be;
Rauchbier – 'smoke' beer made with barley malted over a beechwood fire and a bit of an acquired taste, but shows how clever the artificial-flavour manufacturers are because those hickory-smoked barbecue sauces taste just like this;
Schwarzbier – 'black beer', very dark German lager (Köstritzer);
Trube – means troubled, as in cloudy. 'There may be Trube ahead . . .'
Weissbier – the large family of 'white' beer, describing the cloudy appearance and Weizen 'wheat', for its origins in having about half wheat to malted barley. The terms are interchangeable. This group is as big and varied as that of stout but at the other end of the chromatic spectrum, in both draught and bottled versions (Erdinger Weissbräu is huge and Schneider one of the best). Some Dunkel Weissbiers have bits batting about in their roiling, turbid maelstroms (which doesn't seem to me to be a good idea); Kristalweiss, is the clear, filtered version more up my Straße – they sometimes have a touch of tangerine with the bread-dough sourness, but you wonder if the cloudiness is part of the appeal for contrarians and whole-foodies).

German wine – it is important to get one thing straight from the outset: Germany is one of the great wine-producing nations and when it sticks to what it does best the results are the finest of their type to be found anywhere. It is inarguably the spiritual home of arguably the greatest white wine grape, Riesling, and the temporal home of winemakers who can tease from it such a diversity of tantalising styles as to leave one a-tingle with anticipation.

G

But before we get anywhere near any of the tingly bits we have to confront the problem that German wine comes with rather a lot of 'previous' – the three-pronged fork on which their export market impaled itself in the 1970s and 1980s. Firstly, there was misleading labelling – where the names of quality villages were expropriated for the purpose of labelling inferior wines from their outlying regions (called Bereich or Grosslagen). Doesn't sound too bad until I mention the leprous likes of Piesporter Michelsberg and Bereich Bernkastel. Second of this unholy trinity were the brands of Liebfraumilch (Our Lady's Milk – a rather offputting notion in itself). People who were appalled by Black Tower and the long-established Blue Nun will be equally appalled to know that they're still here – and thriving – but probably not much mollified to know that the wines are at least somewhat improved. (Research needs to be done about the significance of female religious figures in the marketing of German plonk, I feel.)

Whatever, thirty or forty years on it seems impossible that the creation of these brands should have been in response to the phenomenal popularity of German wine. Unused to wine, British servicemen stationed in Germany after the Second World War had taken a shine to the sweeter German styles and brought the taste home with them.

The third villain of the piece was the grape that many of these wines were themselves made from: Müller-Thurgau. A botched crossing of Riesling and Sylvaner, this overproductive Frankenstein's monster among grape varieties makes flaccid, flabby sugar-waters – by which I mean that they lack any of the acidity that is the very essence of upstanding German whites (and the very thing that will soon get that tingle thing going).

In terms of official classification, Tafelwein, the lowest quality level, thankfully accounts only for a few per cent of production and should generally be avoided. The next – and largest – rung accommodates the QbA wines (Qualitätswein bestimmter Anbaugebiete, if you must), a very mixed bag that should be approached with caution unless one is familiar with the individual grower's output. In general it can be said that it is not easily possible to find good German wines in the supermarkets (in the UK, Waitrose is the very honourable exception) and only with difficulty on the high street or in the mall. Having said this, one of the biggest producers, Kendermann's (their Black Tower brand notwithstanding), have moved up a gear and meanwhile two of the best and biggest independents, Ernst Loosen (pronounced 'loh-sen') and Johannes Leitz, are rapidly morphing into the sort of quality-conscious brands that could really move German wine up the agenda.

So we'll need to get in touch with an independent merchant to lay our hands on some of the wines to be found of the five-rung Qualitätswein mit Prädikat (QmP – literally, 'distinction') quality-rating ladder, which is based on increasing levels of natural grape sugars. We need help anyway, because traditionally there have always been a large number of part-time, smallholding producers who used to hand over their harvest to the local co-ops but who now tend to do their own thing.

*GET A HANDLE...

RIESLING KABINETT-LEVEL WINES (THE LOWEST AND LEAST SWEET QMP RUNG) TYPICALLY PROVIDE A FIRST WAVE OF LUSCIOUS, SWEETLY RIPE FRUIT WHICH IS MOMENTARILY LICKED INTO SHAPE BY A RUSH OF LINGERING, CLEAN, GREEN ACIDITY. IDEAL FOR GRATUITOUS DRINKING (AS MOST DON'T MARRY WELL WITH FOOD) AND COMING IN AT AROUND 9% ALCOHOL, THEY ENSURE THAT NOVITIATES CONTEMPLATING OVER A COUPLE OF LEISURELY GLASSES THIS TINGLING SYNTHESIS OF THE SWEET AND THE DRY WILL HAVE STARTED TO UNDERSTAND GERMAN WINE.

Next up, Spätlese ('late harvest') designates significantly sweeter wines of the type Hugh Johnson has unimprovably described as 'throbbing with fruit'. Sweeter yet, Auslese ('selected harvest') and seriously sweet Beerenauslese (made from individually selected 'berries') put us in pudding territory, although again they are perhaps best sipped unencumbered by any food.

On the top rung (if we exclude the tiny quantities of Eiswein, made from grapes left out until the first freezes of winter arrive) is Trockenbeerenauslese (often unambitiously abbreviated to TBA). The additional two syllables contribute 'dry' (in the sense of 'dried out' or 'shrivelled') to the foregoing and the partial desiccation of the grapes serves to concentrate the sugars to an even more overwhelming extent. These are rare and expensive nectars and although the honey, apricot and marmalade comparisons may sound cloying it is essential to remember that everything is kept fit and balanced by that same sergeant-major of acidity that spends all day running up and down the ladder.

The Gothic nature of German labelling – one of my own breakthrough German wine experiences springs to mind with a half bottle of Bürklin-Wolf Wachenheimer Gerumpel Trockenbeerenauslese Riesling from, I think, 1983 – is nothing like as mad as it seems and, approached methodically, it can be our friend. They are the most informative labels of any country and generally name the producer (here, Bürklin-Wolf), the village (Wachenheim) and, for the better wines, a specific vineyard (Gerumpel) and the level of ripeness as well as the grape and the vintage. One problem is knowing which of the first three is which (a clue is that the suffix 'er' is often added to the village name) and another is that idiosyncratic German winemakers tend to do things their own way and one man's idea of exactly what a Gerumpel Auslese should be may be rather different to his neighbour's.

Geographically, Germany's wine-producing regions are clustered in the south-west of the country. If I conjure for myself a quintessential and uniquely German white wine – a delicate, poised, ethereal thing, with fruit pure to the point of chastity, innocent of any oak of course but with a seriousness and a clarity of purpose expressed by the straightness of its spine of minerality and acidity – I'm probably thinking about a Riesling Kabinett from the Mosel-Saar-Ruwer, the most prestigious region. The slopes that tumble down to the river – some so steep that the grapes have to be winched up at harvest time – are what most people probably think of when they picture a German riverside vineyard. The villages of Graach, Wehlen, Ürzig and Erden on the bends of the river north of the main town of Bernkastel are home to the greatest concentration of the country's most illustrious winemakers. Among them are JJ Prum [3] (their austere, haunting wines may be the best) and the expansive and expanding unofficial ambassador for the German cause, Dr

Ernst Loosen [1], who has footholds on many of the slopes and further afield. Other notables include Selbach-Oster [2], Willi Schaefer [2], Kurt Hain [2] and Reinhold Haart [3] (both Kurt and Reinhold make some of the real Piesporter to shame those flagrant label abusers), Meulenhof [2], Fritz Haag [2] and Willi Haag [3]. Some of the other Middle Mosel names to conjure with are Max Ferdinand Richter [1], Schloss Lieser [2] and Kerpen [2], and the Moselland [1] co-operative should also be added to the roll of honour.

Like the wines themselves, everything about the Mosel is elegant and elongated, including the tall green *flute* bottles and the stems of the traditional glasses. There is a growing feeling in the area that the recent sequence of excellent vintages may owe something to rising temperatures, which, combined with the natural shelter provided by the surrounding hills, have allowed the grapes to ripen fully far more frequently than used to be the case. Some odd words crop up here and there on labels – Priesterseminar, Gymnasium and Konvikt (less worrying than it sounds – it means 'seminary'). In the tiny Saar area, Egon Müller [2] rules, with Van Volxem [2], von Hövel [2] and Hanno Zilliken [3] in attendance while von Kesselstat [1], von Schubert [2] and Karthäuserhof [3] are the names to drop when talking about the even tinier Ruwer (but far better to walk the walk and buy some of the wines).

Heading east, the good folk of the Nahe region have pulled up the vast majority of their Müller-Thurgau vines (it accounts for about only ten per cent now) and replaced them with Riesling and the red Dornfelder. Schlossböckelheim, Oberhausen, Niederhausen and Norheim are the best villages and although the name that rings loudest by far around the hillsides is that of Dönnhoff [2], others like Emrich-Schönleber [3] and Schlossgut Diel [3] can also be heard.

Along the north bank of the Rhine, the villages either side of

Wiesbaden once produced the river's most prestigious wines. To the west, around Rüdesheim, J Leitz [1], Georg Breuer [2] and Johannishoff [2] still keep the flame burning and the Beerenauslesen and Trockenbeerenauslesen are among Germany's most prized wines. Other names to look out for are Peter Jakob Kühn [2], Robert Weil [1] and, to the east, Domdechant Werner [2] in the town of Hochheim, which gave us the name 'hock' (which, if used at all by anybody – except me – now seems to apply to any Rhine wine in a tall brown bottle).

Across the river in the Rheinhessen – until recently Germany's most productive wine region, and not always in a good way – there's a lot going on. Many grape varieties are being grown and new ones are being tried out all the time by ambitious young winemakers for whom the drowning of the reputation of the hallowed vineyards of Nierstein in an ocean of crap Niersteiner Gutes Domtal is history. Brüdersberg and Hipping (and Rothenburg, further downstream in Nackenheim) are some of those vineyards; Heyl zu Herrnsheim [2], Guntrum [1] and Gunderloch [1] are some of the best names of the old guard who farm them. The upstarts are doing interesting things as well – often under organic and, in some cases, biodynamic regimes – with Silvaner, Scheurebe, Huxelrebe, Rieslaner, Weissburgunder (Pinot Blanc) and also Riesling. They include Dreissigacker [2], Keller [3], Wittmann [3] and Stefan Winter [2].

This new wave of winemakers often look south to the Pfalz region – principal usurper of the Rheingau's throne and now also the most productive – for their inspiration. This is the sunniest, driest part of the country and it shares those characteristics, and the capacity to produce excellent wine from a wide variety of grapes, with Alsace across the border in France. Scour the shelves for labels showing the villages of the best area, the Mittelhardt: Forst, Wachenheim,

Deidesheim, Ruppertsberg are what we're looking for and if our reward is wines made by the likes of Müller-Catoir 2, Bürklin-Wolf 2, von Buhl 2, Kurt Darting 2, Basserman-Jordan 2, Knipser 2 and Schloss Vollrads 2 then happiness will be the result.

Baden Württemberg is the southernmost region and covers the largest area – these two factors make it completely different from the rest of Germany. Warmer temperatures make for riper, fuller, food-friendly wines from all the Burgunders: Spät, which makes most of the forty-five per cent of the Baden wines that are red and the seventy per cent in Württemberg (but where Lemberger – the Austrian Blaüfrankisch – is also successful); Weiss, and, most importantly, Grau, which is the Pinot Gris that also thrives across the Rhine in Alsace. Heger 3, Salwey 3 (especially for reds), Karl Heinz Johner 2, Metternich 2 and Aldinger 2 are a few of the leading producers who have reduced the percentage of wine produced by the co-operatives from ninety per cent to less than seventy per cent.

Best to confront straightaway the fact that Franken wines are usually bottled in a *Bocksbeutel* – a shape most familiar from Mateus Rosé and apparently modelled on the shape of a goat's scrotum – and move on. The Silvaner grape gets its chance to prove it's the dog's bollocks here, making wines of intense minerality in the capable hands of growers like Horst Sauer 3 (in the worryingly named Lump vineyard in Escherndorf), Wircher 2 and Fürst 2 (who also make some of Germany's best Spätburgunder). There are some sensational sweet wines, too, if you can get your hands on them.

Brief mention here of the tiny Ahr region, largely devoted to red wine chiefly from made from Spätburgunder. Meyer-Näkel 3 are generally reckoned to be the leading exponent.

One of the great joys in the whole world of wine (and a possible upside of the general Anglo-Saxon disdain for Hock and Mosel) is that the basic or 'estate' wines made by these Wagnerian giants of winemaking can be had – if people take the trouble to look – for Lilliputian prices, often for less than ten pounds per bottle. From there, it's a small step up to the Kabinett wines; thereafter, a happy land of diversity is opened.

Another great joy is the result of stashing away a steely Riesling or twelve for a few years (although sometimes merchants will come up with mature vintages at prices that, at Kabinett or Spätlese level, can be lower than the cost just of commercial storage for a few years). When they emerge, the steeliness has been given an extra edge and glint with something unmistakably like petrol or kerosene – some people don't like it up 'em but those that do are mad for it.

The three mortal sins commited by Germany's wine industry have not been entirely expiated (although Müller-Thurgau is in retreat) but they are at least offset by three cardinal virtues, which should bode well as far as exports are concerned. They are, respectively, the appeal of the naturally low-alcohol wine styles described above; the growing global interest in the sleeping giant that is the Riesling grape; and a style of wine, confusingly called 'Trocken', which has exploded in popularity within Germany but is yet to catch on outside. At its best, Trocken, which now accounts for some sixty per cent of production including most reds, maintains the luscious fruitiness of traditional styles such as Spätlese but vinifies them to a level of dryness that will be satisfactorily familiar to drinkers weaned on Aussie Chardonnay before cutting their teeth on South American Sauvignon Blanc.

Germany's vineyard is situated at the very northern extremity of where it should be possible to produce palatable red wines, though at this latitude it's fairly hit and miss whether the grapes ripen fully; nonetheless, an astonishing forty per cent of German wine is now red, with the percentage growing. Those of the best producers of white wine who also make some reds apply the same fanatical levels of attention to them but they have a bigger problem in that they are, in many cases, flogging a dead horse. Mostly the results are on the thin side, or on the tart side, and all too often on the thin, tart side. The expired animal can sometimes be maintained in the upright position by means of close confinement in a tight-fitting structure of expensive new oak, but like a racehorse in the stalls awaiting the start, when the gate is sprung the deception is revealed and the beast defiantly stays put.

As in England, poor old Pinot Noir – here called Spätburgunder – has to shoulder much of the misplaced burden of hope. There are exceptions such as Knipser [2] in the Pfalz; Lang [2] in the Rheingau; Salwey [3] in Baden; and Loosen's Villa Wolf [1], for a rare example of a good, inexpensive red wine. There's also the odd exceptional wine, such as Fürst [3] in Franken. But buying German Pinot Noirs speculatively is likely to lead to disappointment or worse. Dornfelder, a crossing developed in 1956, is often a better bet for fleshier, fruitier and notably silky if unsophisticated wines. The other major red grape is Portugieser (aka Blauer Portugieser), which is neither Portuguese nor by any means a 'diamond geezer', making as it does mainly dull rosé *Weissherbst*.

The Germans are the biggest consumers of sparkling wine, the vast, inexplicable bulk of which is their own frequently one-dimensional, frothy Sekt. It is possible to get your hands on one or two standouts from conscientious producers such as Dr Loosen [1], Solter [1] or von Buhl [2] but comparatively little is exported, leastways to the UK, which appears to have adopted an unofficial policy of 'no Sekts please, we're British'.

Gewürztraminer – spicily distinctive, pink-skinned grape that doesn't mind whether its name has the umlaut or not. Why would it, having spread out from Alsace to every self-respecting winegrowing country in a matter of a decade or two? None of them have yet improved on Alsace, whose fat, rich, rose-petal-and-lychee-scented wines – and that's the dry ones – are well-matched with oriental food, while the luscious, late-harvest, sweet versions are best contemplated in splendid isolation.

Gimlet – one part lime juice cordial to two parts gin shaken with ice and strained through the eye of a needle in to a cocktail glass.

gin – in essence a vodka principally flavoured with juniper, gin's origins are in the medicinal cordials of the Middle Ages when the flavourings were themselves remedies and the alcohol both preserved them and helped the medicine go down. Later on, it was the flavourings that were used to help the alcohol go down. In its modern form, gin originated in seventeenth-century Holland, where soldiers who had derived 'Dutch courage' from it during the Thirty Years War then brought it back to Britain. London Dry Gin – now a meaningless phrase except to denote an unsweetened product – was the result and it, in turn, led the way to Gin Lane ('drunk for a penny, dead drunk for twopence'), the Gin Act of 1736 (quadrupling the price and curbing the sale of it) and the Gin Riots (the understandable response). Plymouth Dry Gin is a legally defined style but with only one, excellent and eponymous, producer.

The other principal botanicals (and flavourings) that have survived into the modern age are almonds, angelica, anise, caraway, cardamom, coriander, lemon peel, liquorice, orange peel and orris root. Dutch gin 'jenever', either 'oude' (aged for a minimum of one year) or 'jonge', is a less alcoholic, consequently heavier, more viscous style, usually strongly flavoured, invariably drunk neat and without any of the dodgy connotations that 'Mother's Ruin' has in the UK or memories of Prohibition-style 'bathtub gin' in the US.

Quality producers and brands – some brand new – are reinventing gin in the UK. Bombay led the way and there are now an array of others such as Blackwoods, Caorunn, Chase, Geranium, Greenall's, Hayman's, Hendrick's, Juniper Green, Martin Miller's, No.3, Old Raj, Oxley, Pink 47, Sacred, Spismith, Whitley Neill and Zephyr. If it's G&T you're after, remember that the quality of the 'T' makes a huge difference and as a refreshing contrast to any old crap gin mixed with a saccharine-filled supermarket tonic, try one of the above mixed with Fentimans or Fever-Tree. Of the other major manufacturers and brands of gin, Boodles, Gilbey's and Tanqueray are excellent; Beefeater (especially 24) and Booth's are good but Gordon's is so rough it would send a shiver up the spine of even the marinated minger in the middle of Hogarth's etching.

Gin knows no borders these days and good ones are made worldwide, in Austria (Monopolowa), France (Blue Ribbon, Citadelle, Nouaisor, Magellan – which is blue), Germany (Schlichte Steinhäger – in its earthenware bottle), Holland, obviously (Bols, Damrak, Doornkaat, Van Gogh, Zuidam), Ireland (Cork), New Zealand (South), Spain – Europe's largest consumer (Larios), Sweden (Right) and in the USA, where they may not do the three-martini lunch so often these days but they do still love their gin, as the proliferation of brands shows (Bardenay, Barton, Bluecoat, Burnett's, Death's Door, Ethereal, Fleischmann, Glenmore, Jackelope, Karkov, Leopold's, McCormick, New Amsterdam, North Shore, Port of Barcelona, Rogue, Organic Nation, Seagram Extra Dry – the brand lives on although the company is long gone) as does the presence of

UK brands such as Baffert's and Quintessential, which are sold only in the US. The Philippines is the Gin Lane *de nos jours* – they now consume forty per cent of the world's total (over 200 million bottles of San Miguel – yup, same people as the beer).

Gin Fizz – one part lime juice to two parts gin, simple syrup to taste, shaken with ice, strained in to a highball glass and finished with soda; known to travel under the alias of Tom Collins, whose brother John disguises himself with bourbon instead of gin. Rum, cousin of John and Tom, uses something else entirely – rum, indeed.

glassware – a huge amount of the pleasure of booze is transmitted via our sense of smell, especially when it comes to better quality booze. Go-faster glasses help to amplify this and it is especially important for wine glasses, which don't have to be expensive but do have to be a) quite big; b) in-curving, tulip-like, towards the rim to keep the aromas in; and above all, c) clean.

The best wine glasses are made in Austria by Riedel and of their heroically, insanely huge range, the extraordinary, hand-blown 'Sommelier' cost upwards of fifty quid a stem so you feel quite sad when you break them. The much cheaper 'Vinum' range are safer and still mighty fine. The glass is very thin and I've come to the conclusion that the principle here is basically the same as with condoms – the lining of a sheep's intestine may have done the job for the Elizabethans but, for my money, the less there is between you and the object of your affections, the better. Wine glasses must be held by the stem – not by the bowl because it looks barbarous, nor by the base, as I sometimes do, because it looks pretentious.

If you 'do' cocktails, you probably already do the glasses (and know that between short, squat 'shot' glasses; tall, straight-sided highball glasses, tumbler-like short, straight-sided rocks and the iconic long-stemmed, slope-sided cocktail glass itself you've covered most of the bases).

With beer, as with life generally, 'a glass' is more important than 'which glass' and if you find yourself talking about the advantages of nonic glasses, or asking 'mein host' to keep your pewter stein behind the bar of your local, it's already too late for you. As for the other sort – beer goggles – it's just too broad a subject to cover here.

Glenfiddich – the ground-breaking daddy of single malts, the first one to become a brand in its own right and still the biggest-selling, owned by William Grant and located on Speyside. The older malts can compete with the best, but its basic twelve-year-old (unrecognisably improved recently) has probably done more to spread the malt gospel than anything else.

Glenlivet, The – one of the biggest-production single malts offering similarly good value at the basic level to the other two Big Gs. Founded on Speyside in 1824 and now owned by Pernod Ricard.

Glenmorangie – flagship whisky brand (pronounced glenMORanjy) of France's LVMH, rapidly expanding both its production and its repertoire to include lots of different wood finishes and other experimental 'expressions', but without any compromise in quality.

Glen Moray – low-key Speyside distillery sold by LVMH to fellow frogs La Martiniquaise in 2008 and currently offering a good-value introduction to the world of malt whisky; however, the new owners sell a lot of 'yeah-but, no-but' whisky in France, which may make the future of this brand unclear.

Godello – (aka Gouveio in Portugal) classy white-grape variety of north-western Spain. Could become a contender in the zesty-whites division when Sauvignon Blanc-fatigue eventually sets in.

Goldkapsel – literally a gold-coloured capsule around corks used by some German producers as a means of designating which of their wines they, subjectively, feel are especially good within a designated, regulated category – usually at the Spätlese to Beerenauslesen levels.

Graciano – (aka Tinta Miùda in Portugal) fine, red-wine grape of northern Spain, the reputation of which as low-yielding and susceptible to disease almost led to its disappearance as a constituent of the best Riojas. A few growers have kept the faith – or acquired it in the case of Brown Brothers of Australia – and addressing such lily-livered behaviour with a regime of five-mile runs at the crack of dawn followed by brisk cold showers are a number of single varietals (CVNE, Contino, Zorzal) that foreground the characteristic damsons, liquorice and mulberries.

grand cru – literally 'great growth', a term applied to the best vineyards and by extension the wines made from the grapes grown in them, specifically in Burgundy, including Chablis, Bordeaux's Right Bank (the left has a somewhat different system) and, more recently, in Alsace. Translated as *Grosses Gewächs* in Germany.

grand vin – applied to the principal wine produced by a Bordeaux château, when more than one wine (i.e. a second wine) is made.

gran reserva – traditionally the top classification for wines in various *Denominaciónes de Origenes* (DOs) of Spain, notably Rioja, where red wines – theoretically only from superior vintages – are required to be aged in oak for a minimum of two years and held back until five years after the vintage (four for whites, which are required to spend six months in cask). Still a reasonable indication of what to expect, if not always of quality, and not appropriate for all styles these days now that some producers are prepared to forego the honours to produce more modern, fruit-led wines.

grappa – any nineteen-year-old who traverses Italy on an InterRail trip and finds himself in want of funds to finance the purchase of any but the cheapest industrial grappa, and only gaggingly manages the consumption thereof because, 'It's all we've got, so neck some!' will be surprised to find that – at its best – grappa is one of the (if not *the)* finest and most complex fruits of the distiller's loom. My first encounter put me off for twenty-five years so I know the problem. My second encounter – with Tignanello grappa – was a revelation of citrus, almonds, red meat, toffee and coffee – pretty much everything you could delightfully come up with.

Grappa is Pomace brandy – distilled from wine fermented from the leftover skins and pips in the same way as the French marc. Different grapes make very different grappas, especially in different hands. In this respect, it's the most multifarious of spirits – the leavings of a big red, like a booming Brunello di Montalcino, make a very different grappa to those from a feathery, sparkling white Moscato d'Asti. Quality is variable and still shocking for the cheapest. It's best to head straight to the top – thankfully never desperately expensive – including those made from other SuperTuscans. Sassicaia and the feral, yellow peril of ash-wood-aged Ornellaia are equally extraordinary, but there are many fine ones for the cost of a decent single malt. Try Castello di Banfi, Julia, Marzadro, Morellino di Scansano Co-op, Nardini, Poli, Suprema and Tosolini.

Grasshopper – equal parts light crème de cacao and green crème de menthe and two parts single cream shaken with ice and strained directly down the drain or into a cocktail glass if you're still curious.

Greco Bianco – southern Italian white grape of ostensibly Greek origins and excelling as one of the holy trinity of Campania whites (with Fiano and Falanghina) in making similarly sappy, succulent, big-boned wines, which are on the lookout for a roast chicken, but round enough to drink on their own in Greco di Tufo. Thought to possibly offer a glimpse of Roman-era wines and deservedly gaining popularity.

Greek wine – given that they started in the seventh century BC, it's disappointing that it took until the end of the twentieth century AD for Greece to start making good wine. With such hot summers, fitting the right grape to the right climate has been the key (big surprise) and it's refreshing that growers have kept faith with so many traditional and indigenous grapes and added international varieties only sparingly. The biggest companies (Boutari 1, Kourtaki 1) operate nationwide, maintaining high standards, and there have been lots of encouraging start-ups, from major investors to enthusiastic minnows.

Retsina (resinated wine) is a great testament to the power of holidays to make people, including me, happy with anything. The real stuff starts in the relatively cool north-eastern Macedonia – in Halkidiki, then for some crisp, sophisticated whites from Assyritko (try Biblia Chora 2 or Tsantali 1). The Naoussa region especially produces heady reds from Xinomavro (Boutari 1, Kir-Yanni 1), but the Peloponnese is the best region, notably around Nemea for some serious oak-aged reds from Aghiorgitiko grown at cooler altitudes (try Gaia 2, Megapános 2 and Spiropoulos 1). In the north you'll find sweet, fortified reds from Mavrodaphne of Patras. Around the islands, Santorini grows the best Assyrtiko (Gaia 2, Hatzidakis 2, Sigalas 2) on its wind-blown volcanic heights; Samos makes luscious Muscats (the cooperative is the only producer, especially of Nectar 2 from semi-dried grapes) and Moraitis 1 in Paros makes some fine rosé from the local Mandilaria.

green issues – seem to fall in to two categories as far as wine particularly is concerned and the first, what's actually in the bottle, is dealt with elsewhere under organic (and biodynamically produced) wines. Painting green with a broader brush, the issues are of climate change, how the wine came to be made in the first place, and the wine-miles question of how the bottle found its way to your table.

Presentation is everything in the world of wine and big, heavy bottles are *de rigueur* especially for showboating New World wines but it seems bonkers that some chest-thumping organic producers are using bottles that are three times the weight of their contents. The problem is – curse my cloven carbon hoofprint – that it feels good to pour wine from a bottle with a bit of gravitas to it. The new lightweight glass bottles say 'cheap', as much as the plastic bottles say rain-sodden camping 'holidays' in Brittany. So dire are they that I may even prefer the reconstituted orange juice Tetra Paks.

Oddly, the pouches that are starting to appear may be the way ahead. They're a clean break with the past and all its burdens of association and expectation. They weigh virtually nothing so the carbon footprint of the contents is reduced by twenty per cent compared to a glass bottle, they can be chilled in minutes and you can squodge them into a tight corner of the fridge or picnic basket.

As for climate change, there may be a great deal to be learned from viticulture, perhaps more than from any other form of agriculture, because winemaking is now so precise, and there's so much research and science involved, and so much passion and so much . . . money. The grapes for some of the best wines in the world are grown at the absolute climatological limits of where they will (usually) ripen fully. Leading winemakers in places as diverse as Champagne, Burgundy, the Mosel and Australia's coolest climate areas believe they are seeing changes and adapting to them and now anticipating them on a year-by-year basis.

Grenache – some grapes have all the luck while others have to grind it out. Grenache is the fourth most widely planted grape variety and wines of the stature of Châteauneuf-du-Pape and Rioja would be unrecognisable without it. And are we grateful? Do we say, 'Well done, son?'

Grenache thrives in the poorest soils, where it needs to send its roots way down in search of the precious minerals that mark its serious side and offset the eager-to-please, 'Juicy Fruit' part of its character, which comes from being relatively low in tannins. Unblended, it makes ripe, round wines with a touch of sweetness often described as 'jammy'.

The rosés that taste so good on a sweltering Provençal hillside (and never quite the same in November in Bognor) are mostly made from Grenache and in Tavel, Lirac and Bandol are among the world's best pink wines, surprisingly complex but with plenty of stuffing, too, for high-testosterone barbecues. To the west, in Maury and in Banyuls, a stone's throw from the Spanish border, Grenache makes complex, chocolate-friendly, age-worthy fortified wines that are all about nuts and toffee and spice.

Across the border the Spanish know it as Garnacha, or Garnatxa in Navarra (where no Basque-ified word is complete without at least one 'X' and preferably a 'Z' or two for good measure). It's the cornerstone here and in up-and-coming Priorato and receives the award for best supporting actor in Rioja, where it provides the richness that broadens out the darker, denser tones of Tempranillo.

The Aussies grubbed-up acres of Grenache to plant yet more Cabernet Sauvignon in the 1980s. Now they cherish what remains and are even replanting with promising results. And in Sardinia, under the alias of Canonau, grenache makes the island's finest red wines in a darker and uncharacteristically macho style.

grog – five parts dark rum to two parts lemon juice stirred with boiling water to taste. Serve in a rocks glass with a clove, a piece of cinnamon and one lump of sugar. What shall we do with a drunken sailor?

Grüner Veltliner – noble white signature grape of Austria (aka 'groovy', so I'm told) offering – where yields are kept low – a full-bodied, Germanic purity of fruit allied with serious minerality and often finished with a twist of what is usually characterised as white pepper.

hangover hárslevelü harvey wallbanger health and alcohol home-made booze hungary huxelrebe

health and alcohol home-made booze hungary huxelrebe hangover

hangover hárslevelü harvey wallbanger health and alcohol home-made booze hungary huxelrebe

H

hangover – aka *gueule de bois* (wood-mouth) in France; evocatively *Kater* (tomcat) in Germany and Holland; ominously *resaca* (the taking back) in Spain; the Italians are so sensible (in this respect) that they don't have a proper word for it. Most of the problems of hangover are to do with dehydration and there are no cures – whatever Jeeves says – only reparations and offerings to the gods and the dogs that bit you.

Hangover management, especially prevention, is the best course – a way of life, for some – and the consumption of plenty of food (before and during) and water (during and after and at least an equal proportion to booze) can mitigate the effects of all but the most heinous self-abuse. The plan is to avoid waking up feeling like Lucky Jim: 'His mouth had been used as a latrine by some small creature of the night, and then as its mausoleum. During the night, too, he'd somehow been on a cross-country run and then been expertly beaten up by the secret police. He felt bad.'

Harvey Wallbanger – build two parts vodka over ice in a highball glass with orange juice to taste and float one part Galliano on top to finish. Then again, don't (see hangover, above).

health and alcohol – as far as chronic abuse is concerned (as opposed to the acute issues – again, see hangover), let's not mess about: alcohol is an addictive poison and if you consume too much of it regularly, it'll fuck you up. Over a long period, it'll kill you. Cirrhosis, psychosis, depression and suicide are some of the undesirable outcomes and even trying to avert these can kill you as, uniquely, alcohol withdrawal, unless carefully managed, can be fatal. The horrors of *delirium tremens* – the DTs – include hallucination, tachycardia, diaphoresis, seizures, diarrhoea, paranoia, tremor and formication, and carried off as many as a third of sufferers before the advent of modern tranquillisers and they still kill five per cent of sufferers.

Even if it's under control, booze makes you fat and beer makes you very fat, very fast. But there are a few upsides and in general very moderate regular consumption, especially of red wine, is now considered to be of benefit to good health. Specifically, resveratrol, a phytoalexin found in the skin of red grapes, has been the subject of bold claims for its anti-inflammatory and anti-cancer properties, not least by the growers in south-western France of the Tannat grapes in which it is particularly abundant. The healthful effects of wine drinking are foregrounded in the 'French paradox', which draws attention to the fact the French consume large amounts of saturated fats as well as wine and yet have a relatively low incidence of coronary heart disease.

As with most issues relating to diet and health, it is not rocket science to work out that all things in moderation are fine and anything in excess is not.

Highland Park – Orkney distillery owned by the Edrington Group, whose eighteen-year-old whisky has been serially called the 'Best Spirit in the World' by a US spirits review, and – for the money – I'm not about to argue the toss.

homemade booze – moonshine made out of any old rubbish distilled any old how is especially popular, aka *changaa* in Kenya where, especially when contaminated with methanol, it kills hundreds of people a year. In India it is known as *tharra* which, when contaminated with methanol, kills . . . wait a minute, could there be some connection here?

Pruno is not distilled but fermented in Ziploc bags filled with mashed fruit, water, bread (for the yeast), sugar and ketchup to make it taste nice. Popular in US jails despite apparently tasting of vomit, with which it has a surprising amount in common.

The home-brew beer people make the point that beermaking began like that (with such reasoning they should live in caves). Home-brew is not usually even properly homemade as the wort is bought in big cans, sold by manufacturers who doubtless saw the home-brewers coming. Making beer is complicated and best left to experts, some of whom, it must be admitted, did start out at home, but just don't do it, OK? Homemade wine is not nice either (except sometimes elderflower).

Hungary – 'H' has been rather a depressing letter so far so clap hands for Hungary. It has the usual international grape varieties but, more interestingly, lots of unusual ones such as Furmint and Hárslevelü, which make manly dry whites (from the likes of Dobogó [2] or Hilltop [1]) that wear leather trousers and slap their thighs before taking on all that incredibly heavy food. Those grapes are also responsible for Hungary's unique contribution to the Great Wines of the World (drum roll) – the sumptuous sweet Tokaji – graded in order of sweetness from three to six *puttonyos* (after the number of buckets-full of super-sweet *aszu* wine added to the drier base wine). Best producers of the 'wine of kings and king of wines' include Disznókö [3], Dobogó [2], István Szepsy [3], Királyudvar [3], Oremus [3], Royal Tokaji [3], Tokaj Classic [3]).

Essencia – the only wine I've ever been served in a spoon – is made for the gods. A tiny, ageless amount of this barely liquid, barely alcoholic (as low as 3% abv), expensive essence of sweetness can have the equivalent of a bag of sugar in a bottle but plenty of acidity to keep the extraordinary treacle-sponge-and-custard flavours alive.

Reds from Kardaka (aka Gamza in Bulgaria) and Kékfrankos – which is Austria's Blaufränkisch – (try Attila Gere 3 or Weninger 2) can be delicious if not exactly complex and, to the country's great credit, it's hard to find a bottle of Bull's Blood these days, although it's renascent in its original, prestigious form known as Bikavér (from Tibor Gal 2).

Huxelrebe – productive cross-bred white-grape vine developed and grown in Germany and, to a small extent as an early ripener, in England. Try: Darting from Germany, Frome Valley from England.

ice wine iceland international bitterness units india inzolia irish coffee israel italy ice wine inzolia

Iceland – nothing good here, only some of the world's most expensive imported booze sold by the state monopoly and the vile, strongly caraway-flavoured akvavit called Brennivín (aka locally 'black death'), which does, however, help to drown the flavours of some of the vile traditional foods. Anyone for sour rams' testicles? Putrefied shark? The frozen food supermarket chain isn't up to much either, so I hear.

ice wine – Canadian term for their ultra-late-harvest sweet wines and in common usage in English to refer to the similar *Eisweins* of Germany and Austria.

India – it's always difficult for a booze industry to thrive in a country that has as one of its founding aims that of the total Prohibition of alcohol. Despite a tradition of wine running throughout 2000 years of its convoluted history right up to the end of the colonial period, India has had to start again and did so with a decent sparkler in the early 1980s called Omar Khayyam. The baton was passed to new investment and some good stuff (try Grover [1] or Sula [1]) is being made to satisfy rapidly growing domestic demand from the burgeoning middle classes and industry expectations are for rapid expansion. On the grain side of things, India's proud beer industry has been augmented by the new quality strand in the production of whisky such as Amrut.

International Bitterness Units (IBUs) – sounds like a method for dividing assets in rich people's divorce proceedings (or is it the Duckworth-Lewis method?), but is in fact the standard measure of bitterness in a beer.

Irish beer – Ireland is the only country where stout is the dominant style of beer, exemplified by Guinness, which exists in several versions: the draught is creamier and sweeter than the dry 'basic' bottled beer, which is itself outshone by the excellent, more full-bodied Foreign Extra and Foreign Export (mainly in Nigeria – and partly made of sorghum). Both are 7.5% abv. Beamish and Murphy's are the main competition while most Irish bitters and lagers are – for most British hopheads – like a waking nightmare of how our beer was in the 1970s.

Irish Coffee – one part whiskey to four parts hot coffee and a teaspoon of sugar in an Irish-coffee glass (with a handle) and topped up with a layer of thick cream poured over the back of a spoon. Sod 'em and begorrah – I'll have two!

Israel – has a legitimate claim to being the birthplace of wine (but the paternity suit is a complicated one). The modern industry is making great strides with international varieties and smaller producers such as Binyamina [1], Clos de Gat [3], Dalton [1], Tishbi [1] and Yarden [2], and new independents in the Golan Heights and Upper Galilee are keeping the established players such as Carmel, who have fifty per cent of the market and Barkan-Segal and Golan Heights Winery, who share the next thirty per cent between them, very much on their toes.

Italian beer – surprisingly, Italy is the most exciting and rapidly expanding country in Europe (maybe the world) for craft brewing. From a stagnant situation in the late 1990s, when only the big brands and Italy's own Peroni and Moretti – themselves now owned by Big Beer – were available. There are now in excess of 150 microbrewers and brewpubs making every conceivable type of beer, often to a very high standard, and more are starting every month.

As elsewhere, the movement has grown out of home-brewing, mainly in the north, and particularly in Lombardy and Piedmont. The prime movers have been Agostino and Stefano Arioli's Birrificio Italiano, Teo Musso's Le Baladin and the Sangiorgi brothers' Lambrate and many an Italian brewer has earned their stripes in one or more of them. Exports are in their infancy but watch out for Birrificio Artigiano, Montegioco, Panil and Zahre.

Italian wine – yes, there are nearly one thousand different grape varieties. Yes, one of them is Montepulciano, which makes the wine called Montepulciano d'Abruzzo but doesn't make the one called Vino Nobile di Montepulciano. Yes, some of its finest wines have had to be labelled *vino da tavola* and yes, I still go there and find wines made from grapes I've never heard of, from places I've never heard of. But I stay calm and remember what Lorenzo the Magnificant sang: 'chi vuol essere lieto, sia' – whosoever wishes to be happy, shall be happy – it's all part of the *gioia*.

Italian wine is changing as fast as everywhere else and all for the better – especially with whites. The once farcically abused D[enominazione di] O[rigine] C[ontrollata] system was so badly *controllata* that – in what seemed an abject admission of defeat – the authorities decided to tack a G (for *garantita*) on the end for the better wines, and in a stroke condemned the rest to being somehow less so. It's a much more robust system now, though, and supplemented by a vibrant I[ndicazione] G[eografica] T[ipica] category, based on France's *vin de pays* system, which has run so far so fast that it is in danger of leaving behind the value-for-money aspect that presumably should be fundamental to it.

'*Parole, parole, parole!*' ('Words, words, words') is the Italian lament about the national need to be voluble before all else. Yet there are many times when one wishes for a few more *parole* on some of their wine labels – what do you do with one that says 'Maculan Breganze di Breganze 2007' and not another word – no back label – nothing? (The answer, in this case, is buy it, as Fausto Maculan is one of Italy's best white winemakers – maybe *the* best – and Breganze is yet another hidden, regional gem, so good they named it twice, but the problem remains and when there are more words they don't necessarily tell you any more.)

Italy has only been unified (more or less unified, anyway) since 1860 and the best way to get a handle on its wines is to look at the regions that represent the individual kingdoms, principalities, fiefdoms and whatever else that came together to form the country. The intense regionalism that still exists has prevented them from doing that French thing of catering for every vinous need of its citizens within each winemaking area, but there's plenty to keep us busy.

*GET A HANDLE...

EMBRACE THE JOYFUL, ANARCHIC DIVERSITY OF IT ALL (RATHER LIKE WITH THE COUNTRY ITSELF) – A CACOPHONY OF GRAPES AND NAMES AND STYLES OF WINES ARE IMPROVING BY THE YEAR (ESPECIALLY FOR WHITES) AND ARE READY TO TAKE ON THE WORLD FOR PROVIDING GREAT VALUE.

North-Western Italy

Top left, the only time to think about the wines of the Valle d'Aosta is if you're there – as well you might be if you're a skier or you're driving back to the UK from elsewhere in Italy. Small amounts of typically lean, fresh Alpine wines – like those of Savoie – are made and consumed almost exclusively locally from their own Petit Rouge and Fumin black grapes in Torrette (local mover and shaker Costantino Charrère [3]) and Enfer d'Arvier and from Petite Arvine and Blanc de Morgex (Co-op [2], Champorette [3]) for crisp, clean breath-of-fresh-air whites.

> **DRINK LIKE A KING with ...**
>
> Adria
> Alasia
> Ca'di Ponti
> Gran Sasso
> Leonardo Co-op
> Pasque
> Ponte del Diavolo
> Ponte Pietra
> and just about anything from Sicily
>
> **... FOR THE PRICE OF JUST DRINKING**

Down a bit to Piemonte – Italy's Burgundy – where the names to remember are three more 'Bs': the areas of Barolo and Barbaresco, where they make beefy, bold, baronial reds from the Nebbiolo grape, and the Barbera grape, which makes generally lighter, easier-drinking reds for lunch. With Brachetto and Bonarda broadening the picture – Piedmont (the English spelling) is clearly the Bs knees.

Barolo's Nebbiolo vines, planted on small, carefully selected, individually named and endlessly subdivided slopes south-east of Alba, give up tiny amounts of ethereal, woodsy wines which make you feel you should knock the soil off them, so umbilically do they seem to be connected to the mushroomy earth that bore them. With maturity – an underrated quality, and not just in wine – blooms the perfume famously and accurately described as of tar-and-roses and which is not to be nuzzled without some expense and planning. Try Altare [3], Ascheri [2], Bava [2], Borgogno [2], Burlotto [2], Cavallotto [3], Clerico [3], A Conterno [3], G Conterno [3], Conterno-Fantino [3], Fontanafredda [2], Grasso [2], Manzone [2], Marcarini [3], Marchesi di Barolo [3], Mascarello [3], Massolino [3], Pio Cesare [2], Poderi Colla [2], Rocche dei Manzoni [3], Sandrone [2], Scavino [2], Vajra [2] or Vietti [3].

As in Burgundy, producers are everything and most of Piedmont's great names make wines, often both red and white, in a number of different areas – and are listed by the one they are best known for – of which Barbaresco (Ceretto [3], Cigliuti [2], Gaja [3], Giacosa [3], di Gresy [3], Moccagatta [3], Produttori del Barbaresco Co-op [2], Prunotto [2], A Rocca [3], B Rocca [3]), whose riserva wines require four years' ageing, compared to Barolo's five, is the one best able to hold a candle to the latter. Pre-eminent among those producers of similarly intense, tannic and age-worthy wines, Angelo Gaja is one of those dynamic souls capable of reinventing a region, the soil having been tilled both by his father and Bruno Giacosa, to the extent of manhandling it from relative obscurity to a credible rival to Barolo within a generation. Now, because he wants to blend some Barbera in with his Nebbiolo, he sells most of his wine under the relatively lowly Langhe DOC label. Things hereabouts are complicated, needless to say, and other leading growers sometimes declassify wines in to the Langhe Nebbiolo and Nebbiolo d'Alba DOCs. Another good source is the Roero DOC (Ca'Rossa [2] or Correggia [2]).

Of Piedmont's other red grapes, the widely planted, hugely versatile and variable Barbera is the most serious and has the enormous advantage of not necessarily requiring long ageing. Barbera d'Asti (Araldica [1], Braida [2], Ca' del Matt [1], Ca' Solare [1], Coppo [3], Terre da Vino co-op [1]) is generally preferable to Barbera d'Alba (Germano [2], Mascarello [3]) but, as ever, the producer is paramount and the pinky-but-perky, young-drinking Barbera del Monferrato (Bera [2], Tacchino [2]) is a different animal altogether.

There are classy whites as well, especially Gavi, made from Cortese, which when good (which it is not always) has plenty of stuffing and is best with food. Try La Battistina [1], Broglia [2], Casa Sant'Orsola [1], Castellari Bergaglio [1], La Giustiniana [2], Produttori del Gavi Co-op [1], La Scolca [3] or La Zerba [2]. Vermentino – known locally as Favorita (try Deltetto [2]) – and often excellent Arneis from Roero, is catching on fast (try Almondo [2], Malvirà [2], Porello [2], Sorilaria [2]).

For fizz, Moscato d'Asti (Cascina Fonda [2], Chiarlo [1], Contero [2], Saracco [2]) – entirely preferable to plain Asti – comes in at a featherweight 6% abv, more *frizzante* than fully sparkling and is like a bowlful of luscious, skinned, chilled grapes.

The same producers everywhere make lighter lunchtime reds, and as names of grapes are prefixed to place names, a kaleidoscopic profusion of DOCs results: the 'little sweeties' Dolcetto d'Alba (Alario [2], Ca' Viola [2], Oberto [3]) and Dolcetto di Dogliani (Bricco Rosso [2], Pecchenino [2]) – not sweet at all but bitter-cherry dry and Piedmont's answer to Beaujolais; the strawberry-ish, usually *frizzante*, love-it-or-hate-it reds in Brachetto d'Acqui (Alasia [1]), Freisa di Chieri and Freisa d'Asti (Brovia [2]). Light, bright, bitter-almond Grignolino is Piedmont's 'other' light-red grape (but with none of the come-hither cherriness of Dolcetto). It makes wines the colour of a cardinal's cloak – I've seen many a darker rosé but none have the austere, aquiline gravitas of a good Grignolino, which might be thought of as an ascetic, *asciutto*, even *amaro* version of Beaujolais:

try Grignolino d'Asti (Duchessa Lia 1) and Grignolino del Monferrato Casalese; around Verduno 2 the Pelaverga grape makes strawberry-scented reds (Alessándria 2); the Colli Tortonesi (Barbote 2, La Colombera 2, Massa 3) is getting attention for Barbera and whites from Timorassa, as are improving, appley-dry whites, *spumante* and some sweet *passito* whites from the eponymous Erbaluce di Caluso DOC to the north.

A whiff of Nebbiolo glory can be had in the outyling areas, where the grape mostly assumes the name Spanna, notably in Gattinara (Antoniolo 3, Travaglini 3), Ghemme (Cantalupo 2, Torraccia del Piantavigna 3), Lessona (Sella 3, Sperino 3), Fara (Dessilani 1), Colline Novaresi (Vallana 2) and Carema (Ferrando 3). The broad Monferrato (La Spinetta 3) and Piemonte DOCs give rein to producers experimenting with non-traditional grapes.

North Central Italy

Heading west, Lombardy is a hodge-podge of a region with nothing like the reputation of Piedmont but does benefit from some isolated spots of excellence. Franciacorta makes what are by far Italy's best sparkling wines to the east of Brescia. The best producers (Bellavista 3, Berlucchi 3, Ca' del Bosco 3, Cavalleri 3, Montenisa 3, Pizzini 3) make wines that look Champagne in the eye (price-wise, too) while Terre di Franciacorta is the DOC for variable still whites and reds.

Thus, for reds, towards the Swiss border, Valtellina – Lombardy's outpost of the Nebbiolo empire (called Chiavennasca here) – is their piece of what all the fuss is about in Piedmont (and only Valtellina Superiore will do, from Fay 3, Nino Negri 3). Should a little local difficulty break out, they could look south of Pavia to the Oltrepò Pavese – not a rave DOC but working with lots of grapes, and making some some good Pinot Nero (Frecciarossa 2, Isimbarda 3),

Moscato and Barbera (Casteggio Co-op [1]). Next door, in Emilia Romagna, the Colli Piacentini specialise in *frizzante* reds and a blend of Barbera and Bonarda in Gutturnio (Castello di Luzzano [1], La Stoppa [2]).

On the Ligurian coast the Rossese grape thrives in Dolceacqua (and Riccardo Bruna [3] has a mini-cult following for it and for his Pigato, i.e. Vermentino) but the most interesting stuff is to be had from along the coast towards La Spezia in Cinque Terre. It is if you go there anyway, as its lip-smacking whites seldom leave the area, let alone get exported, and seeing the extraordinary slopes on to which the vignerons and their indigenous Bosco and Albarola vines cling you can understand why they want to keep them at home. Some very good Pigato is, however, starting to escape from adjoining Colli di Luni (Fosso di Corsano [2], Lunae Bosoni [2]).

North-Eastern Italy

On a map, the outlines of the myriad demarcated wine regions of the north-east resemble the leavings in a bowl of day-glo spaghetti – a little too rich for even the heartiest Italian appetite to finish. There is no more exciting or diverse wine-producing area in the world and they've been doing interesting things here for centuries.

The northernmost of *Le Tre Venezie* (The Three Venices) is the mountainous Trentino-Alto Adige, the latter bit of which (aka the Südtirol) borders Austria. The altitude shows in the clean lines and ringing, Alpenhorn acidity of the whites that are produced with Germanic precision from Pinot Grigio, Pinot Bianco, Chardonnay, Riesling and even Müller-Thurgau is invigorated here by such as Cesconi [2], Haas [2], Hofstätter [3], Kuenhof [2], Lageder [1], Niedrist [3], Tiefenbrunner [3] and Walch [2]. Exceptional Sauvignon Blanc is made on the lower slopes, much of it by the outstanding co-ops Abbazia di

Novacella [2] – a twelfth-century abbey, so a sort of co-op – Andriano [2], Colterenzio [2], San Michele Appiano/St Michael-Eppan [2], Terlaner [2], Valle Isarco [2]. Gewürz also feels at home here, especially around Termeno (quite literally, if you know the place is called Tramin in German). Things are looking up for the local Nosiola white, which has been rescued from the brink of oblivion by a few good producers such as Pojer e Sandri [3] or Vallunga Vivallis [1]. For reds, most of the same people make characterful, glossy, Austrian-seeming wines from Lagrein (Niedermayr [2]) and, even further north, a smattering of top Pinot Noir is made in Val Venosta (Falkenstein [3]).

Another local red-wine grape (purple-wine, more accurately) getting some exposure outside the region is Trentino's big-boned Teroldego Rotaliano (the former is the grape), the best of which Endrizzi [2], Foradori [2], Mezzacorona Co-op [1], San Leonardo [3]) have an intense, berry fruitiness allied with high natural acidity that needs careful handling if it is to make old bones. The Marzemino grape makes light, plummy, sometimes slightly *frizzante* flibbertigibbets of wines in the Marzemino Superiore d'lsera DOC, a glass of which Don Giovanni calls for before descending to the abyss. It is the Marzemino and other local varieties that are holding their own against the international grapes, represented by some fine Pinot Nero and lots of Merlot (which, in fairness, has been around for ages) but anything that elbows out the rather dull Schiava (aka Vernatsch) is good news – local isn't always best. Trentino also excels with fizz, much of it Chardonnay-based (Cavit [1], Ferrari [3]) and sweet vin santo (see p.398).

To the south, into the second Venice, the Veneto itself, stretching west from Lake Garda (and itself a catch-all DOC – try Ponte Pietra [1], Zeni [1]), the reds are fresh and light – very light in the case of Bardolinos (such as Buglioni [2], Corte Giara [1], Guerrieri Rizzardi [2],

Monte del Fra [1], Montresor, Tantini and Zenato), a region which is rehabilitating itself after decades of shamelessly selling out to the supermarkets' bottom shelf. Some of the best reds are lighter yet, in the dark rosé *chiaretto* style and all are made from the same Corvina grape (with some Rondinella and Molinara) as Valpolicella, the biggest name in reds hereabouts, which carries similar baggage to Bardolino although thankfully most of it these days is crammed full of cheery, cherry fruit. Try Allegrini [1], Alighieri [1], Altarol [2], Bolla [1], Buglioni [2], Bussola [3], Campedelli [3], Corte Sant' Alda [2], Dal Forno [3], Pasqua [1], Quintarelli [2], Le Salette [2], Tedeschi [1], Tommasi [2] or Valpantena Co-op [1]. The 'c' in Valpolicella is a 'ch' (as in what else but cherries?) and the stress is distinctly on the penultimate syllable – saying it a few times while waving your arms about makes you feel surprisingly Italian.

Some of the same producers go the extra mile and make the red pride and joy of the region, burly Amarone della Valpolicella, from semi-dried grapes, which at 15–16% abv used to seem shockingly alcoholic. It doesn't any more but here's hoping it may do so again one day; meanwhile, the wines are the essence of bitter cherry and bitter chocolate loveliness, as the name suggests ('amaro' means bitter and 'one' is the augmentative). There's a sweetly seductive, sometimes *frizzante* version called Recioto, the leftover skins from the making of which are sometimes resourcefully added to regular Valpolicella during fermentation to give extra body – a process called *ripasso*, resulting, with luck, in good value, mini-Amarones (Capital della Crosara [2], Masi [1]). The rather forbidding black grape Raboso makes acidic, tannic wines and is best blended (with Merlot by Il Saporito, for example) or used for making sparkling *rosato* (usually with Prosecco).

There are sleek whites now, where before they were to be avoided

– they used to send us the rubbish (at our request) but hopefully nobody born after 1980 will share the trauma. On the southern and western shores of Garda the DOCs of Lugana – the local name for Verdicchio – and Riviera del Garda Bresciano are attracting attention for the best of their zappy whites (Ca' dei Frati [2], Costaripa [2], Tomassi [1], Zenato [1]) and decent reds and rosés from Gropello. Rapidly improving Bianco di Custoza (Cavalchina [1], Custoza Co-op [1]) is a blend including some of the Garganega grape that makes the big name in whites – Soave. Careful selection is still called for here, and unlike Valpol the DOCG '*superiore*' and '*classico*' wines ain't necessarily so, but citrus, almond and minerals are married in the best of them (Alpha Zeta [1], Anselmi [2], Coffele [2], Gini [2], Inama [2], Pieropan [2], Prà [2], Tamellini [2]). Recioto di Soave is made by the same process referred to above for Valpolicella and the result is one of the most distinctive and delicious sweet whites of the world, a liquid baklava of nuts and syrup that nonetheless keeps hold of its essential dryness and minerality. Try Cantina di Soave [3], Nardello [3] or Quintarelli [3].

Of the outlying constellations of DOCs barely visible to the naked eye, Colli Berici is doing well with international varieties (Casa Defra [1]). Whites from local Vespaiolo (literally 'waspish' but making dry wines that are anything but; although wasps might like the outstanding dried-grape sweet wines) and Friulano thrive alongside incomer reds from Cabernet Sauvignon and Merlot in Breganze on the other side of Vicenza, notably in Fausto Maculan's [2] profoundly mineral dry wines and ravishing dried-grape sweeties. Sample also Breganze Co-op [1].

Sparkling Prosecco is on a roll at the moment; the good stuff is from the newly elevated DOCG of Prosecco di Conegliano-Valdobbiadene to give it the full tongue-twisting honours (and also, while we're at it, some from the IGT Prosecco dei Colli Trevigiani). The best is all tingly and round and peachy – a classy glass of wine with some bubbles in it (Adami 2, Bertiol 1, Bisol 2, Ca' Morlin 2, Carpenè 1, Malvolti Cipriano 1, Fabiano 2, Frassinelli 2, Mionetto 1, Ruggeri 2, Sergio 2, Trevisiol 2, Vinvita 1, Zonin 1). Prosecco is the name of the grape, by the way, and if it's from Cartizze, it's from the best site and the best wine from it is Superiore di Cartizze and will be somewhat sweet (they call it *seco*, or dry, so that's all nice and straightforward, isn't it?).

You'll find Italy's Alsace top right, tucked under the the cuff of Italy's pantomime boot. It is the third of the Venices, Friuli-Venezia Giulia, and runs right up to the Slovenian border (and beyond, as far as vineyards are concerned). The styles are generally drier than those of Alsace but as a diverse source of toothsome, full-bodied whites with similarly high standards I don't think I'll regret the comparison – the biggest disparity is in the quality and variety of the reds here (maybe I'll regret that bit).

The Colli Orientali is the hub and the local Friulano grape (formerly known as Tocai Friulano – but which has, like Tokay d'Alsace, had to drop the 'Tocai' bit to avoid confusion with the Hungarian sweet wine, Tokaji – as if!) is the mainstay for whites with a flash of green to them – somewhat similar to Sauvignon Blanc but with a silkier finish (Due Terre 3, L Felluga 3, Meroi 3, Midolini 2, Specogna 2). Here, and in next-door Collio (M Felluga 2, Gravner 3, Keber 2, Primosic 2, Princic 3, Schiopetto 2), other local grapes – big-boned Verduzzo (making succulent, dry wines, fizz and good sweeties) and tart, refreshing Ribolla Gialla (which has a history that even extends to having been name-checked by Boccaccio) – line up alongside high-kicking Sauvignon Blanc and Pinots Grigio and Bianco to provide the limelight-hogging whites.

In the wings, the reds are limbering up for the world stage – from Merlot (Borgo del Tiglio [3]) with ample local support from Refosco (Ponte del Diavolo [1], Tenuta S. Anna [2]), Pignolo (Vigne di Zamò [3]) and Schioppettino (Ronchi di Cialla [3]). Light, floral *passito* (dried-grape) and late-harvest sweet wines made from Picolit (Torre Rosazza [3]) provide the finale and are considered locally more as *vini da meditazione* than as dessert wines.

In the north-west, the IGT category is considered to be whatever the Italian for naff is, but here in F-VG – although not on the same scale as in Tuscany – many good winemakers flirt with the IGT category and a few of the best have thrown its flag around their shoulders, with Zyme [3] in Valpolicella and in Friuli especially Silvio Jermann [3], whose abilities with grapes more than compensate for his infelicities with words – two of his top wines are 'Were Dreams, now it is just wine' and 'Red Angel on the Moonlight'.

To the south, the hilly bits of Friuli-Isonzo can produce whites to match (Blason [1], Borgo San Daniele [3], Lis Neris [2], Lorenzon [2], P Pecorari [2], Roncus [2], Vie di Romans [3], Zanusso [3]) and reds to outshine those of their northern neighbours including the Refosco, known as Terrano in the Carso peninsula that sticks out towards Trieste (Zidarich [3]). Heading back towards Venice, the flatter parts of Friuli, namely Grave del Friuli (Di Lenardo [1], Plozner [1]), Latisana (Anselmi [1]), Piave (Villa Sandi [1]) and Lison Pramaggiore (Bosco di Merlo [2]) are names to watch for their future potential for volume production of both reds from Merlot and Cabernet and whites from Pinot Grigio and Friulano.

The Po Valley foams red with Lambrusco (often the Po is the best place for the worst stuff) and there are good, gushing, grapey ones – there are always good ones in Italy – from the DOCs of Grasparossa di Castelvetro and Salamino di Santa Croce (Cavicchioli [1], Ceci [2],

Donati [3], Graziano [3], Pederzana [2]). South of Bologna, the Albana di Romagna DOCG – Italy's first for whites – makes excellent sweet *passito* wines (Cesari [1], Fattoria Paradiso [2]) as well as appley dry ones preferable to the oceans of Trebbiano di Romagna. The Colli Bolognese (Terre Rosse [2]) is up-and-coming but, more importantly, we get our first taste of the red grape that dominates central Italy in Sangiovese di Romagna (La Berta [1], Castelluccio [1], Zerbina [1]).

Central Italy

Tuscany: If there were only one archetypal image of Italian wine it would be a straw-covered bottle of Chianti and that would be a fiasco. Not because it's so absurdly out of date and generally rubbish but because that's what those bottles are called. The contents were frequently calamitous but rapidly rising standards in the region have rescued it from farce. Sangiovese (aka Morrelino, Sangiovete, Brunello and a hundred more) is the most widely planted grape in Italy. Tuscany and Umbria are its back yard and Chianti has been – for better or worse – the face it showed the world. It's a huge region – 150 km from tip to toe – and while some good wine is to be had throughout, the vast majority are concentrated in the central Chianti Classico area, the rumpled candlewick bedspread between Florence and Siena and one of the most distinctive and delightful landscapes anywhere. If the label says 'Riserva' the wine is part of the twenty per cent of total production aged for two years or so before being released and is generally more likely to have some of the stewed bitter-cherry, almond and dark chocolate we're looking for.

Chianti is Italy's Bordeaux, very much château- (or, rather, castello-) based and with much debate between modernists and traditionalists. Modernists frequently plump up their wines with

Cabernet Sauvignon and/or Merlot, using the 20 per cent allowed for grapes other than Sangiovese; the purists, increasingly using 100 per cent Sangiovese and maybe a little local Canaiolo, realise that when the wines of a region lose their identity the region risks losing everything. Try Ama [3], Antinori [2], Badia a Coltibuono [3], Le Boncie [3], Bossi [3], Brolio [2], Cafaggio [2], Castellari di Castellina [2], Cecchi [1], Le Corti [3], Da Vinci [1], Felsina-Berardenga [3], Fonterutoli [2], Fontodi [2], Isole e Olena [2], Melini [1], Monte Bernardi [3], Paneretta [3], La Pieve [2], Querceto [2], Querciabella [3], Rampolla [3], Riecine [3], Rocca di Castagnoli [2], Rocca di Montegrossi [3], Ruffino [2], San Felice [2], Terreno [1], Vicchiomaggio [2], Vignamaggio [2] or Volpaia [3].

Of the sub-regions and satellites Chianti Rufina is by far the most important, producing some wines of comparable quality to good quality Classico (Basciano [2], Farnetella [3], Grati [2], Montesodi [3], Nipozzano [2], Selvapiana [2]), while the Colli Senesi (Geografico [1], Innocenti [2], Panezio [1]), Colli Fiorentini (Corzano e Paterno [3]) and Montalbano (Leonardo Co-op [1]) can provide good value. The last adjoins Carmignano, to the west of Florence, first demarcated at the same time as Chianti in 1716 and always worth seeking out – it may be the most reliable in the region for quality (Ambra [2], Capezzana [2], Vannucci [3]) and the outlying Barco Reale di Carmignano DOC can offer good value junior wines. On the other side of Florence the little DOC of Pomino is largely in the hands of the ancient Frescobaldi family and suitably swanky wines are made along with some good value ones such as Castello di Pomino.

Around the southern edges of Chianti, some of Italy's grandest reds are made in the Brunello di Montalcino and Vino Nobile di Montepulciano DOCGs. The former, one of the great wine towns of Italy, perches atop its hill, contemplating the concentrated, age-worthy, brick-tinged wine that will emanate from the vineyards below: Argiano [3], Banfi [3], Barbi [3], Biondi-Santi [3] – the first quality producer who kick-started the whole thing in the 1980s after tilling the ground decades earlier – Campo del Drago [3], Caparzo [3], Casse Basse [3], Castelgiocondo [3], Castiglion del Bosco [2], Col d'Orcia [3], Costanti [3], Eredi Fuligni [3], Fanti [3], La Fiorita [3], Fossacolle [3], Lisini [3], Luciani [3], Cantina di Montalcino Co-op [2], Pacenti [3], Pertimali [3], Piccolomini [3], Pieve di Santa Restituta [3], Poggio Antico [3], Poggione [3], Poggio San Polo [2], Renieri [3], Salicutti [3], Santa Maria [3], Sesti Uccelliera [3]. For a glimpse over the fence, the lesser wines from the best producers, labelled Rosso di Montalcino and made from the younger vines and less favoured sites, although often surprisingly light and pink, can still have power, length and depth. The new Sant'Antimo DOC, mopping up pretty well everything else, is worth watching.

On another haughty hilltop, Montepulciano is the unreconstructed face of Tuscany, but this may yet prove its strongest suit as the subtle, complex, patience-rewarding wines from some of the old boys are, when they are good, a stern reminder about babies and bathwater when it comes to converting to modern styles of winemaking (Bossona [3], La Braccesca [2], Canneto [2], Le Casalte [3], Poliziano [2], Romeo [3], Salcheto [3], San Agnese [2], Valdipiatta [3], Villa Sant'Anna [3]). To the east, the Cortona DOC (d'Alessandro [2], Il Castagno [3]) is attracting attention and the local *vin santo* (see p. 398) are among the best.

The SuperTuscan phenomenon, starting in the late 1960s and led by the experienced (all 600 years of it) Antinori family at Tenuta San Guido, saw top-class producers turn away from the absurd strictures of the DOC system – which, for example, *required* a certain usage of white grapes in Chianti – and start using varieties like Cabernet Sauvignon and Merlot to make fine wines, which, as a result, they had to sell as *vino da tavola*. The wheel turns and the original wines (still among the best – Ornellaia [3], Sassicaia [3], Solaia [3] and Tignanello [3], later augmented by Guado al Tasso [3] and Masseto [3] and labelled as IGT Toscana) have been joined by yet more serious money from Gaja of Piedmont (Ca' Marcanda [3]), Frescobaldi (now owners of Ornellaia) and Ruffino, to name a few, and have a DOC of their own in Bolgheri (Grattamacco [3], Le Macchiole [3], Poggio al Tesoro [2], Satta [3]) in which Sassicaia has its own sub-zone. Throughout the region many fine winemakers continue to work within the IGT system to produce the likes of Caiarossa [3], Capannelle [3], Graetz [3], La Massa [3], Montellori [2], Montevertine [3], Petrolo [3] and San Giusto a Rentennano [3], while most mix and match with different wines. The problem is that everybody wants to be a SuperTuscan now and there is some very bad value around.

The SuperTuscan effect has been seismic and new DOCs are springing up all along Italy's shapely thigh, between Chianti and the coast. Morellino di Scansano (Belguardo [2], Magliano [2], Moris Farms [2], Podere 414 [2], Poggio Argentiera [2], Le Pupille [2], Scansano Co-op [1], Terre di Talamo [2]) has been the most successful and, with the Maremma IGT (Camillo [1], Marsiliana [2], Sassotondo [3], Val di Toro [2]) has transformed a swathe of Tuscany's formerly carrot-crunching coastal littoral into a dynamic, some would say overexploited, Sangiovese powerhouse in little more than ten years. Abutting Bogheri are the Val di Cornia (Petra [3], Russo [3], Trinoro [3]) and Suvereto (Montepeloso [3], Tua Rita [3]) DOCs, tipped for great things, and money from the old guard is pouring into the newest areas of Monteregio di Massa Maritima (Coliberto [3], Macchiaiolo [2]), Montescudaio (Terriccio [2]) and Montecucco (Potentino [2]) – veritably the full monty.

So dedicated to Sangiovese have winegrowers traditionally been that there are still only pockets of white-wine loveliness – savoury, grapefruity Vernaccia di San Gimignano are the best (II Casato 2, Cesani 1, Falchini 1 – also fine reds, Guicciardini Strozzi 2, Mormoraia 2, Panizzi 2, Pietrafitta 2, Teruzzi e Puthod 2), are the best and sometimes even age-worthy, but some might rudely say *faute de mieux* and suggest that much of it tastes as if it were made to be tossed back by incurious tourists who will never be seen again. Seldom-exported Montecarlo (Buonamico 1) and Bianco di Pitigliano (Montauto 1, Pitigliano Co-op 1) are worth seeking out if you're on the spot. The prevalence of the rather dull Trebbiano Toscano grape is a major factor although it does OK supplementing Malvasia in making the dried-grape, sweet (or semi-sweet), amber-coloured and sometimes excellent *vin santo – vino da meditazione*, which, alternatively, is drunk with almond *cantuccini* biscuits as a simple dessert if meditation is secondary to delectation.

Umbria: Strangely, Umbria – so similar to Tuscany in so many ways – excels with whites. Grechetto is the grape of Orvieto (Barberani 1, Bigi 1, Castello della Sala 2, Sportoletti 1, Trappolini 1) and good ones are rounded and mineral-rich in either *secco* or semi-sweet *amabile* styles.

Traditional reds are also more varied than in Tuscany and the best by far is from the Montefalco Sagrantino DOCG – the latter is the grape – and good ones (Adanti 2, Antonelli 3, Arnaldo-Caprai 2, Bea 3, Colsanto 3) seem old-fashioned in the very best possible sense: austere, *asciutto, amaro* even. None of them are cheap, mind you, so some producers make a junior Rosso di Montefalco version, which is still a little expensive.

By comparison, Umbria's Chianti-style Sangiovese-and-Canaiolo combo Torgiano is a bargain. Try Antigniano 2 or Lungarotti 2 – they started it all. There are lots – too many? – of up-and-coming little DOCs – Colli Martani (Madonna Alta [2]), Colli Perugini (Chiorri [2]), Colli del Trasimeno – and the IGT Umbria scene is vibrant (La Carraia [2], Lamborghini [3], Poggio Bertaio [2]). Tuscany's many-tentacled Antinori kicked the whole thing off with their Castello della Sala Cervaro Chardonnay [3] – one of Italy's best whites.

Le Marche/Abruzzi: Lots of good reds are to be found along the muscular calf of the Adriatic coast, and some of the best are from the Rosso Conero DOCG around Ancona. Based on the Montepulciano grape – nothing to do with the town – they are the first taste of the south with aromas of crackling herb-scrub under foot and dark fruit, shimmering in the heat haze (Piantate Lunghe [3], Le Terrazze [3]). Using less Montepulciano and more Sangiovese, the larger Rosso Piceno DOC area encircles Conero but there is a smaller *superiore* zone in the south producing some of the best stuff (Accattoli [2], Ciù Ciù [1]).

The Lacrima di Morro d'Alba DOC makes highly distinctive, myrtle-scented wines that can be rather alarming at first but the intensely herby, syrupy fruit grows on you (there's a sweet version, and *lacrima*, the tear, refers to the drops of juice that the super-ripe grapes leak). A number of good producers make wines all over The Marches (Fazi-Battaglia [1], Garofoli [1], Monte Schiavo [1], Moncaro Co-op [1], Umani Ronchi [1]) including the the rather obscure Colli Pesaresi (Mancini Focara [3]) and Falerio dei Colli Ascoloni (Saladini Pilastri [1], Solaria [1]) DOCs. Such attention to detail under that system doesn't leave so much scope for IGT (Boirà [1]) but there are pockets of non-local grapes (Boccadigabbia [2]).

Whites are good from the versatile Verdicchio dei Castelli di Jesi where it is shaking off the corny packaging (Colonnara [2], Mancinelli [2],

Santa Barbera 1, Sartarelli 2) and, for preference, those of the hillier Verdicchio di Matellica (Belisario 1, Colle Stefano 2, La Monacesca 1) are standouts.

Things are admirably straightforward to the south in the Abruzzi: there are full-on, fruit-powered reds from Montepulciano (Adria 1, Caldora 1, Il Faggio 1, Frentana Co-op 1, Gran Sasso 2, Masciarelli 2, Montipagano 2, Nicodemi 1, Roxan 1, Terrana 1, Valentini 3), the ballsy rosé versions are called Cerasuolo and some decent whites are made from Trebbiano (additionally Ancora 1, Barba 1, Rocca 1, Vetriano 1). When they're good – as they often are these days – they make it seem our lives have become too complicated. There are also some rather high-falutin' wines (Inama 2, Valle Reale 2) and the new DOCG of Montepulciano d'Abruzzo Colline Teramane (Illuminati 1) is taking off. The Malvasia can be good (Farnese 1) as can the Pecorino (Tollo 1) and the IGT Colline Pescaresi (Castorani 2, Trulli 2).

Head south to Lazio and there are only a few distractions on the shin side of Naples. The only amusing thing about the Est! Est!! Est!!! di Montefiascone DOC is the story of its novelty name – and it's not amusing enough to relate; however, it is home to noted oenologist Riccardo Cotarella, who, with his brother, Renzo, has the good-value Falesco 2 venture and is very active here and in Umbria. Dodgy DOCs abound, but there is occasional treasure to be had in light reds – Cesanese del Piglio (Poggio le Volpi 2) – and Frascati whites to take the heat out of a Roman holiday: Fontana Candida Santa Teresa 1; Villa Rufinella 1; Villa Simone 1. Big reds come from Velletri.

Southern Italy

The south has traditionally been the place for strong, rustic-and-ready wines but quality is improving here as rapidly as anywhere. Plenty of history in Campania, north of *la bella Napoli*, and lots of lovely, well-upholstered, complex whites from the Greco di Tufo and Fiano di Avellino DOCGs and the Falanghina di Sannio DOC – the first is the grape in each case. This is where you'll find one of Italy's chewiest, longest-lived reds – Taurasi, another DOCG, from the Aglianico grape derived from Ellenico i.e. Greek (Caputo 2, Ferrara 2, Feudi di San Gregorio 2, Galardi 3, Grotta del Sole 2, Mastroberardino 2, Montevetrano 3, Terredora 2, Vesevo 2). There are mini versions in the coastal Cilento DOC (De Conciliis 2, Maffini 2) and the IGT Beneventano, which is also good for cheaper whites (Bellamico 1, de Falco 2). The Falerno del Massico DOC (Villa Matilde 3) – named after the most famous wine of the ancients – is a thoroughly modern Milly now. The Coda di Volpe grape (literally 'fox's tail', describing the way these grapes grow in long, narrow bunches) makes the white version of the variable local Lacryma di Christi (literally 'tears of Christ', after the fertility those falling tears bestowed on the piece of heaven – the Bay of Naples and the slopes of Vesuvius – that the newly fallen Satan made off with. If you made this stuff up nobody would ever believe you . . .)

Puglia, occupying the heel and the Achilles tendon area, makes a vast quantity of wine and is catching up with the quality-beats-quantity idea fast but there are more pointless DOCs stuffed down there than there are socks down Iggy Pop's pants. With its powerful Primitivo (aka Zinfandel) and native Negroamaro (literally, and accurately, 'blackbitter') reds this is the source of strapping, manly wines, so don't argue about it, though most don't make it out of region anyway. The sunburnt wines that do make a break for it from the Salice Salentino, Brindisi, Primitivo di Manduria and Copertino DOCs are worth exploring from regional generalists and local specialists alike (A Mano 1, Antinori's Vigneti del Sud 1, Apollonio 2, Bella Modella 1, Candido 1, Cantele 2, Carpentiere 2, Castel di

Salve [2], Conti Zecca [1], Copertino Co-op [1], Leone de Castris [2], Li Veli [2], lynch-pin Puglia figure Severino Garofano's Masseria Monaci [1], Masseria Trajone [1], Racemi [1], Rocca [1], Sampietrana [1], San Giuseppe [1], San Marzano [1], Taurino [1], Terre Allegre [1], Tormaresca [1], Vallone [1]). Among them are some excellent Rosato del Salento, and seldom-seen grapes like the aristocratic Nero di Troia in Castel del Monte (Longo [2], Rivera [1], Zagaria [2]), Malvasia Nera and Aleatico for sweet *passito* reds. The IGTs do well – Salento (La Casada [1], Surani [2]); Puglia (Longo [2]); and Tarantino (Tatu [1], Trevini [1]) in particular.

Little Molise's only claim to vinous fame is the Biferno DOC and more importantly, within it, the brightly shining star of Di Majo Norante [1] who, now I think about it, sell most of their wines as IGT anyway. Basilicata – the instep – also has, appropriately enough, a sole claim on our time with Aglianico del Vulture, from the extinct volcano on whose flanks bask the vines of the stern aristocratic reds (Alovini [1], d'Angelo [3], Paternoster [2]). Two of Calabria's toes wiggle: Ciró for tannic reds from the Gaglioppo grape and good whites from local varieties and, in a final fourish of this madness of names, the sappy Greco di Bianco so-called not because it's white but because that's the name of the town (Librandi [2], Santa Venere [2]).

Islands

To call Sicily the 'new California', as some have, has the hollow ring of hype but the Sicilian wine industry has certainly had some work done in the last decade or so. State-of-the-art wineries full of gleaming stainless steel are sprouting up all over the place. As in Portugal, the fact they didn't have the wonga in the 1980s to rip up all their interesting indigenous vines and replace them with Cab Sauv and Chardonnay turns out to have worked in the largest Mediterranean island's favour. The equation is completed by raising standards and lowering yields and the world has beaten a path to Sicily's door for her sultry, sapid whites – from indigineous Inzolia, Grecanico and Grillo – and her sultry, smoky reds – from Nero d'Avola, Nerello Mascalese and Frappato.

Nero is the signature grape and makes astonishingly different wines in different locations on the island but – however daft it sounds – all seem to have some sort of volcanic quality to them, along with a distinctive minerality, a crackle of scrub-fire smoke and bags of lip-smacking, wild, red berries: Barbera [2]; Cusumano [1]; Donnafugata [2]; Ca' di Ponti [1]; the pivotal Planeta [1] family, who also head the excellent and enormous Settesoli Co-op [1]; Tasca d'Almerita [1] and Villa Tonino [1].

A lot of Sicily's white wine was traditionally blended and fortified in the making of Marsala but table wines from Grillo (Adria [1], Duca di Castelmonte [1], Fondo Antico [2], Lamura [1], Montoni [2]) and Inzolia (Borgo Selene [1], Terra Firma [1]) show promise where producers fully realise the grapes' potential but there are quite a lot of cabbagey stinkers, too, so don't say I didn't warn you.

The white grape behind Sicily's sometime major contribution to Europe's wine lake, Cataratto, has given ground both to other Italian varieties (Pinot Grigio and, notably, Campania's Fiano) and imports (Chardonnay and Viognier shine) although, again, dedicated producers (Anthilia [2], Montalto [1], Ferrari [2]) seem to be able to make decent wine with it. Shiraz shines among the 'international' reds and they can afford that Cabernet Sauvignon now.

Sicily's hot summers mean irrigation is a must but the cooler slopes of Etna are ringed by vineyards up to 1000 m and it is here that Nerello makes some of the island's best reds (Benanti [1], Cornelissen [3], Duca di Castelmonte [1], Passopisciaro [3]). It also thrives in the top-right Faro DOC (Palari 3), while the southern DOCG of Cerasuolo di Vittoria makes blends majoring on Frappato with softer strawberry-ish tones and something of excellent Beaujolais about them (Cos 2, Valle dell'Acate 2). Lots bottled as IGT (Angelo 1, Cottanera 2, Fazio 2, Majus 1, San Mario 1).

The tiny island of Pantelleria, to the south and at the same latitude as Algiers, makes zesty, orangey *passito* sweet wines from semi-dried Moscato, which they call Zibibbo (Murana 2).

The vast empty dockside warehouses of Marsala are testimony to the neglect of the island's once mighty fortified wine of the same name – it's hard to find a bottle in the town itself – but there are stirrings (Arini 2, Buffa 2, De Bartoli 3, Florio 2, Rallo 2). How often an effective monopoly producer (Pellegrino 1) actually raises its game I don't know, but these complex Madeira-style wines wines are a great bargain.

Sardinia doesn't have quite the winemaking back-story of Sicily and has been a bit of a slow-coach but the best producers, such as Argiolas 2, Gabbas 2, Pala 2, Santadi 2, Sella e Mosca 1 and Turriga 3, can compete on the world stage. Vermentino is Sardinia's flag-carrying white grape. The best are from the Vermentino di Gallura DOCG (Capichera 3, the Gallura 2 and Vermentino Co-ops 2), the rest are Vermentino di Sardegna and there is good white from local Nuragus with sherry-like Vernaccia di Oristano (Contini 2) adding more local colour.

For reds, cannonau (aka grenache) is the workhorse and has a crackle it doesn't have elsewhere (Loi 2); the world's best (some would say only good) carignan – from old bush vines – is in the Carignano del Sulcis DOC. There are local grapes too: monica generally making undistinguished, often rather 'hot' wines which are sometimes labelled Monica di Sardegna. If the heat thing can be kept under control it can be more of the aromatic, crackling hillside herd-scrub type than that of burning tyres and is just the thing with a pungent Putanesca. There is inward investment, which is not afraid to put it's money behind an IGT Isola dei Nuraghi label, especially as some of it's from Sassicaia (Punica 3, also Isola del Sole 2). For Heaven's sake don't forget that bovale sardo is aka muristellu hereabouts (Mandrolisai Co-op 2) . . . but *basta, basta* with the *parole*, already!

japan jacquère jahrgang jerepigo john collins judgement of paris jug wine japan jacquère jahrgang jerepigo john collins jug wine

J

Japan – Japan has been more important as a consumer (especially in prosperous times) of fine wines and spirits than as a producer (in which terms it is far more important in sake and increasingly good whisky than in wine). It has been in the space currently occupied by China during more than one boom in the prices of first-growth claret.

Judgement of Paris – iconic wine-tasting arranged in 1976 by Steven Spurrier, a British wine merchant in Paris (now turned luminary) where top clarets and white Burgundies were tasted blind against California Cabernet Sauvignons and Chardonnays. The result – a near whitewash for the Americans – was of seismic significance in securing a seat for the upstart 'New World' of wine at the top table. The initial French reaction was to sniff that the real test for the red wines would come in thirty years' time when they would be fully mature but when the re-match took place in 2006 the results were much the same.

jug wine – traditionally, the most basic level of California wine, sold in large jug bottles with handles that facilitated carriage as well as not infrequent consumption directly from jug. The precursor of the modern bag-in-box.

Jura, Isle of – comparative baby, only going since 1963 and owned by Whyte & Mackay, a subsidiary of India's United Breweries. Has earned a deserved reputation for the quality and delicacy of its whiskies.

kadarka kamikaze kerner kir kiss-me-quick klevener de heiligenstein klevner kosher booze kamikaze

kamikaze kerner kir kiss-me-quick klevener de heiligenstein klevner

kir kiss-me-quick klevener de heiligenstein klevner kosher booze kadarka

K

Kamikaze – three parts vodka to two parts triple sec and one part lime juice shaken with ice and strained in to a cocktail glass in the cockpit.

Kir – one part crème de cassis to ten parts Aligoté built in a wine glass (or use Champagne in a flute glass for a Kir Royal).

Knockando – fine Speyside distillery in the ownership of Diageo and notable as my wife's favourite dram during the (now long-past) whisky years (today she prefers Knockandon't).

Kosher booze – the Jewish dietary law, or Kashrut, requires that there be strictly and only kosher ingredients in booze and, more relevantly, that the people making it be Sabbath-observant Jews. As far as wine is concerned it seems to have provided an excuse for low standards – very low particularly for *mevushal* wines that are cooked as part of a belt-and-braces approach to make them permanently kosher by rendering them 'unfit for idolatrous purposes' (or any other purpose I would imagine).

Things are on the up, though, as competition is itself cooking nicely especially, but by no means exclusively, among Israeli producers of both kosher and non-kosher wines. Peisachovka is a dodgy-sounding 'raisin-infused' kosher vodka but, in fact – regardless of whether or not they have a *hechscher* symbol denoting suitability – many of the best brands of vodka are acceptable, as are many top gins, single-malt whiskies and craft beers, the reason being that it is easier to research exactly what is in them. Mazeltov!

labels lactic acid lagrein lebanon l'en de l'el lagar licoroso liquoreux liquoroso liqueurs long island

loureiro los angeles low-alcohol drinks luxembourg

labels – are important. They function on two levels: the first is the information they give (or don't) about the wine inside the bottle; the other is the way in which they do it.

The question we really want the label to answer is simply this: 'Is it any good?' Life's not like that but by understanding what a label tells us – hopefully, but by no means always, what it is, and where and when and by whom it was made – we can get closer to correctly predicting the answer.

The 'where' part is the most bewildering and the key is to understand the various systems of appellation – the naming of specific places where wine is made – and the three levels that operate in most European countries: controlled appellation; regional wines; and table wine, introductions to all of which are provided in the sections on French wine, German wine, et cetera.

Table wines can be made of any grape, anywhere, by anyone and (if, as often, no vintage is specified) at any time . . . in France or in Italy or Spain. But with wine at this level it's not really the roll of the dice it sounds because although good wines can come dressed in the plainest clothes (this is more likely in Spain than in France or Italy) it's not advisable to try to find them by a process of trial and error. What awaits much of this wine is a further declassification to 'Product of the EU', and the ignominy of distillation into industrial spirit or, at rock bottom, ethanol (perhaps to fuel the machines that will harvest next year's crop).

Most European wine-producing countries have French-based systems of AOC and *vin de pays* and it is important to understand that while the different systems can sometimes partially cover the same areas, those of the regional wines are much more extensive (and it's also useful to understand that the table wine category covers the gaps in between these areas as well as the most basic wine made within them). In general, provided it meets the various criteria, most producers would rather label their wine AOC than VdP because it usually sells for more money, but if they are keen to experiment, for example, with a grape variety not allowed under the AC regulations they'll take the VdP route.

All straightforward enough but what confuses the shit out of people is that wines from the same grape variety grown in the same field can be labelled under two (or more) different appellations. Getting your head around what makes this apparent anomaly possible means you're starting to crack the whole labelling labyrinth. Here is an example: a grower near the town of Loupiac, and who is perhaps more interested in red wines, makes some simple dry whites from Semillon that he labels under the most basic AC Bordeaux classification. When the authorities tighten the rules for using that name it starts to look as though he may have to start calling it *vin de pays* de l'Atlantique. He's not too happy about that and spends a sleepless night thinking about the social death that would result should the rules be tightened again a couple of times and he has to start labelling it *vin de table*. So, he resolves to pay a bit more attention to the Semillon and soon finds that the grapes from the best part of his vineyard meet the criteria to make wine that can be labelled under the more specific AC of Entre-Deux-Mers. His interest in white wine grows and one year, when the conditions look right, he decides to leave the grapes on a few vines for a late harvest in order to try making some sweet wine. It turns out to be pretty good and he bottles it under the basic sweet wine AC of Prèmieres Côtes de Bordeaux and determines that the next time he makes it he will try to meet the criteria for the better, more specific (and more expensive) local, sweet AC of Loupiac.

One grape variety in one vineyard making wines with potentially six different names is an extreme example but it makes the point that these systems are not just about where a wine comes from but about the quality and the style of the wine being produced, which in itself is often down to the decisions of the winemaker.

All demarcation systems operate rather like the zoom function on an internet mapping system and move in from the general to the specific. Start by looking at the whole of France and any half-decent wine produced in the Switzerland-size swathe of the country that runs up to 100 miles either side of the Loire river eastwards from the Atlantic to within 100 miles of Switzerland itself would qualify to call itself *vin de pays* du Val de Loire and you would expect it to have a friendly price tag.

Zoom in and you'll see, within it, eleven *départements* – the French equivalent of counties – each of which may have a VdP with its name on it. Press zoom again and the most detailed level – the zonal areas – within the *départements* becomes visible. With each narrowing of focus, the demands on the winemaking process become somewhat more rigorous.

The same principle applies to the AOC system, which zooms

inwards from a whole region (Burgundy, say) to a sub-region (maybe the Côte de Nuits) and then to levels that VdP doesn't run to, namely a specific village (Morey-Saint-Denis takes my fancy) and then, at the max, to an individual vineyard maybe a few hundred yards across (how about Clos des Roches – which, as it's Burgundy, might itself be divided between numerous owners). In general, the closer in you zoom, the higher the quality should be (and the price) – the problem is that sometimes, albeit decreasingly, it's only the price that goes up.

It's all about specifics but they don't need to be too specific to make a big difference, as the village-people know. Buying a Côtes du Rhône Villages wine (i.e. from a designated group of the best villages) for a couple of quid more than a plain old Côtes du Rhône increases the chance of loveliness exponentially because much of the lowest-level stuff has been taken out of the equation and the same often applies to the *villages* suffix in Anjou, Roussillon, Macon, Beaujolais, the Côte de Nuits and, to a lesser extent, de Beaune.

The 'what' part on a label means grape varieties and there can be problems – especially in France, Italy and Spain – but we can always do what they do and forget about the names of the grapes sometimes. If you like claret (oops! you'll almost never see that name on a label outside of a supermarket), i.e. red Bordeaux, you don't really need to know what it's made from, do you? It's more useful to know where to buy them and the names of some of the châteaux that make wine you want to drink at prices you're prepared to pay. The Rhône is more of a mix but reds are usually variants on the GSM theme (Grenache, Syrah, Mourvèdre), without the 'G' or the 'M' in the northern part. Burgundy is easy-peasy as it's basically Pinot Noir for reds and Chardonnay for whites.

The same 'read no evil' approach can help in Italy and Spain, especially outside the main regions. Somebody who knows they like good Rioja or Chianti is more likely to be concerned with how they can get consistently better wines than with the percentage of Tempranillo – and rightly so – and they need to concentrate on finding the best 'whos' (see below). In the UK, if you come across a wine from an unfamiliar region, suck it and see – the logic being that the market is already so diverse and the competition so ferocious that even to get a look-in means a region must have something going for it (hopefully in addition to being cheap). In 2009 the EU passed legislation to allow producers in all regions to specify grape varieties on labels and this may (or may not) simplify things for consumers because the legislation certainly doesn't require it.

The 'when' part means vintages and, although it's heresy to say so in some quarters, they don't seem to be *quite* as important as they used to be. Winemakers are more skilled and able to turn things around and make better use of what they've got than before. At one end, there are still stinkers – 2002 in much of Italy for example – and at the other, to be presented with 'The Vintage of the Century' not once – 2000 – not twice – 2005 – but, with 2009, three times in a decade is rather wearing. Who knows? One day we might not believe them.

In some New World winemaking regions – South America and South Africa in particular – the weather is consistent to the extent that, for low-to-average price wines, especially reds, vintages are largely meaningless. Meanwhile, in the same places, and additionally in Australia, New Zealand and the USA, in quest of freshness, some of the best people are gambling at the cool altitudes and perimeters of where their favoured varieties will ripen at all and where the weather in any given vintage can make the difference between great wine and no wine at all. If vintage information is available by all means use it and remember a few recent standouts like 2000, 2005 and 2009 in France generally and 2007 in the Rhône in particular, but also remember that the 'when' counts for nought when compared to the paramount, the *sine qua non*, the nitty gritty of the 'who'.

Everywhere, always, it's the 'who' that counts for everything (and I'm not talking about the geriatric rock 'n' rollers). There is no wine label in the world that doesn't show the name of the maker and if I see the name Zind-Humbrecht or Cesare or Ridge or Loosen or any of the many, many choice souls like them that are listed in this book then I'm a happy, complacent bunny. I'd trust these makers with my life, let alone to make some nice wine. I'd buy anything they put into a bottle regardless of the what, the where and the when. It's as simple as this – get to know some of their names.

Good wine is made by passionate people with one goal – to make good wine. Biodynamists make good wine but I suspect it's not because they're biodynamists – that's a symptom, not a cause – but because they're quality-obsessives who sweat all the details, including the labelling. It's usually simple enough: crap label = crap wine. What we want is a confident, understated, less-is-more approach with strong designs on good expensive paper (textured is especially good). We don't want any animals (except insects), or jokey names (there are one two exceptions – Goats do Roam, Chat-en-Oeuf), or primary colours (strong yes – bright no).

Winemakers seek to emulate (or, at least, grab some reflected glory from) their most successful neighbours. Perhaps this is why, for example, so many Sauternes labels have the white and gold theme familiar (I should be so lucky) from d'Yquem. Tuscany's IGT boom has – on the back of the SuperTuscan boom – spawned dozens of good, overpriced imitators of the originals, which all look brilliantly, absurdly, shamelessly alike with lots of strong-but-muted powder blues and browns, lots of horizontal lines and sections, lots of glittery gilt, Roman type and lots of made-up names ending in 'aia', 'aiolo' and the like.

Beware bullshit terms on labels – a lot of them may have originated in good faith but it's best to be suspicious when you see phrases like 'Family Reserve' – let's face it, if there were any truth in it, what's it doing on a supermarket shelf? Other words to avoid are 'personal', 'private', 'winemaker', 'cellarmaster', 'selection', 'reserve', (but not reserva or riserva) and so on.

There are some useful non-legal terms: *vieilles vignes* (old vines) wines are often a notch up; specific names of *cuvées* (particular batches or blends) suggest a careful winemaker, as does the name of a particular part of the vineyard that is not part of the legal name.

L

lagar – large, low stone trough in which grapes are trodden, still in use for making some premium port and pronounced with the emphasis on the second syllable (which avoids any lager/trough confusion).

Lagavulin – as with most whisky distilleries on Islay and elsewhere, the first production here was illegal and only made honest in 1816. Ownership of the distinctive iodine twang of the sixteen-year-old is now with Diageo.

Lagrein – red-wine grape of north-eastern Italy's Trentino-Alto Adige, the part of Italy that (rightly) thinks it's Austria, making quite tannic, mineral wines with high acidity and the deep, uniform colour and sheen more recognisable in Austrian reds. This is not to do it down – I'm a big fan of it, especially lightly chilled – but the green, myrtle, sometimes cough-syrupy edge is not to everybody's' taste, especially if the fruit is not sweetly ripe.

Laphroaig – (pronounced 'la-froyg') quintessential Islay whisky distillery combining quantity with quality and notable for the smokiness of its liquid (now property of Fortune Brands of the USA).

Lebanon – It wasn't only the scorching sun that made pickers at Gaston Hochar's Château Musar break into a sweat; harvests were regularly interrupted by shelling in the Bekaa Valley during the worst of Lebanon's civil war. Musar [2] has the highest profile but there are a number of producers including Kefraya [3], Ksara [1] – established in 1857 – Massaya [2] and Tourelles [3] making first-class Bordeaux- (and some Rhône-) style wines. The vines are grown at altitude to keep things fresh and there are some interesting white varieties such as Merwah and Obiadeh making good whites, some of them rather old-fashioned (in a good way).

liqueurs – mainly for girls, obviously, liqueurs originated in mediaeval monastries as a way of preserving medicinal herbs and what-not. When people realised that the herbs didn't do much good they carried on making – and consuming – the drinks because they tasted quite nice and got them drunk. The names and types and styles of liqueurs are as fuzzily confusing and strangely, sweetly comforting as the drinks themselves. A liqueur – as distinct from any brandy, flavoured vodka or schnapps (in the European sense) – is defined by the fact that it is sweetened. (In America, schnapps are sweetened and are, as such, liqueurs.)

Some of the first booze I ever tasted was in the come-hither form of liqueurs and, oddly, my parents ingulged my brief enthusiasm for collecting miniatures – presumably they thought I wasn't going to drink them. Re-tasting them, some of which I hadn't tried since, has been hard but nostalgia-tinged work. They're still cloying and generally weird but at least I haven't tried to shag my sister this time.

Herbal liqueurs are doubtless much as those original medicines used to be and recipes remain secret albeit some of the main ingredients are obvious or noted in brackets. Bénédictine (with twenty-seven botanicals in the recipe, none of which predominates) and Chartreuse (likewise, but with 130) are the most famous and interestingly (well, I think it's interesting, anyway) more 'Benny' is consumed in the working-men's clubs of Burnley than anywhere else. I'm not making it up – the East Lancashire Regiment was stationed near Fécamp during the First World War and they got a taste for it that endures to this day. German and Austrian monasteries still make lots of vile herbal liqueurs (Andechs, Ettal) that seem designed to taste as if they're doing you good; other multi-herb concoctions include Elisir du Dr Roux (a recently devised drink, so the tradition remains alive), Alpen Wolf, Fior d'Alpi (which has a Bonsai-like tree in the bottle), Galliano (with anise and vanilla), Izarra and Radeberger. Bitters – including the sweetened versions – are dealt with under a separate heading (see p.45–46).

Of the herbal liqueurs that advertise a predominating flavour, these are notable: anise, including Sambuca Romana (with elderberries); Herbsaint, pacharán, as well as ouzo, anisette and pastis, (including Pernod and Ricard, as well as Boyer, Bardouin, which, as they are sweetened, are strictly speaking liqueurs); caraway (Brennavín, Kümmel – with cumin and fennel); cinnamon (Goldschlager, which, like Danzig Goldwasser, has flakes of gold leaf floating about in it – so who says liqueurs are not girly?); coca leaf (Agwa); damiana;

L

génépy; gentian (Suze); ginger (Canton, The King's Ginger) green tea (Zen); honey (Drambuie); liquorice (Dr McGillicuddy's, Jägermeister); mastic (Mastichato Chio); mint (Dr McGillicuddy's, Menta, Strega); tea (Aurum); thyme (Farigoule); verbena (Verveine du Velay); and violets (Parfait Amour).

The vast spectrum of *crème* liqueurs (as opposed to cream liqueurs) are not creamy and some of the fruit ones are also known as cordials, although some definitions of cordial insist on a non-alcoholic nature. See what I mean about the names? *Crème* liqueurs provide the core of the mixologists' palette – every conceivable fruit seems to have a *crème* made from it. Some of the best are those made from bitter oranges, collectively known as Curaçao (after the island where they originated in rum-based form, although they are now mainly made from grape brandy), with the finest known by brand name such as Grand Marnier and Mandarine Napoléon. The colourless version is called triple sec (Cointreau, Licor 43 – 'cuaranta-y-tres'). There also exist blue, green, red and yellow versions (for mixology purposes), and a South African incarnation called Van der Hum.

There's big money in liqueurs. If they get noticed, they can sell all round the world. Where there's money there's innovation, and where there is innovation there is quality, be it from established brands that are reinvigorated (Boudier, Rossi d'Asiago) or from new ventures (Chase, Stock, Zuidam – new*ish*, anyway). The big liqueur companies such as Bardinet, Bols, Cusenier, De Kuyper and Marie Brizard have large ranges and are not further referenced, and include those sometimes referred to as 'liqueur brandies' made from cherry (Luxardo, Heering, excluding maraschino – the 'sch' is pronounced 'sk' – and which are drier and colourless), apricot and peach (Archers).

Others fruits (and names . . . so many names) range from the obvious – blackberry (aka mûre), blackcurrant (aka cassis), lemon (aka limoncello), mint (aka menthe, both green and colourless), pear (aka poire williams, with a pear grown inside the bottle), pineapple (aka ananas), raspberry (aka framboise), sloe (aka prunelle), strawberry (aka fraise) wild strawberry (aka fraise de bois) – to the unusual . . . banana, bilberry (aka myrtille), lychee (Kwai Feh, Soho), passionfruit (Alizé), melon (Midori), black raspberry (Chambord Royale) and rhubarb (Chase).

The *crèmes* encompass coffee (Kahlua, Starbucks, Touissant, Tia Maria – literally 'Aunty Mary'), chocolate/cacao in both white and dark versions (After, Droste, Godiva, Sabra – with orange; Vandermint – with mint) and vanilla (Tuaca). Finally, nuts are another important category, with almond (aka amaretto – Disaronno), hazelnut (Frangelico), coconut (aka batida de coco – CocoRibe and the massive selling Malibu) and a mix including pistachio (Pisa) making good things.

Cream liqueurs are the girliest of the girly and though easy to scoff at, they're even easier to scoff. It's unfair that they're dispensed in such tiddly measures in pubs when I want to glug them like a great big manly milkshake. Maybe it's just as well as otherwise I'd probably drink enough to make myself sick. Whiskey-based Bailey's Irish Cream, launched by Gilbeys in 1974 and now one of Diageo's best-sellers, is the archetype and has spawned a hundred imitators. Additionally flavoured with cocoa, vanilla, caramel and sugar (probably best not to dwell on the vegetable oil that keeps the emulsion stable) it is, like the others, best served simply over ice.

Everything has been tried: peanut – Peenie Wallie; pears – Lauria; praline – Guylian, and that's just the 'p's. Some, including Cadbury's and Grand Marnier, have thankfully been consigned to the spitoon of oblivion. Apart from whisky (Arran Gold, Carolans, Columba,

Coole Swan, Drumgray, Edradour, Heather, Merlyn – with Welsh whisky; Norfolk Cream – with English whisky), there are cream variations based on other spirits including rum (Cruzan, Sangster's and Key – made with cane rum), tequila (Baja Rosa, Tequila Rose) and vodka (Jago's, Paris Rose – with strawberry, apparently . . . maybe I'll just be sick now anyway). Some obscure notions have been successful such as chai tea – Voyant; lime – KeKe Beach; marula fruit – Amarula; and there are some cream versions of other liqueurs such as sambuca (Luxardo) and coffee (Dooley's, Starbucks) and chocolate (Droste, Vermeer), which work well in small doses.

Advocaat (aka advokatt) is a one-off, apparently confected from Soviet-era tank anti-freeze and Bird's Custard Powder but, in fact, made from eggs. The strapline from the 1970s advertisements, 'Eefninks and morninks – I trink Warninks!' seems admirably decadent now but the drink's moribundity is terminally advanced, in the UK at least. When dropped in to a layered mixture of equal parts crème de bananes over melon liqueur, advocaat usefully solidifies into a substance known in certain drinking games as 'Gorilla Snot Number Two' and is consumed as a forfeit. Don't say I didn't give you fair warnink.

Liqueurs based on other types of booze have long been popular, especially whisky (Drambuie, Glayva, Irish Mist, Yukon Jack and Southern Comfort – with peach) but also with gin (Hayman's) while Spain's *ponche* (Osborne, Soto) – something of an acquired taste – is made from brandy and aged sherry and, in a cruel twist, also comes in cream and flavoured versions. Enough with the liqueurs, already!

Long Island Iced Tea – equal parts vodka, light rum, silver tequila, gin, triple sec, lemon juice and simple syrup shaken with ice, strained in to a highball glass and finished with cola to taste. Remember what Anthony Burgess said – only have as many cocktails as you have nostrils.

Los Angeles – shake one egg (i.e. one part) and one part lemon juice to three parts whisky, half a part each of sweet vermouth and simple syrup with ice and strain . . . every sinew to make good your escape (or use a cocktail glass).

low-alcohol drinks – every now and then, circumstances arise which call for such things so it's important to know the good from the bad and it's the natural, rather than the contrived, that are the good. If you ferment grape juice you usually get a liquid with an abv somewhere between 7.5% and 15% and thankfully there are many good things to be had at the lower end. Many top German Rieslings are in the 8–9% abv slot, classy Semillon – picked before full ripeness – from Australia's Hunter Valley is usually 10–11% abv, and rapidly improving *vinho verde* from Portugal is in the same range.

Lower still, an elegant, lacy Moscato d'Asti comes in at around 5-6% abv – the wines are chilled to stun the yeasts and prevent them fermenting all the luscious fruit sugars into alcohol. Lowest is Tokaji Escenzia but with residual sugar of a-bag-a-bottle and a price tag of around 300 quid (and both figures are for a 50cl bottle) its 3% abv is the only thing that's low.

Reds are a problem (but McGuigan produces a notable 9.5% abv Shiraz) and obviously putting a thimbleful of *crème de cassis* into your white wine or Champagne to make it a Kir or Kir Royal isn't going to fool your palate or your liver. Adding one-third soda-water to make a spritzer will do the job, though.

Low-alcohol beers don't seem to work – there's a big hole in the palate – but bitter flavours seem best able to cope with serious dilution. An old favourite rehydrator is a Financial Times – simply a small measure of gin with a good jigger of Angostura Bitters and filled to the brim with soda-water. So named for the colour, it has much in common with another get-out-of-jail card, the Campari and soda (with a generous slice of orange).

Alcohol-free wine is a contradiction in terms and an affront to everything we hold dear. The wrong-headed thinking that gives rise to a product such as the 'still, alcohol-free aromatised wine product' offered in a UK supermarket (sounds enticing, doesn't it?) should be resisted at all costs. The particular abomination I tried smelled like a mixture of bodily fluids. Most low-alcohol Lambrusco Bianco that advertises itself (if that's the right word) as 'partially fermented grape must' tastes like sugared water. Frankly, I'd rather stay upright . . . or even have a glass of water.

Luxembourg – is most interesting as a wine producer as the next-coolest and next-smallest European producer after England. They are getting rid of their Müller-Thurgau and Elbling and replacing these grapes with the various Pinots and, like England, make good sparklers such as Massard 2 and Clos des Rochers 2. AB InBev-owned Brasseries de Luxembourg Mousel-Diekirch also make some rather nice beers.

Lychee Martini – equal parts gin, lychee liqueur and lychee syrup shaken with ice, strained in to whatever glasses sit best on the side of the bath (assuming there are two of you) and garnished with a lychee.

manseng marechal foch margarita marsanne marzemino mauresque mauzac mavrodaphne mavrud

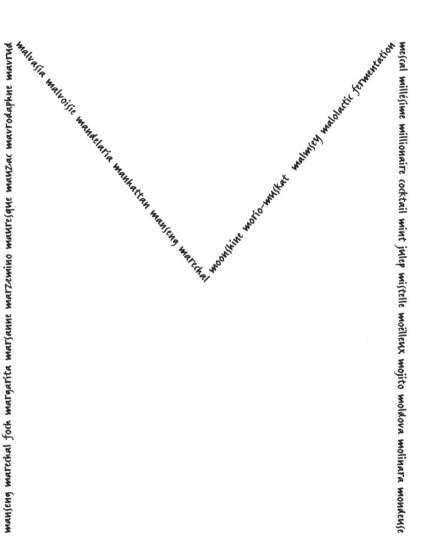

malvasia malvoisie mandelaria manhattan manseng marechal

moonshine morio-muskat malmsey malolactic fermentation

mescal millésime millionaire cocktail mint julep mistelle moëlleux mojito moldova molinara mondeuse

Macabeo – (aka Viura) lip-smacking white grape in Rioja, where it accounts for ninety per cent of white plantings (Allende [2], La Báscula [2], CVNE's Monopole [1], Marqués de Càcereb [1], Marqués de Murrieta [2], Muga [1]). A major ingredient in cava (with Parellada and Xarel•lo) and, unblended, perfectly in step with la *marcha* of the 'new' Spain in fresh 'drink-me-I'm-yours' but still food-friendly wines from Yecla (Castaño [1]), Campo de Borja (Gran Tesoro [1]), Calatayud (San Alejandro [2], Virgen de la Sierra [1]), Utiel-Requeña (Fuenteseca [2]), Castilla-La Mancha (Roqueta [1]) and Navarra (Lasierpe [1], Principe de Viana [1]). Also in southern France, in the Languedoc, where it is usually blended, except in some *vins doux naturels*.

Macallan, The – Speyside whisky distillery dating from 1824 and owned by the Edrington Group. Traditionally uses sherry casks for ageing its well-balanced liquids – and, as such, a precursor of today's many wood-finish products – now with a wide range of single malts and with reserves dating back to the 1920s (the 1926 sold out at $38,000 per bottle).

Macedonia – wine-producing region divided between Greece and the independent former Yugoslavian republic. From the latter, reds from local Vranac and white Smederevka grapes can be good and tentative exports are led by the Tikveš Co-op.

maderization – the practice of allowing controlled oxidation of fortified wines through exposure to moderate heat, as with Madeira. The process imparts a pleasant baked, raisiny character and a deep colour to the wines and renders them effectively immortal – to the extent that it's not even necessary to stopper an opened bottle (but it looks a bit crap if you don't).

made wine – wine made from reconstituted grape concentrate, usually sourced from Cyprus. The result is park-bench staples such as VP British Wine and 'Cyprus sherry'. Still sells steadily.

Mai Tai – two parts each light rum and dark rum, three parts lime juice, one part each orange curaçao and orgeat syrup shaken together and poured over crushed ice in a rocks glass. Garnish with a ladyboy.

Malbec – red-wine grape best known for making meaty, meat-friendly wines in Argentina. Once widespread in Bordeaux and still important in south-west France (where it is generally aka Côt), especially in Cahors (where it is aka Auxerrois).

malmsey – historically any sweet, strongly alcoholic wine such as the one in a butt of which the Duke of Clarence is said to have been drowned in 1478 in the Tower of London. Also refers to the sweetest style of Madeira made from Malvasia (and of which the name is a corruption).

malolactic fermentation – important, usually elective process in wine-making in which harsh malic acid is converted into softer lactic acid. Half the debate about white wine these days seems to be about malo or no malo or, increasingly sensibly, the blending of the two.

malt – 'barley or other grain that has been prepared for brewing or distilling by steeping, germinating and kiln-drying' (OED) – good to know that. Also shorthand for single malt whisky.

Maltese beer – good ones like Cisk are made by Simonds Farsons, which was established in 1928 to sustain the British troops stationed there.

Malvasia – confusing family of grapes (red and white) grown mainly in Iberia and Italy. In the former, refers to the sweetest style of fortified wine of Madeira (called malmsey in England) and to sprightly, new-fangled dry whites from Toro in Spain. In Italy, the dry wines from north-central regions (specifically Colli Piacentini), the far north-east around Isonzo and, down south, in Abruzzo are the ones to look for. Good sweet Malvasia delle Lipari is made in the Aeolian islands off north-eastern Sicily. Monterey, California, also produces some excellent Malvasia Bianca.

Manhattan – five parts bourbon or rye whiskey, two parts sweet vermouth and a dash of bitters stirred with ice and strained in to granny's handbag (or a cocktail glass) with a cherry to garnish. Called a Rob Roy if made with Scotch.

Manseng – characterful double-act of white grapes (Gros Manseng and Petit Manseng) in south-west France, especially in the small, high-quality Jurançon AC. The bigger sister (literally, and in every sense) makes zippy, sappy dry whites, notably with a tang of grapefruit, while the smaller one outshines her with luscious, late-harvested, *moëlleux*. Gradually spreading, deservedly, from their home turf to all points and a hot tip for the inevitable onset of Sauvignon Blanc fatigue.

Margarita – six parts tequila, two parts triple sec, three parts lime juice (and none of your Margarita-mix rubbish, thank you very much) shaken with ice and strained in to a cocktail glass with a salted rim, please. Might as well start making the next one straight away (but try to stop else your stomach will feel like an acid bath).

Marsanne – sturdy white grape branching out from its base in France's northern Rhône to all points, notably California and Australia (Tahbilk have the oldest vines, from 1860). Makes minerally, deeply coloured, often seriously dry, nougat-scented wines on its own and adds backbone to blends. Sample this with Paul Mas 'La Forge'.

Mauzac – important white grape in south-west France, usually blended with Len de L'el in Gaillac and with Chardonnay and Chenin Blanc in Limoux. Makes a variety of styles from dry to semi-sweet and from still to sparkling, most notably the latter in Blanquette and Crémant de Limoux.

Mavrodaphne – black grape used almost exclusively for making sweet, fortified Mavrodaphne of Patras in Greece's northern Peloponnese. The cheap ones are quite nasty but the expensive reserve and grand reserve wine are highly regarded locally.

mead – fermented honey, diluted with water and likely to be the earliest form of hooch (in colder latitudes), presumably having been the product of spontaneous fermentation. Has beard-and-sandal issues as far as marketing is concerned. Not tasting very nice doesn't help either.

Mencía – (aka Jaen in Portugal) promising red grape in north-eastern Spain's Galicia and Castilla León. As elsewhere in Spain, the sleeping giant of plots of badly managed but well-established old vines has been woken by young Turks who are making very good, very intense stuff in Bierzo, Valdeorras and Ribeira Sacra.

meritage – (pronounced to rhyme with heritage) American term coined in the 1980s for Bordeaux-type blends of grapes (both red and white) almost exclusively in California.

Merlot – 'I'm not drinking any fuckin' Merlot!' So ejaculated Paul Giamatti's lugubrious character Miles in the 2004 tasting-room-buddy film *Sideways* and thus was the tranquil life of a grape variety pitched into a tailspin. Not quite, but sales figures of Merlot-based wines were under much scrutiny for a couple of years and the rebranding as Carmenère of the large part of Chile's vineyard that had been assumed to be Merlot certainly seemed to quicken its pace. Ironically, the treasured bottle that the lovelorn Miles drinks park-bench style from a plastic cup is of Château Cheval Blanc – the top Saint Émilion, which is made from a blend including approximately fifty per cent of the detested varietal.

Like most grapes, Merlot will make exciting or dull wines depending on where and by whom it is grown and what they choose to do with it. On Bordeaux's Right Bank, Merlot makes some of the world's most sought-after wines and names like Château Pétrus have become bywords for extravagance. The wine itself, like many in Pomerol – one of Merlot's twin Bordeaux power-bases – is characterised by an expansive opulence that is in marked contrast with the more severe (some would say serious) traditional style typical of its other base up the road in Saint Émilion. Pomerol, made from a very high percentage of Merlot (with some Cabernet Franc) is about accentuating the intense, lush primary fruitiness that characterises sweetly ripe Merlot, whereas Saint Émilion (with more of the austere, mineral influence of Cab Franc) tends towards more evolved fruitcake and warm, stewed-plum flavours. Other taste comparators for Merlot include mint (as a sort of high-pitched green note on the back-palate), cherries, blackcurrants and vanilla (which is probably more about the expensive oak in which the better stuff is invariably aged).

From Bordeaux, Merlot has spread across the world to make itself the second-most widely planted red grape after Cabernet Sauvignon. The Californian examples upon which Miles directed his baleful gaze were perhaps sulking because their second-string role is so obvious there. They are something of a mixed bag (it seems to do better further north in Washington state), and cheap ones – in California as everywhere else – tend to be rather green, sour and monosyllabic. There are good examples from the southern hemisphere but in general Merlot seems to function best when blended as many, especially from hotter regions, do take on that infernal burnt character.

Merlot makes white and rosé wines too. In Ticino, the southernmost bit of Switzerland (where it's Merlot or nothing), I have dined with a little carafe of each hue as an object lesson in the diversity of what a grape can do (acknowledging the fact that grape juice is white, and wine is only ever red or rosé because the skins are left in to macerate in the juice for however long). Across the border in Italy there are some good crisp, light (expensive) wines in Trentino-Alto Adige and Friuli-Venezia Giulia and further south Merlot is an important grape in a number of even pricier SuperTuscans, of which Ornellaia's Masseto, Frescobaldi's Lamaione and Castello di Ama's L'Apparita are the notable single varietals.

methanol – (aka methyl alcohol and, weirdly, wood alcohol). The Mr Hyde to our friend ethanol's Dr Jekyll (no pussycat himself). The simplest alcohol (present naturally in tiny quantities in wine and spirits) and the stuff people with an unhealthy interest in after-shave, antifreeze and so on are looking for. Drinking a thimbleful of pure methanol brings the risk of blindness, a small glass and you could be on the drag-racer to eternity (it's used to fuel them).

meths – (aka de-natured alcohol) methylated spirits made to taste disgusting by various nasty additives (for revenue protection as much as anything else) but still consumed by terminal alcoholics. At around 2p per unit of alcohol, liver destruction, blindness and death are assured.

Mexico – wine has been made in Mexico since the arrival of the conquistadores but it has taken getting on for 500 years for the potential to be realised (particularly of Baja California, that strange withered appendage of land that hangs limply down from below the belly of the 'real' California and, within it, the Guadalupe Valley). Beyond the Americas, Mexican wine effectively refers to those of one company – LA Cetto 1 – whose strapping reds, notably from Zinfandel and Petite Syrah, are excellent ambassadors.

mezcal – is to all intents and purposes the tequila made in the Mexican state of Oaxaca from somewhat different types of agave and by a somewhat different process. Who cares, if it tastes even worse than 'normal' tequila? '*Con gusano*' means it has a worm in it, which some people think is a good idea. It's not even a worm apparently, but the larva of a moth.

millésime – the French term for vintage.

Millionaire Cocktail – depends on the mixologist. Either three parts bourbon whiskey, one part pastis, one part orange curaçao, one egg white and a teaspoon of grenadine shaken thoroughly with ice and strained in to a cocktail glass; or, the other one, in which equal parts sloe gin, rum and apricot brandy, a dash of grenadine and the juice of a lime are shaken with ice and served likewise.

Mint Julep – a few sprigs of mint muddled in a rocks glass with a teaspoon of sugar dissolved in water, shaved ice and 6–9 cl usually of bourbon whiskey (but brandy, apple brandy, gin, et cetera are also used) but don't bother if you don't have a verandah (or at least a jacaranda).

mistelle – (aka *mistela* in Spain) made from adding a spirit, usually brandy, to grape juice to prevent fermentation. Normally around 16–18% abv, after some ageing it can be drunk chilled as is (like Pineau des Charentes or jerepigo in South Africa) or used for blending in fortified and *liquoreux* wines.

moëlleux – (literally 'mellow') the French term, mainly used in western parts, for medium-sweet wine.

Mojito – three or four wedges of lime muddled with a couple of springs of mint, two teaspoons of sugar, 6–9 cl light rum, then shaken with ice and strained on to crushed ice in a highball glass. Topped up with club soda and garnished with mint leaves, a droopy moustache and a sombrero (for urban cowboys).

Moldova – most promising wine producer of the former Soviet republics, situated between Romania and Ukraine; thus, part of the greater geographical region of Moldavia. Wine here is made from a wide range of grapes, across the board in terms of styles and from a vineyard area approximately the same as that of South Africa. Their booze industry is diverse, with vodka, brandy and cordials seeing some export. If Moldova can get the technology and hygiene sorted (and generally be a bit less Moldovan) it could be a major force.

Morning Glory – one part each lemon (or lime) juice and orange curaçao, two parts brandy (or whisky), two dashes each of pastis (or anis) and bitters and a teaspoon of simple syrup shaken with ice, strained into a highball glass and topped up with soda water to taste. That'll keep your pecker up.

Morocco – formerly significant producer of rustic reds for export to France (mainly for blending) but the EEC, as was, put paid to all that in 1967. Now ambitious producers like Celliers de Meknès (Domaine Riad 2) and Thalvin-Ebertec 1 (both under the same near-monopoly ownership) are making good wines (especially in the Beni M'Tir region) and are starting to make inroads into foreign markets. French giant Castel is taking Morocco seriously, and leading French growers like Bordeaux's Bernard Magrez and

Alain Graillot from the Rhône are involved in partnerships (usually a good sign).

Moscow Mule – the drink that made Smirnoff's name (but still not a good enough reason to use it). Build two parts of any other vodka with one part lime juice over ice in a copper mug, topped up with ginger beer to taste. Dark rum in place of vodka makes it a Dark and Stormy.

Mourvèdre – (aka Monastrell in Spain, and Mataro in Australia and USA), black grape making rugged, alcoholic, tannic wines of varying quality. In the southern Rhône (including Châteauneuf-du-Pape) and Bandol it is valued for adding tannic structure to blends. In Australia it is the 'M' in Rhône-style GSM blends – Grenache and Syrah being the first two, with a few single varietal bottlings (Cascabel 2, Rusden 3). Blending with just Shiraz is also common and it is similarly used in California's Central Coast's Rhône-Ranger wines and sporadically as a quality single varietal. As Monastrell, there is a buzz around the grape in Spain's Yecla, Jumilla and Almansa regions where, in common with other regions, plots of established vines are being identified and exploited to much greater effect than ever before through the use of modern techniques.

mulled wine – (aka *Glühwein* in Germany) the mistake people make is to ignore the fact that if you mull crap wine, you get crap mulled wine. For each bottle of big, fruity red that you pour in to a large pan and heat at the lowest possible setting, add: one star anise, a bit of cinnamon, a cup of seriously strong Earl Grey tea, a small cup of dark rum, a heaped tablespoon of demerara sugar, a couple of peeled mandarins, clementines or satsumas or an orange studded with a few cloves – the peel itself is too bitter. The other mistake is overheating, which is a disaster because alcohol boils at 78°C/173°F and it will all have disappeared long before the wine itself has boiled. The temperature should be around 55–60°C/130–140°F at which point you'll see nothing more dramatic than a few elegant whisps of steam coming off the pan as you ladle it into sturdy heat-proof glasses.

Muscat – diverse (and I mean diverse) family of grapes, aka Moscatel (Iberia), Moscato (Italy), Muskateller (Germany), making white, rosé and red wines that range from steely dry to sumptuously sweet. Can be still or sparkling, have an alcohol content that varies from 5–18% abv and are made all over the world, from Alsace to Australia. Only the Pinot family is anything like as diverse.

Muscat Blanc or, with full punctilio, Muscat Blanc à Petits Grains, is the kingpin. It makes the richest and roundest Muscat wines across southern France, Alsace and northern Italy. Among the best are the luscious *vin doux naturel* dessert wines (though the locals often prefer them as aperitifs) of Beaumes-de-Venise, Rivesaltes, Frontignan and Saint-Jean-de-Minervois, which have a lightly honeyed, orangey elegance and offer excellent value.

In Alsace, Muscat Blanc (known as Muscat d'Alsace) is usually blended with Muscat Ottonel and is a good introduction to the dry style that is catching on in the Pays d'Oc and in Australia it is grapey but still full and round. Muscat makes the only wines that actually taste of grapes and the Muscat of Alexandria is one of the few varieties that are eaten as well as used for making wine.

Ottonel is the mainstay Muscat in Austria and in the right hands, the *Trocken* wines are a hauntingly, smokey-citrus dry counterpoint to the opulent sweet versions.

In northern Italy Muscat Blanc (Bianco) makes grapey, feather-light (around 5% abv), *frizzante* Moscato d'Asti and the amount of work that goes in to producing it makes the lowly price a bit of a mockery. On Sicily and the tiny island of Pantelleria to the south-west, Muscat of Alexandria is charmingly called Zibibbo and makes equally charming, aromatic, orangey *passito* wines from semi-dried grapes.

On the Greek island of Samos you'll find excellent-value sweet wines. It was across the Med in ancient Egypt and Mesopotamia where some of the earliest experiments in winemaking involved the ancestors of today's Muscat grapes. Rather later, one of Napoleon Bonaparte's consolations during his exile on St Helena was the odd case of Constantia, the fabled South African dessert wine that is being made again (since the early 1980s) by Klein Constantia. I expect he would have liked the fortified and figgy liqueur Muscats that the town of Rutherglen in the baking hot north-east of Australia's Victoria sends out to the world at an average of 18% abv.

Muscadet is no relation, but the dark and silky, raisin-rich Moscatel sherries are close cousins. These in turn are not to be confused with the generally cheap, sugary and characterless Moscatels de Valencia again made from Muscat of Alexandria (aka Alejandría).

There aren't that many reds made from the Black Muscat, which thrives in California mainly as a table grape, used for eating, but these sweet, lip-smackingly redcurranty wines have a great affinity with chocolate desserts – a notoriously difficult food match for wine. Muscat's musky, perfumed wines are believed to have aphrodisiac qualities, as a wine of up to 20% abv (and brimming with energy-giving sugars) consumed after a long, boozy dinner might well be.

M

nebbiolo négociant négrette negroamaro negroni cocktail nerello mascalese nero d'avola neuberger

nerello mascalese nero d'avola neuberger neutral spirit new world wines new Zealand noble rot non-vintage norton nosiola

nebbiolo négociant négrette negroamaro negroni cocktail nerello mascalese nero d'avola neuberger

Nebbiolo – noble black grape of northern Italy, the pride of Piedmont, producing the country's finest and longest-lived wines in Barolo and Barbaresco. To most people it is probably the least familiar of the great red-wine grapes because the Piedmont authorities restrict plantings to the best, sunniest, hillside sites and the quantities produced are minuscule when, for example, compared to Cabernet Sauvignon in Bordeaux. Even Burgundy's production of Pinot Noir (perhaps the best wine with which to compare it) is many hundreds of times the size. The fact that it is expensive will not come as a surprise, but your money would buy one of the most ethereal of wine experiences, where the rustle of dried rose petals mingles with tar and tobacco and flavours of strawberry, chocolate and something of the deep woods that predominates in mature wines. A glimpse around the door can be had in wines from conscientious producers in the Nebbiolo d'Alba DOC, similarly from nearby Gattinara (where it is aka Spanna), Lombardy's Valtellina (aka here as Chiavennasca), and some leading Barolo and Barbaresco winemakers sell declassified wines under the Langhe Nebbiolo DOC approved in 1995. Needless to say, winemakers the world over are trying to cajole this least cooperative of grapes into reprising its Piedmont performance elsewhere but with no notable successes.

négociant – the French term for a wine merchant who, most likely, is involved in making the wine they sell, sometimes from the product of their own vineyards and also from grapes or wine purchased from other growers. Bordeaux and Burgundy have large numbers, some of whom have been in business for over 200 years, and *négociant* wines can be a good choice for reliable, if unspectacular, quality.

Negroamaro – (literally 'black bitter', but that's a little harsh) black grape making tannic, often hot wines in the Brindisi, Copertino Salice Salentino and Squinzano DOCs in Italy's heel. Blending with Malvasia Nera or Primitivo makes it a different, better proposition.

Nero d'Avola – (aka Calabrese) signature red grape of Sicily mainly from the south-east, making wines with a smoky, mineral core that are (usually) saved from being overly hot by the intensity of their red-berry fruit.

Neutral spirit – the almost pure (190° proof or above) alcohol that is the collected and condensed vapour released during the distillation process. It is the base for clear spirits such as gin and vodka, in blending dark spirits such as whisky and rum and for fortifying wines such as port.

New World wine – an oddly unsatisfactory term that is increasingly irrelevant. Used as shorthand to describe wine as a kind of alcoholic fruit juice, heavily bolstered by oak (in some form or other) that is thankfully going out of fashion; also unfortunately applied to wines from the southern hemisphere plus northern Americas despite the fact that some of these countries have a long history of winemaking (in the case of South Africa for over 350 years). The subtext is that these upstart wines lack the subtlety and complexity of the wines of Europe.

Meanwhile – even if only since the mid-1990s – the Old World has finally woken up to the fact that the combination of quality and value offered by, for example, Australia, is the most effective weapon in a ferociously competitive and globalised wine market. Things are looking better, though, due to the success of what has become rather clumsily known as the 'New Old World' – regions like the Pays d'Oc, Sicily and parts of southern Italy and Spain, where thousand of acres of plonk-producing vines have been grubbed up and replaced with varieties that make wine that people actually want to drink.

In the 'New New World' of the BRIC countries, the flames of growing oenophilia seem to be fanned by the allure of the traditional – the terroir, the *vins de garde*, the nuance – as exemplified by China's thirst for Château Lafite. Europeans are (shortsightedly) rarely contemplating the likely future impact of wines from thousand-acre vineyards in Brazil and China. It will be fascinating to see if the Europeans have learned their lessons from competing with what I can only apologetically refer to now as the 'Old New World' of Australia, New Zealand and parts of the Americas. If so, perhaps it may help them in the battle for market share to come with the 'New New World' of Asia. It may be that the real lesson to be learned is that, as in so many other areas of commerce, what we Europeans should do now is sell expertise and experience, not horny-handed tilling of the soil. Top-flight winemakers have been scouring the earth to find suitable terroirs to make the wine that the world wants to drink and the results are trickling toward the tasting tables.

New Zealand wine – 1982 wasn't just a great year for Bordeaux. It was memorable for New Zealand too as it was the first year their wine-makers sold their wares overseas. They cadged some space for a few cases on a New Zealand Royal Air Force plane heading for RAF Brize Norton and, from there, the precious cargo made its way to a tasting in London in a clapped-out Cortina.

The wines went down well but their kind of quality never comes cheap and, what with the cost of transporting the wines halfway around the world, sales were a bit slow to, ahem, take off. But New Zealand is the ultimate can-do country and has always punched (and kicked, and cover-driven) above its weight so if it's broke they'll fix it. As recently as the 1960s there were just a few hundred hectares of vines, predominantly of Isabella (nope, me neither) and I'm not sure how many of the thousands of acres of Müller-Thurgau they planted in the 1970s are left (and I don't care as long as I don't have to drink any). But they cracked it in the 1980s and lift-off soon followed. The average price for one of their bottles is now higher than for any other country's sold in the UK. Australia has overtaken the UK as their biggest customer (the USA is third) in an export market that in 2009 topped the NZ$ 1 billion mark for the first time.

1982 was a good vintage for me, too, because at some point in that year a girlfriend and I purloined a Sancerre from her dad and it was my *Eureka!* bottle – the one that made me understand that wine could provide a lot more pleasure than merely the effects of its alcohol. It was a Sauvignon Blanc, of course – the grape variety upon whose narrow shoulders the whole of New Zealand's initial success has rested. I was alarmed by Kiwi Sauvignons at first – they jumped out of the glass, sprayed some sort of gooseberry essence in your face, happy-slapped you a bit and ran screeching out the door with your wallet. A lot of them have calmed down now and have kept that zingy, cut-grass freshness but with more of the restrained, mineral style that my bottle of Sancerre (hopefully) had.

Pinot Noir is the great hope if New Zealand is to continue its dizzying growth in the fickle world of wine trends – total wine production doubled in the late noughties and alarmingly led to the first £3.99 bottles of Sauvignon in UK supermarkets (at below the average UK price for a bottle of wine). As with Sauvignon, I wasn't initially enthusiastic. They were pleasant (if somewhat 'green') wines that were never going to be able to hold a candle to Burgundy. Again, they've grown up into very well-mannered, balanced wines indeed and I dare say there have been a few sleepless nights of late in Beaune. The best have intense raspberry and strawberry fruit offset by creaminess; also, the excess of enthusiasm for oak in the early days is much better managed now.

The producer that has done more to put New Zealand wine on the map than any other has been Cloudy Bay. Started up by David Hohnen of Cape Mentelle in 1985 and now owned by LVMH, Cloudy is now, for me, more impressive as a marketing story than as a wine-making one. The sustained illusion of scarcity (to the extent of creating a website – cloudybaylocator.com) that surrounds what I speculate is the biggest-selling white wine of any at (or above) its price has been brilliantly managed. Meanwhile, the 'other' Cloudy Bay Sauvignon, Te Koko, is aged in expensive new oak – like the great dry-white Bordeaux made from that grape – and is one of the best value wines in the world.

Montana (owned by Pernod Ricard), the biggest New Zealand producer, make over a third of the nation's total and are almost twice as big as their nearest rival, Nobilo (now part of Constellation Brands). Quality is refreshingly high among the big firms. Privately owned Villa Maria and Oyster Bay have also both nailed the quantity/quality conundrum, the former particularly for its Pinots (although, as often in the southern hemisphere, I prefer the cheaper and mid-range wines to the 'best') and the latter for straightforward Sauvignon.

Meanwhile, the influences – and the alumni – of Cloudy Bay have spread out across the country. New Zealand is now a very brave New World of over 500 small producers who make wine at a general standard that is superior to that in any 'old world' wine nation, and sell it in a more ambitious way, too. No flogging your grapes to the local co-op and heading off to the pub – everybody has seen the power of branding and, with this in mind, virtual winemaking as well as contract winemaking is growing.

Having cracked Sauvignon Blanc and Pinot Noir, your average overachieving New Zealand winery obviously wasn't about to rest on its laurels. They're making some fine Chardonnays in a wide variety of styles across the different regions and Viognier, Gewürztraminer and Riesling that can hold their own against all but the very best of their northern hemisphere counterparts. They've also been hedging their bets against any outbreak of Sauvignon Blanc fatigue by planting plenty of Pinot Grigio, much of it alongside the Pinot Noir in Marlborough. The results are a fascinating mix of the lean, crisp Italian style with some of the roundness and richness of Alsace.

As for the reds, Cabernet Sauvignon, Merlot and, above all, Shiraz are making wines that, again, seem to have much more in common with their far-away French cousins than with their Australian neighbours' blockbuster versions. Being further from the equator, the wine-growing regions have a cooler climate than most of the major

Oz regions and as a result the wines are leaner and fresher and have better acidity (a fact not lost on their Antipodean cousins who are now planting, in droves, in their coolest areas).

The biggest wine-producing area is Marlborough, at the north-eastern corner of South Island. Its 11,000 (and rising) hectares of wall-to-wall vines comprise half of New Zealand's total – an extraordinary figure given that there was not a single vine there prior to 1973. The secret is the climate, which is cooler than across the Cook Strait. It keeps in place the acidity without which nobody would ever have heard of Marlborough. It's not all Sauvignon, of course – there is good Chardonnay and Riesling, rapidly improving Pinot Noir and Pinot Gris is also picking up speed.

The big firms all make wines from Marlborough Sauvignon Blanc and Pinot Noir (whether from their own or from bought-in grapes or juice); names to look out for include Astrolabe [2], Boreham Wood [2], Churton [2], Clos Henri [2] (being Henri Bourgeois of Sancerre), Clos Marguerite [2], Cloudy Bay [3], Culley [1], Delta [2], Dog Point [2], Forrest [1] (especially late-harvest Riesling), Framingham [2] (owned by Portugal's Sogrape), Fromm [2], Greywacke [2] (Cloudy's founding winemaker Kevin Judd's new baby), Hans Herzog [3], Isabel [2], Jackson [2], Kumeu River [2], Lawson's Dry Hills [2], Mansion House Bay [2], Saint Clair [2], Allan Scott [2], Selaks [1], Seresin Estate [2], Southbank [1], Tindall [2], Tinpot Hut [1], Wither Hills [1] and Yealands [1].

Hawkes Bay, halfway up the east coast on the North Island, is the second-largest region and home to lots of smaller-scale producers making a diversity of wines in a diversity of soils and microclimates – thankfully, the one unifying characteristic is a quality-conscious approach. Merlot and the Cabernets (Sauvignon and Franc) set the pace for reds in the 1990s looking to make wines in the image of Bordeaux, *barrique* ageing and all, but – to my taste – there seemed to be square-peg-and-round-hole issues, especally concerning ripeness. So it is with much relief that I welcome the roll that Syrah is now on, notably in the Gimblett Gravels sub-region. There is good, even very good, Chardonnay, but – as with the reds – the real stars are only starting to emerge now and Viognier and Pinot Gris are beginning to shine. Among the galaxy of good producers are Alpha Domus [2], Babich [1] (also in Marlborough), Bilancia [3], Church Road [3] (now owned by Pernod Ricard), Clearview [2], Corbans [1] (Pernod Ricard), Craggy Range [2], Kim Crawford [1] (now owned by Constellation), Distant Land [1], Esk Valley [1] (owned by Villa Maria), Mills Reef [2], Mission [2] (making wine since before the dawn of history, i.e. 1851), Mount Nelson [2], C J Pask [1], Redmetal [3], Sacred Hill [2], Sileni [1], Te Awa [2], Te Mata [2], Terravin [3], Trinity Hill [2] and Vidal [1] (owned by Villa Maria).

Martinborough, at the southern tip of the North Island (part of Wairarapa – itself not to be confused with Waipara, below), with lots of small, individualistic growers, is slugging it out with Central Otago for the Pinot Noir bragging rights. Notable producers include Ata Rangi [2], Dry River [3], Escarpment [1], Martinborough Vineyard [2], Palliser [1], Schubert [3] and Danny Schuster [3].

Central Otago is the world's most southerly wine region and necessarily edgy wines are made by appropriately edgy people whose lives (and livelihoods) revolve largely around one question: 'Will the Pinot ripen?' That question is asked (often by bearded young men in woolly hats) on getting on for 100 farms (a five-fold increase in a decade) including Amisfield [3], where, as almost everywhere, some of the Alsace whites are also successfully grown, Chard Farm [3], Felton Road [2], Lowburn Ferry [3], Mount Difficulty [2], Peregrine [3], Quartz Reef [3], Rippon [3], Wild Earth [2]. They don't come cheap – why would they?

The Canterbury region around Christchurch is outshone by one of its offspring, the sub-region of Waipara to the north of the city. Pinot is the staple, as elsewhere, with Chardonnay, Riesling and Pinot Gris for treats. The climate is cool, and so are the winemakers: among the names to seek out are Bascand [1], Bell Hill [3], Mount Brown [1], Mountford [3], Mud House [1], Pyramid Valley [3] and Whitestone [2].

The area around Auckland, New Zealand's largest city, is divided into a number of zones of which Waiheke Island (try Stonyridge [3] and Goldwater [2]) and Matakana (try Providence [3]) have some high-end producers vying to produce New Zealand's most expensive red. The city is the base for Montana's classy sparkling wine production (try Deutz [2] and Lindauer [1]).

Gisborne, up from Hawke's Bay, has the third-largest production – much of which is for the large firms – and majors on whites grapes (Vinoptima [3], Kim Crawford [1], Millton [2], Pegasus Bay [2] and Cooper's Creek [2], who also have NZ's only Arneis). Likewise, back on the South Island, east of Marlborough, whites do well in Nelson – Neudorf [2] and Seifried [1] both make a wide range (the former also excels with Pinot Noir).

***GET A HANDLE...**

HAVING MADE ITS NAME WITH ZIPPY SAUVIGNON BLANC, NEW ZEALAND IS GETTING READY TO TAKE ON ALL-COMERS ACROSS A WIDE RANGE OF GRAPES FROM SVELTE PINOT NOIRS TO STYLISH GEWÜRZ – AND EVERYTHING IN BETWEEN.

noble rot – see *Botrytis.*

non-vintage – (aka NV) refers to a wine – often Champagne – made from a blend of different vintages and always sold more cheaply than the producer's vintage-dated wines.

original gravity oak old-fashioned cocktail old vines orange muscat organic booze original gravity oak old-fashioned cocktail old vines orange muscat organic oak old-fashioned cocktail old vines orange muscat organic booze original gravity oak old-fashioned cocktail old vines orange muscat organic booze

oak – used for barrel-making. It's impossible to overstate the influence of the various species of the genus *quercus* on shaping the taste of modern booze. Few of the world's best wines (and little of what we drink every day) would be recognisable without 'new' oak. Without it, whisky would be vodka and cognac would be schnapps.

O

That warm vanilla aroma in your silky reserva Rioja? It's oak (*roble* in Spain). The come-hitherish, toasty edge to your favourite Chilean Chardonnay? Yep – oak. The cedar cigar-box thing people talk about with fine claret? You've guessed it (it's *chêne* in France as in *fûts de chêne* – oak barrels).

In Europe the best oak for ageing wine comes from the Allier and Nièvre *départments* in France's Loire region (specifically, the Tronçais forest). Brandy producers, who, like whisky and rum producers, rely on oak to impart flavour, prefer their wood to be from Limousin. In the US it's *quercus alba* (the white oak) that gives bourbon such powerful vanilla aromas and in Spain it's the same American white oak that makes Rioja the most overtly oak-influenced red wine of all.

The romance that occurs between fermented grape juice and the charred inside of an oak barrel is as complex as any love affair and, as such, sometimes people do strange things to get what they want. The 225-litre *barriques* preferred by winemakers are expensive; even so, France makes about 200,000 of them annually (so cooperage isn't going to be a lost trade any time soon). To age a wine in such a barrel works out at a cost of between one and two pounds per bottle for the first use, when the effect is at its most powerful (sometimes overly so and the wines are blended with others which have been in second-year barrels, and so on).

The effect is so desirable that resourceful winemakers decided that if they couldn't afford to put the wine in oak, why not put the oak in the wine? So they chopped up some toasted oak and chucked the oak chips in to their stainless-steel tanks during fermentation and Bingo! – oaked wine. The industry is still coy about it but if you're drinking a modestly priced wine that has noticeably oaky characteristics you'll know where they come from (whole staves are also used). If you don't like the sound of it, don't read the section on additives in wine (but if you do read it, you'll probably feel better about the chips).

Originally distillers of Scotch whisky would put their liquid in to any old barrel they could find lying around the port of Leith – if it didn't leak it was good enough – but now we know that if you put good spirit into bad wood you get bad whisky. In the 1930s they started using barrels from Kentucky's bourbon-whiskey producers, mainly for reasons of economy. The Americans wanted new oak to give the characteristic toasty flavour to their whiskies but after the barrels had been used a few times they didn't have enough welly – I forget the technical term – left in them for Yankee tastes, but they were perfect for the subtler Scottish accents of whisky-without an 'e'.

In the late 1980s distillers started experimenting with barrels that had been used for maturing different sorts of booze. The result was the launch in 1994 by Glenmorangie of a whisky that had been 'finished' by a six-month spell in a cask that, in its previous life, had been used for ageing ruby port. Other wood finishes – sherry and Sauternes – soon followed and now, like most trends in booze, it has reached the out-of-control phase.

Old-Fashioned – half-teaspoon of sugar, two dashes of Angostura and minimal water to melt the sugar built in a rocks glass with 6–9 cl bourbon, ice cubes, a maraschino cherry, orange slice and lemon wedge to garnish and served with a blending stick (or a walking stick).

Orange Muscat – unrelated to the Muscat family and planted in tiny quantities, I nonetheless suspect that the half-bottles, consumed at dinner parties, of the wines made by Andrew Quady (pronounced 'kwaddy') in California and by Brown Brothers in Australia, have successfully inducted more Anglo-Saxons into the world of pleasure offered by sweet wines than everything else put together.

organic booze – booze is not necessarily any good – or any better, or less bad, for you – just because the ingredients were grown under an organic regime. Meanwhile, a lot of excellent booze, including some of the world's most acclaimed wines are produced organically (and biodynamically) but producers – winemakers in particular – don't want to advertise the fact. Oh, yes, there are any number of knotty problems buried in the rich organic soil. Give me the choice of a bag of organic carrots or a bag of conventionally grown ones, and I'll usually spring the extra for the former in the reasonable hope that they might have a bit more flavour – in essence, they'll have more carrotiness, which probably isn't that difficult for the grower to achieve. The number of factors involved in trying to make a better wine or beer or spirit – and the number of things that can go wrong – is a very different ball-game. For a start, most organic regimes extend only as far as the winery, brewery or distillery door because the actual production methods and the addition of all sorts of additives is not under the oversight of the organic authorities but of the local bureaucrats.

In itself, the idea of a 'healthier' form of a product that contains an addictive and potentially lethal drug is a bit strange, to say the least, and it's probably best not to go there. Meanwhile, it seems reasonable to assume that there is some benefit for our fragile planet in choosing booze that has not contributed to the accumulation of fungicides, fertilisers and pesticides in the environment. The big question, though, is what's the cost to the well-being of the fragile (and confused) drinker if it doesn't taste very nice?

Thankfully, the counterparts of the rogues who spatter a few flecks of muddy straw on to bog-standard eggs and flog them as organic seem to be in a small minority. Most of the producers who are prepared to jump through all the hoops required for organic certification apply the same passion and rigour to the production part of the process as well. For the small but growing demographic for whom everything has to be organic the supermarket own-brand organic offerings are a straightforward option, but only if your expectations aren't too high.

As with all booze the best policy is to stick with good producers. The soil of such hallowed vineyards as Domaine Leflaive in Burgundy, Jean-Louis Chave in Hermitage and Zind-Humbrecht in Alsace is their principal asset and the best way to keep it in prime condition is by maintaining nature's balance through organic methods. Meanwhile, not all of these illustrious winemakers want to do the hoop-jumping – and they certainly have no need or, perhaps desire, to align themselves too closely with the flag-wavers in the organic movement.

In wine it's the mid-range that presents the biggest challenge for producers and consumers alike. Committed organic producers Michel Chapoutier [2] (Rhône), Bonterra [1] (California), the Fairtrade brands Stellar [1] and The Ruins [1] (South Africa) and Albet i Noya [1] (Catalonia) all manage to make the tightrope walk of balancing quantity and quality with style.

For small-scale producers, the specialist organic merchants come into their own. The range is excellent at Whole Earth branches in the USA (and the UK branches are catching up) while specialists like Vintage Roots and Vinceremos, who stock only organic and biodynamic wines (as well as ciders, beers and spirits) have plenty of experience. The real goodies, as usual, are to be had from the top independent merchants, all of whom have as good a range of organic and biodynamic wines as they have of everything else. Ask your favourite merchant about the Perrin brothers of Château de Beaucastel [3] in Châteauneuf, Jean Thevenet [3] in Macon or Nicolas Joly [3] of Coulée de Serrant in Savennières and watch their face break into a big, biodynamic smile.

original gravity – measures the potential alcoholic strength in beer based on the content of fermentable sugars, perhaps named for how much (or little) you'd need to drink before the effect of gravity would return you to your origins.

pacharán país palomino paradise cocktail parellada park bench drinks pastis periquita pedro ximénez pH phylloxera picolit picpoul pignolo pimm's piña colada cocktail pineau d'aunis pineau des charentes pink gin pinotage pisco sour

Paradise – one part each apricot brandy and fresh orange juice to two parts gin with a dash of lemon juice shaken with ice and strained into a celestial cocktail glass to the sound of earthly angels laughing dirty.

park-bench drinks – a niche market, specifically concerned with providing more bangs for the bum buck (as a consequence, the approximate cost is indicated in pence-per-unit of alcohol). Not long ago, Cyprus sherry and 'British wines' like VP and QC were the staples of the 'wino list', but things have changed fast. VP Medium (at 27ppu) is Medium what, exactly? It has quite a strong nose of lime pickle (and that can't be right, can it?) and also something that whisked me back thirty-five years to some murky liquid that emerged from my first chemistry set. I'm glad I didn't drink whatever it was all those years ago because it might well have tasted like it. VP Rich tastes of vomit, which may go down – and come up – well with the target audience. It's made by Constellation Brands, the world's largest wine company. Carlsberg Special Brew (27ppu) spawned a hundred imitators in the stupor-strength lager category but none have the same slight whisp of honey and the malty, creamy taste. The sheer weight of alcohol means it tends to stick in the craw somewhat after the first few tinnies. Tennent's Super (25ppu) has not just the same alcohol content (9% abv) but something of the floral characteristics of many better German wines as well. It's cleaner and drier than Spesh but with that same maltiness – rather lovely, really.

The foregoing are the red squirrels to the monstrous grey that has now established the realm of Ciderspace. Unlike the people who drink them, the white ciders are almost odourless and colourless and are almost as tasteless as this item, though guaranteed to leave the consumer completely legless. Nobody ever drank these because they liked the taste. In fact, does anybody who isn't a wino ever drink them? But White Star Cider it is, folks: at 19ppu it's the bum's rush with the alcohol content of a small town and notes of saccharine dissolved in vinegar – it's the cheapest hit out there.

pastis – star-anise and (crucially, as anisette does not contain it) liquorice-flavoured liqueur, first sold in 1932 by the Ricard company and popular as an apéritif in France. Like all the anis family, becomes cloudy when diluted with water (typically 5:1).

Pedro Ximénez – (often aka PX) pronounced 'he-MEN-eth', white-grape variety of southern Spain, best for making dark, raisiny, intensely sweet, fortified wine in Montilla-Moriles (and in Australia) and showing promise when used in a blend for dry whites.

Petite Sirah – red-wine grape, correctly aka Durif, but often loosely applied to true Syrah and others in California. Historically an unsung blender but now getting more attention as a single varietal there and in Australia and Mexico.

petits châteaux – the five-odd thousand 'little castles' that produce the vast bulk of château-bottled Bordeaux. Although they occupy the lowest rungs, beneath the various *cru bourgeois* and *cru classé* levels – the 'petit' applies to status rather than size – they can offer excellent value when purchased advisedly.

Petit Verdot – black grape of Bordeaux well regarded there, albeit as a rich and tannic blender, but beginning to shine in some single varietals in Australia, Argentina, Portugal and showing promise in Spain's Jumilla region.

pH – scale for measuring acidity, all-important in wine, on which most are in the range 3 to 4 (1 is highly acidic, 7 is neutral, like water, and 14 highly alkaline). Very important in the armoury of winemakers who will often be aiming for a particular pH value in the overall profile of the wine they are producing.

P

phylloxera – a small aphid that attacks the roots of vines and destroys the root system. An outbreak beginning in the mid-1860s had disastrous consequences in France, killing some 2.5 million hectares of vines. Wine production in France fell by nearly three-quarters over the next twenty-five years and the blighters spread throughout Europe. The solution came from across the Atlantic in shipments of millions of phylloxera-resistant rootstocks of American vine varieties on to which new vines of the traditional European varieties were grafted. It remains standard practice to this day for the great majority of the world's vines.

Pimm's – gin- or vodka-based fruit cup dating to the 1820s used for a mixed drink that should resemble a boozy fruit salad in a glass. Indelibly associated with summer in England. If you don't want to drink the whole bottle at a sitting then be sure not to add pieces of strawberry, cucumber and a few leaves of fresh mint to the usual stuff (orange, lemon, apple). I know that raspberry and watermelon do excellent random service, especially if zippified with a squeeze of lime, as does basil in place of mint – its high-pitched pepperiness makes the whole concoction even more intoxicatingly aromatic.

Piña Colada – equal parts white rum and coconut cream to two parts pineapple juice shaken with ice and strained in to a teenager via a highball glass with a pineapple spear as garnish.

Pineau des Charentes – lightly fermented white, red or rosé juice, from the cognac grapes, fortified with cognac to around 17–18% abv (and produced within an AC covering the same geographical area). Some are aged for five, even ten, years in oak.

Pink Gin – two or three dashes of bitters stirred into 6–9 cl gin in a rocks glass, unencumbered (unencucumbered even) by anything so vulgar as a garnish or as prissy as ice. A certain type of Englishman's version of a Dry Martini perhaps, and a fine thing if the gin's up to scratch.

Pinotage – red-wine grape – a cross between Pinot Noir and Cinsaut. For better or worse South Africa's 'signature' grape variety and one that polarises opinion like no other. The novelist Jay McInerny has characterised the aroma as 'lipstick au poivre' and other terms I have collected include Branston pickle, paint, HP Sauce, burnt rubber, bloody red meat (with a whiff of lipstick), and from a dark corner of the far-left field, 'having a Prince Charles moment'. Volatile esters are responsible for the acetone twang that is sometimes present. This is a lot of baggage to lug around but the last few years have seen improvements in the way the grape is handled, which has changed things sometimes to the extent of unrecognisability – at all price levels. Careful oak ageing that preserves the fruit's natural liveliness can result in genuinely distinctive wines that deserve attention. So maybe they shouldn't pull them up and forget all about it.

Pinot Blanc – underrated and, consequently, under-exploited white grape grown from France all the way through central Europe to Slovakia, aka Pinot Bianco in Italy and Weissburgunder in Germany. The plain sister of the overachieving Pinot family, it nonetheless can make full-bodied, enigmatic, food-friendly wines in Alsace, in northern Italy, where it is widespread, in Friuli-Venezia Giulia, Veneto and, at its best, in Trentino-Alto Adige where they make a fuss of its acidity and give it a nice bit of oak. Has friends in Germany, too, where it makes big-boned wines in Baden and Franken and finally goes to the ball with luscious late-harvest and botrytized wines.

Pinot Grigio – versatile, near-ubiquitous white-grape variety aka Pinot Gris in France and Grauburgunder or Ruländer in Germany and – while we're at it – Rulandské Šedé in the Czech Republic and Szürkebarát in Hungary. 'Wine for people who don't really like wine' is one of the cruellest things said about it although some of the colourless, odourless, taste-free liquids produced in bulk are Exhibit

A. But in the right place, in the right hands Pinot Grigio makes classy, complex wines in a diversity of styles wherever it is planted. At its best, for example in Alsace winemaker Olivier Humbrecht's Rangen de Thann Clos Saint Urbain, it can make some of the world's grandest whites.

Why the disparity? As ever, bad winemakers will make bad wine irrespective of the grape varieties they grow and when quantity is valued over quality a productive grape like Pinot Grigio risks getting a bad name. It is closely related to Pinot Noir and with pinky-grey berries that can be mistaken for black grapes it has enough colour to make some really savoury, sappy rosé styles in the north of Italy. The family resemblance seems more than skin deep though and after tasting the fleshier Alsace examples I have more than once found myself thinking they may *look* like white wines but in their DNA they're red.

The Italians have to own up to producing much of the dullest dishwater Pinot Grigio in the supermarkets, but they also produce some excellent stuff in the Veneto, Friuli and above all (quite literally) Alto Adige in the foothills of the Alps. This is the part of Italy that wears Lederhosen and munches bratwurst, but the lean, crisp wines haven't an ounce of fat on them. They're quintessential mountain wines and the perfect choice if ever there really is a fondue renaissance.

Alsace is the spiritual home of Pinot Gris with a range of styles and prices that showcase everything that can be done with it. The locals often still call it Tokay Pinot Gris although Brussels has decreed they can't use Tokay on the labels for fear of it being confused with Hungary's luscious Tokaji wines, which are made from a completely different grape. The simplest wines from the big co-operative wineries are usually good value while the *vendange tardive* wines have a smoky, honeyed lusciousness that's balanced with tangy acidity. At the top of the tree are the *selection de grains nobles* (fairly self-explanatory, I hope), for which shrivelled, super-sweet berries are individually picked right through to Christmas and made into heavenly, nectar-like dessert wines that go oh-so-well with foie gras. For the good stuff, gird your loins to spend upwards of £30 – for a half-bottle.

In the southern hemisphere, New Zealand winemakers have picked up the ball and run with it, perhaps looking towards a post-Sauvignon Blanc future. The results are never cheap and some sensible producers are labelling them either Gris or Grigio according to style and many are an impressive mix of Alsace weight and north Italian verve. Argentina is making some similar styles in the higher altitude vineyards of Mendoza and, for my money, they're the best bet for making the holy grail of good Pinot Grigio at an everyday price.

Pinot Meunier – black-grape variety of northern Europe, aka Schwarzriesling or Müllerrebe in Germany. Poor Pinot Meunier – it's made a big contribution to most of the Champagne that most people have ever drunk – being the most widely planted grape there – and yet most people have never heard of it. It must also feel a bit weird to be the only red grape that makes almost exclusively white wine. Domaine Chandon in the Napa Valley make the only single-varietal red that I've ever tried – after keeping it for a few years I brought it out as a mystery wine one rain-extended lunchtime at Lord's. It wasn't the first such bottle of the day and I can't remember if it was any good but I know there must be a reason for this grape living its life beneath the radar.

Pinot Noir – red- and white-wine grape, aka Blauburgunder in Austria and Spätburgunder in Germany. Pinot Noir is a very . . . difficult . . . grape. It's difficult to grow. It's difficult to make wine with. It's difficult to write about. It pouts. It flirts. It hurts. Its wines evoke more passion and more poetry than all others. It inspires and infuriates infatuated winemakers in every corner of the world. And why do people forgive it all its inconstancy and waywardness? Simply this – because when it is good, it is very, very good.

And when it is bad it is horrid and, until ten years ago, most of it was, but at least it was easy to avoid. All the red wine of Burgundy, unless you included Beaujolais (and you wouldn't have wanted to do that) was – and is – made from it and was best given a wide berth unless you had the Obi-Wan Kenobi of wine along with you for the ride. Less scarily, it was one of the three Champagne grapes (making the fullest-bodied style, which – with or without some of the region's other black grape, Pinot Meunier – is called *blanc de noirs*). Apart from that, there were a few misguided souls experimenting with it in places that were thankfully flung as far as their wines would inevitably be, for example, in Oregon and New Zealand.

The picture today is unrecognisable. My rule-of-thumb used to be that no bargepole was long enough for any Pinot under a tenner. Now, with minimal research, it's possible to buy wines, even from some of the biggest producers, that provide some of the best value in the £5-10 slot and blow me down if even some of the supermarket own-brands aren't now worth a go.

The success of the wine-buddy film *Sideways* was as good for Pinot's PR as it was bad for marketing Merlot and the former has been riding the wave of its reputation for making the most ethereal of red wines ever since. It's true, Pinot – like Nebbiolo – is different, and most of the vocabulary that Cabernet and Shiraz and the like have taught us doesn't usefully apply. Its most general characteristics can be described in terms of its pale and interesting looks (which often belie a full body), its softness and its perfume and comparators are often about sweetness and ripeness and redness – raspberries and strawberries and boiled beetroot. But they don't get up-close and personal enough and people go down to the woods for terms like gamey and smoky and earthy and comparators like mushrooms and the things of the forest floor. You're sure of a big surprise when things go entirely abstract and words like feminine and animal emerge but there is something to it all and I have lost my head with specifically feminine animal things, and intimate things mingling with perfumed things and, well, just lots of sweaty sex, really.

Pinot doesn't like it hot – it doesn't really work in Iberia, for example, except for Cava – but then it doesn't like its tiny hand to be frozen, either. It's happiest flirting at the edges of the cool-climate regions of every country it's grown in. Of the more widely available, moderately priced Pinots (and I do find it hard to believe I'm writing this sentence) it's now possible to buy the basic wines with some confidence from the major Burgundy *négociants*. In the southern hemisphere Chile leads the way and Argentina's higher-altitude vineyards show promise, and nobody would fling those New Zealand wines any more. In Australia the Yarra Valley provides value while the coolest areas in the Mornington Peninsula and, especially, Tasmania are flexing their muscles.

There are few mainstream bargains, but some serious quality from producers in California and those crackpots in Oregon, it turns out, were right. Back in Europe, off the beaten track, overall quality for reds from Alsace and reds and rosés from Sancerre is on the up while Germany's Spätburgunders are a mixed bag (but the best are superb). Italy's cooler north-east is starting to provide some of the cheapest-but-quaffable examples to the supermarkets.

Pinot wouldn't be Pinot if it didn't still tread on your dreams now and then so it should always be approached with a cool heart.

pisco – grape brandy of Chile and Peru with a history dating to the early years of the Spanish conquest. Any drink having that initial syllable has got problems, hasn't it? But good pisco such as Horcón or Mistral is uniquely itself – it seems to be essentially grape schnapps – and is made distinctive by the grapiness of the Muscat wines it's distilled from. It accounts for eighty per cent of all Chile's consumption of spirits, of which eighty per cent is made by two companies: Control and Capel. Some is left to mellow in American oak and some is packaged in the instantly recognisable bottles based on the shape of the Moai figures of Easter Island.

Pisco Sour – one part lime juice, three parts pisco, a teaspoon of simple syrup, half an egg white and a dash of bitters shaken with ice and strained into a cocktail glass in Chile. And only in Chile. Unless you're in Peru.

Planter's Punch – three parts dark rum, two parts lime juice, one part simple syrup and a dash of bitters shaken with ice and strained into a highball glass over and over again.

plonk – mildly pejorative term for basic wine, particularly that bought from supermarkets, very widely used in the seventies and eighties and thought to have originated in Australia as a corruption of *vin blanc*.

Polish beer – of the major beermaking countries, Poland has been the most efficiently filleted by Big Beer: MillerCoors have Tyskie – the biggest seller as well as Żubr and Lech; Carlsberg has Okocim; Heineken has Tatra and Zywiec. Quality remains high across the board though, and there's a handful of little 'uns here and there such as Brok, Łomża and Witnica.

Portuguese wine – Portugal has ploughed its own furrow as far as wine is concerned and the results are fascinating. Its greatest assets – spectacular fortified wines, especially port – are probably its greatest liability when it comes to selling its rapidly improving table wines, which inexplicably account for just one per cent of the UK market. Sales of basic port are falling but it remains so huge and so indelibly associated with any red liquid from Portugal that somehow people can't seem to see around, through, under or over it.

Portugal's erstwhile biggest liability – shortage of cash – may turn out to have resulted in the preservation of its second biggest asset – the plethora of characterful, indigenous grape varieties. Had the industry had the wherewithal in the 1980s it probably would have dug these up and replaced them with Cabernet Sauvignon and Chardonnay. Leading winemakers are experimenting with varieties that are obscure even by Portuguese standards, while in some of the most remote areas only now are people untangling the mixture of grapes in the traditional 'field blends' – the hodge-podge plantings of numerous different varieties.

So it's an ill wind. Even *vinho verde*, at one time in danger of becoming a national embarrassment, has made the move to the asset side of the balance sheet. And then there's Mateus Rosé 1 (and Lancers 1, similarly successful in the USA), the biggest seller among a raft of rather more serious rosés (and that's a phrase you wouldn't have heard a few years ago) that, taken together, are among the best in the world.

So, let's give them a break by looking at the fortified stuff last and instead set off with the table wines and the regions. Like most European countries, Portugal has a four-tier appellation system with a sensible top rung – *Denominação de Origem Controlada* (DOC) – a seldom-seen, useless and pointless middle rung – *Indicação de Proveniencia Regulamentada* (IPR) – and then a sensible, flexible, self-explanatory third rung *Vinho Regional* (VR) before you hit the table – *vinho de mesa* – with a thump. They are currently making the system a bit worse by replacing IPR with two *Indicação Geográficas* (IG) and IGP – the same as IG but with, reassuringly, *Protegida* – levels.

***GET A HANDLE...**

PORTUGAL IS BRANCHING OUT FROM FORTIFIED WINES BUT USING SOME OF THE SAME CHARACTERFUL, INDIGENOUS GRAPES LIKE TOURIGA NACIONAL AND BAGA TO MAKE SOME OF THE MOST DISTINCTIVE AND GOOD-VALUE WINES THERE ARE.

Table wines

In the teeming open-air market of Braga – bang in the centre of the north-westernmost DOC of *Vinho Verde* – there is row upon gleaming row of squat, stainless steel vats, perched on little legs, each with a small tap at the base. The smallest of them hold just a gallon or two; the largest look semi-industrial. The locals fill them with the pressed juice of the grapes from the vines that run round the edges of their gardens (big or small), wait for a while, and hey presto – *Vinho Verde*! 'Green wine' – the reference is to its youth rather than its colour – is huge in Portugal. There are thousands of commercial labels, not to mention the uncounted millions of bottles filled with the cloudy, still-fizzing wine from the taps of all those gleaming vats and which seldom travels further than the end of the lane.

The grapes for *Vinho Verde* (pronouncing it 'been-your-beard', with a light Scots burr works for me) are the laurel-scented Loureiro (Quinta do Ameal [1]), the yeoman Trajadura and the crisp Arinto (aka Pedernã). Alvarinho, unsurprisingly known across the adjoining Spanish border in Galicia as Albariño, is the principal grape variety around Monção, where it makes arguably the finest, if not the most characteristic, 'been-your-beards' such as Monção [1] from the Co-op, Melgaço [2], Palácio de Brejoeira [3], and Soalheiro [2].

The squeamish export market prefers the likes of Quinta do Ameal [1], Quinta de Azevedo [1], Quinta de Sanjoanne [1] and Azeveda [1] frowns on the cloudiness and the fizz of the 'real' stuff. These 'better' wines go to finishing school to smooth off their rough edges, but, refreshingly, some of the uncouth youth (Casal Garcia [1], Casal Mendes [1], Gazela [1]) still make it on to the supermarket shelves and they are an excellent all-in-one spritzer at around 9% abv. The DOC covers the same geographical area as the Minho VR (Quinta de Paços [2] or Qiunta do Covela [2]).

Any robust survey cannot ignore the red wines of the region, not least because they have only recently been overtaken in terms of production by the whites. The Treaty of Windsor of 1386 enshrining the cordial relations between England and Portugal is the longest-lived such agreement in the world and will not be put in jeopardy when I say that thankfully the red *Vinho Verde* is not generally obtainable in the UK – possibly a clause in the treaty declared it illegal on grounds of tasting so horribly astringent.

Moving swiftly on, the Trasmontano VR, squeezed into the top right-hand corner of the country, is largely for wines made from grapes other than those traditional to the Upper Douro, which themselves are to be found in the Trás-os-Montes DOC (try Valle Pradinhos [2]). The Douro is the ultimate proof that the grape vine flourishes in adversity. The 'golden' river winds through this starkly beautiful landscape, candlewicked with terraces – sometimes with walls fifteen feet high – which often accommodate just a single row of vines, the roots of which will break down rock to get to moisture as they bake in the summer heat and shiver in the bitingly cold winters. World-class table wines are being made here now and such is domestic demand for the best that the concept of *ida e volta* (return ticket) wines has arisen, which are exported and then re-imported and, as such, are to be had cheaper in the UK than in Portugal.

Nonetheless, for the less fêted examples, the price: quality ratio is as good as it's ever going to be – they've got the quality/consistency thing sorted out and it's just a matter of time before the world catches on. Crucially, the grapes and the flavours are blends of the Touriga Nacional, Tinta Roriz (Tempranillo), Touriga Franca, Tinto Cão and Tinta Barroca used in the region's most famous product, port (see below) but they're given a new lease of life without the heft of all that alcohol (and also by an influx of foreign blood in many of the new ventures). White grape varieties struggle in the continental climate here but the ones that prevail celebrate in style. Here's a list to dip into: Barca Velha [2] – made by Ferreira, itself owned by Sogrape, Portugal's largest, and privately owned wine concern and Portugal's most prestigious, and probably best, red; Chryseia [3] – prestige project of the Symington port group and Prats family of Bordeaux – also second wine, Post Scriptum [3] and mass-market Altano [1]; Quinta de Côtto [2]; Quinta do Crasto [1]; Dão Sul – Quinta das Tecedeiras [3]; Lavradores de Feitoria [1]; Quinta de

Gaivosa [3]; Quinta do Infantado [2]; Vicente Leite de Faria [1]; Quinta de Macedos [2]; Niepoort [2]; Quinta do Noval [3]; Ramos Pinto [2] – itself owned by Champagne house Louis Roederer – especially Duas Quintas [1]; Roboredo Madeira [1], Quinta do Côa [2]; Roquette e Cazes [3] – as in the illustrious Cazes family of Bordeaux; Quinta de la Rosa [2] – now making substantially more table wine than port; Sastre [3], Quinta do Tedo [2], Quinta do Vale D Maria [3]; Quinta do Vale Meão [3]; Quinta de Ventozelo [2]; Wine and Soul [3] – part-owned, dodgy name and all, by Sandra Tavares, one of a small-but-growing number of influential women in Portuguese wine.

Bairrada is a traditional source of rather tannic, sometimes age-worthy wines, which at their best have a Barolo-like charisma, from the local Baga grape, some of the best of which are *garrafeira* bottlings (those done and aged by merchants). Substantial whites are from María Gomes (aka Fernão Pires). (Try Câves Aliança [1] – also in Dão, Alentejo, Douro, Terras do Sado; Casa de Saima [1], Dão Sul's Quinta do Encontro [2]; Quinta de Bageiras [2] and Messias [1].)

Dão (unsettlingly, pronounced more or less as 'dung' but I'm sure there's nothing to it) was traditionally the biggest name in Portuguese table wines. Quality is as unevenly spread as the vineyards are in the high, sheltered valleys of the region but is improving rapidly as the cooperative system imposed on the region during the Salazar years has been unwound. Indigenous grapes abound, with Alfrocheiro, Touriga Nacional, Tinta Roriz and Jaen (aka Mencía in Spain) the best for reds and Encruzado making elegant, food-friendly whites. (Try Aliança [1] – including Quinta da Garrida [1], Dão Sul [1] – especially their Quinta da Cabriz [1], Quinta da Giesta [2], Quinta das Maias [3], Casa de Mouraz [1], Quinta dos Roques [1], Quinta de Saes [2], Sogrape's Pena de Pato [1] – an interesting name to choose, it means duck feather and Pato is surely only coincidentally that of the leading winemaker in neighbouring Bairrada.)

Both Bairrada and Dão are located within the large Beiras VR, which is the crucible for experimentation in that, like the other VRs, it is more permissive of international varieties. The estimable Pato family bestride the region with father Luis and daughter Filipa and have much of their production in Bairrada but prefer the flexibility of the VR – try especially their Quinta do Ribeirinho 3, also Quinta da Foz de Arouce 2.

The Lisboa (formerly Estremadura) VR was once the source of abundant plonk, but the Atlantic-influenced region north of Lisbon now produces wines that are both relatively cheap and distinctly cheerful, at least as far as export is concerned (Quinta de Chocapalha 2; Cortello 1; Monte Doiro 2; Quinta da Murta 1; Quinta de Setencostas 2; Sanguinhal 1). The apple-crisp white Arinto grape is making waves with good single varietals in Bucelas (Quinta da Romeira 1). On the other side of the capital the Setúbal peninsula is the eponymous home of one of Portugal's lesser known, but often excellent, fortified wines, based on Muscat of Alexandria, as well as to modern, dry whites and successful reds from Castelão, aka Periquita hereabouts (José María da Fonseca 1; Bacalhôa Vinhos 1 – both of them among the pioneers of modern Portuguese wine).

To the east, the Ribatejo DOC – almost geographically synonymous with the Ribatejano VR – makes some decent reds from Castelão and Trincadeira, and producers are starting to work with Touriga Nacional and Tinta Roriz as well as international varieties. Aromatic whites are made from Fernão Pires (try Quinta da Lagoalva 1 and Quinta de Casal Branco 1). The fertile plains along the Tagus tend to overproduce huge amounts of undistinguished wines mainly made by the cooperatives under the VR appellation, a lot of which is white and some of which is good Fernão Pires. (Try Portal de Águia [1]; João Portugal Ramos's Falua winery sensibly blends international and indigenous grapes in its Tagus Creek [1] range.)

The Alentejo DOC (the 'j' is pronounced) is located within the much larger Alentejano VR, occupying the large part of the wide-open spaces of the south-east of the country, which are in complete contrast to the hugger-mugger smallholdings of the north. It has within it eight mini-DOCs, which (as with most of the sub-divisions in the other main DOCs) are effectively ignored as far as export markets are concerned – there's no shortage of unfamiliar names as it is. One of the fastest-developing regions, growing a mix of traditional as well as international varieties including the red-fleshed Alicante Bouschet, it is also a major source of corks from the bark of the oaks that dot the landscape. Try: Azamor [1]; Bacalhôa [1] – especially Tinto da Anfora [1]; Marquês de Borba [1] – owner João Portugal Ramos does the bestriding in the Alentejano but see also his Falua in Ribatejo [1]; Quinta do Carmo [2]; Cartuxa [1]; Quinta do Centro [2]; Cortes de Cima [2]; Esporão [1]; Eugénio Almeida [2]; Malhadinha Nova [3]; Mouchão [3]; Paço de Camões [1]; and São Miguel [1].

DRINK LIKE A KING
With ...

Altano
Azamor
Bacalhôa
Cortello
Quinta da Côa
Quinta de Gaivosa
Quinta de Garrida
Quinta dos Roques
San Isidro de Pegões

... FOR THE PRICE OF JUST DRINKING

Squeezed between the Alentejano and the sea, the Terras do Sado VR and, within it, the Palmela DOC, are looking promising with Bacalhôa [1] – owned by Aliança, Damasceno [3] and Santo Isidro de Pegöes Co-op [1], but along the hot south coast even the Atlantic westerlies can't cool things down enough in the Algarve VR and quality is patchy (Sir Cliff Richard's Vida Nova [1] is not entirely friendless – see also the entry for celebrity wines, p.79).

Fortified wines

Port is made from the same Douro grapes listed above, grown on those vertiginous slopes the demarcation of which, in 1756, was one of the earliest anywhere. A few top quintas still tread their best grapes underfoot in traditional stone *lagar* (see p. 245) tanks (and a few have reverted to the practice after all sorts of experiments with mechanisation) because the human foot, and the pressure on it, is perfectly suited to crushing the pulp and skin of the grape while the pips and stalks slither out or slip between the toes rather than being crushed, which would make the wine bitter – too much information, perhaps, but still useful to know. Fortification 5:1 with 70–90% abv grape spirit to truncate fermentation was originally intended to keep the wine sufficiently sweet for English palates while working wonders in preserving the wine for the long voyage north to Blighty. The journey began with the boat trip downriver to Vila Nova de Gaia, opposite Porto, where the wines are aged in the lodges of the big – still often British-owned – port houses.

The machinations of the trade are inexplicable to outsiders as well they might be when one considers that the amount of port allowed to be made in any given year by any given grower – the *beneficio* – is allocated in advance by a committee according to a complicated points system that doesn't appear to take into account the actual quantity of grapes likely to be produced. Understandably, with the twin shackles of the *beneficio* and the costly process of ageing their wines, producers are always on the lookout for new opportunities, some in the area of table wine and some within port. Late Bottled Vintage (LBV), white port and now the brazen, but still strangely alluring, hussy that is pink port, are all relatively recent innovations (and all on the part of Taylor's).

The two basic branches of the port family tree are the wines that are aged in wood and those that are aged in bottle, which are generally superior. Of the former, ruby is the bog-standard, matured in wood for two or three years, then blended, filtered and bottled. Surprisingly, most is consumed in France. Up the quality scale a notch to LBV and vintage-character ports, generally made in average-quality years and kept in wood for four to six years before bottling, they don't improve once bottled and usually have no sediment so don't require decanting. The quality of LBVs seems to have been somewhat in decline and, given the choice, I'll take a 'crusted' port every time – they're bottled unfiltered and need to be decanted.

It's the residual solids in the wine that allow it to continue to develop in the bottle (they are also largely responsible for the uniquely vicious hangovers that result from overindulgence). A further notch up are single-quinta ports, made from grapes from a single named vineyard, usually in years that are not declared vintage. Made in the same way as vintage port, after two years in wood they're bottled, unfiltered, and, again, must be decanted. (Dow [2] and their Quinta do Bomfim [3], Warre [2], and their Quinta de Cavadinha [3] and Graham's [2] and their Quinta dos Malvedos [3] are all under the ownership of the Symington Group; Fonseca's Guimaraens [3], Croft [2] and Quinta da Roeda [3], and Taylor's [2] and their Quinta de Terra Feita [3] and Quinta de Vargellas [3], are the property of the Fladgate Partnership.)

Of the wood-aged ports the basic tawnies may be blended with white port to lighten the colour and are usually disappointing. The best stuff emerges after ten, twenty, even forty years in wood as the pale, sophisticated aristocrat of the family – it's often the preferred tipple of the shippers themselves. Colheitas are vintage-dated tawnies released when they are ready to drink. White port is made from white grapes, and makes a refreshing aperitif served chilled, often mixed with tonic in Vila Nova (try Taylor Chip Dry [2]) but aged and vintage versions such as Alves de Sousa [3] and Messias [3] are promising.

Vintage port accounts for just one per cent of total production and the so-called declarations that occur every three or four years on average seem to depend at least as much on likely demand as they do on the quality of the vintage. There are three main problems with it – it's expensive, messy and moreish. To find out what it's about, buy a fully mature wine (for £30–£50) from a good house from, say the underrated 1983, 1985, 1991 or 1992 vintages; stand it upright for a day to settle, open and pour slowly into a clean jug, leaving the last inch in the bottle. Rinse the bottle, then pour it back in. It'll keep for a good few days and at a couple of quid for a dinky little glass of fiery, fruity loveliness, it won't seem extortionate.

The large firms regularly acquire and dispose of individual houses, make wine under licence and do whatever else is necessary. Symington have Cockburn [1], Gould Campbell [3], Quarles Harris [3], Quinta de Roriz [3], Smith Woodhouse [3] (especially LBV), and Quinta do Vesúvio. Sogrape have Ferreira [2] and Sandeman [2] (both, especially tawnies), and Offley [3] (especially vintage Boa Vista [3]). Other leading producers and brands are Cálem [2], especially colheitas [3]; Churchill, especially LBV, also rosé table wine; Delaforce [3], made by Fladgate; Feuerheerd [3]; Krohn [3]; Quinta do Noval [3], especially flagship Nacional [3]; Ramos Pinto from Louis Roederer [3]; Quinta de la Rosa [3]; Quinta de [3], Romaneira [3], Royal Oporto [3] and Quinta de Santa Eufemia [3].

Like port, the wines from the patchwork of tiny vineyards on the volcanic Atlantic island of Madeira are fortified, which is to say that the fermentation process is stopped by the addition of grape spirit in order to preserve some of the sweetness of the fruit. Uniquely, though, Madeira is then heated to around 45°C, a process that occurs both naturally by the sun warming the oak barrels stored in the rafters of the island's wine lodges for the most age-worthy wines and, pragmatically, in large tanks for the ones to be enjoyed as three-year-olds. The result is the same – the wines develop their characteristic, rich flavours of dried fruits, nuts and caramel.

The wine had its beginnings in the mistake of an eighteenth-century merchant, who sent a shipload of the island's regular table wine across the Atlantic to the West Indies in high summer. The wine was baked during its slow progress through the Doldrums and, having been rejected on arrival by the customer, baked all the way back again, too. By then the flavours had been greatly concentrated by evaporation and the merchant, seeing the potential, set about recreating the sweltering conditions of the ship's hold and experimenting with fortification to stabilise the resulting wines. The process – and the flavours – are little changed today.

Unlike port, there are virtually no primary-fruit flavours remaining when the wines are released for sale: everything has evolved by then and the heating process also allows the wines to age more or less indefinitely – even the contents of a bottle left uncorked will suffer no deterioration for at least a year. This is good news because a little of the intense coffee and spice flavours of a 100-year-old wine goes a long way.

The basic stuff is made from the black Tinta Negra Mole (literally 'soft blank ink') grape, while the other main indigenous black grape, Bastardo, is used only for the local rosé. Of the four 'noble' white-grape varieties, which are generally released as reserve wines after a minimum of five years' ageing, Malvasia (aka malmsey, as in drowning in a butt of . . .) makes the sweetest wines – rich, dark and deep (and good with pud, even chocolate ones), while Bual is lighter, with flavours of almonds and apricots and works with all types of pastries and cakes, as well as with cheese. The drier pair are Sercial (sometimes known by its less-than-noble soubriquet of 'dog-strangler' in reference to the extreme acidity of its youth) and Verdelho and they both make lighter wines with crisp, citrus-peel aromas and figgy, marmaladey flavours. Verdelho is delicious as an aperitif with salted almonds or cashews, air-dried hams and aged cheese while Sercial goes surprisingly well with sushi (specifically with the umami flavours of soy). All Madeiras work well in place of port and *vins doux*, especially with nuts and dried fruits.

The next rungs on the quality ladder are the 'special reserve' and 'extra reserve' wines – blends of different vintages with a minimum of respectively ten and fifteen years' maturation in those oak casks. The greatest treasures of the island are, as with port, the 'vintage' wines, made from grapes from a single year's harvest and aged for a minimum of twenty years. They emerge with all those nutty, coffee and dried-fruit flavours deliciously intensified by the effects of evaporation – the 'angels' share' can be as much as six per cent per year so, by my calculations, after twenty years there's, well, not much left. (The Madeira Wine Company, part of the Symington Group, owns Blandys [1], Cossart Gordon [2], Leacock [2] and Miles [2]. Other leading producers are Barbeito [2], Borges [3] and Henriques y Henriques [1].)

poteen – (also poitín, and pronounced 'potcheen') Irish term for illegally distilled liquor, usually made from barley or potatoes in rural areas and of highly variable strength and quality. The better stuff does seem to set off some sort of echo of another time and place in some dark corner of my Celtic soul and has nothing much to do with the newly legalised, commercial varieties of Bunratty and Knockeen Hills. These come in varying alcoholic strengths (the latter up to

90% abv) and complete with EU-sanctioned GI status and admonitions to the consumer to 'drink responsibly' which sets off something else in another dark corner of my Celtic soul.

pousse-café – literally 'push café'. A mixed drink in which the different ingredients are carefully poured (in order from the densest to the least dense) to make layers or horizontal stripes. A party trick really but not a bad one.

Prairie Oyster – surely there's no point in building the ultimate 'kill or cure' of the unbroken yolk of a small egg, teaspoons each of Worcestershire sauce and tomato ketchup and two dashes of Tabasco if you don't then add a goodly measure of gin or vodka? What good could possibly come of it?

premier cru – (first growth) French term that – in the context of the appellation system of Burgundy, for example – distinguishes a vineyard in terms of geography (provided sometimes certain winemaking criteria are also met) from the *village* level wines below it and the *grand cru* wines above it. Also in Bordeaux (and for which the English translation is generally used to refer to the five Left-Bank wines so loftily denominated) with the classifications *premier grand cru (classé)* and *premier cru supérieur* applying to wines from the Right Bank (and in Germany the *Grosses Gewächs)*. So it's all perfectly straightforward . . .

press wine – made from the generally inferior juice produced by applying pressure to the grapes after the free-run juice has been extracted, and traditionally used to make the wine consumed by the wine-estate workers.

proof – confusing measure of alcohol content (expressed in degrees proof, and shown as such in labelling, for example 70° for most whiskies). Based on the proofing of naval rum rations, 100° proof is defined as the greatest dilution in which gunpowder will still combust. I haven't tried that lately myself, but in practice, in the UK it works out at 1.75 times the more sensible measure of abv and in the USA, where it is still in wide usage, as twice that measure.

Prosecco – neutral white-grape variety of the Veneto region of north-eastern Italy which gives its name both to a style of wine and to the newly popular DOC and IGT near Treviso in which the usually (*spumante*) sparkling or (*frizzante*) semi-sparkling wines for which it is best known are made.

quinta qualitatswein quality quinta qualitatswein quality quinta qualitatswein quality quinta qualitatswein quality quinta qualitatswein quality quinta qualitatswein quality quinta qualitatswein quality quinta qualitatswein quality quinta qualitatswein quality quinta qualitatswein quality quinta qualitatswein quality quinta qualitatswein quality quinta qualitatswein

Qualitätswein – the main classification of higher quality wine in Germany: Qualitätswein bestimmter Anbaugebiete (QbA) and, above it, the five-rung Qualitätswein mit Prädikat (QmP) system.

quality – although experienced subjectively, where there is a demand for a beverage of a more than purely utilitarian nature, there are some aspects of quality (or more accurately, likely contributors to its enhancement) that can be measured or predicted. In the case of wine, the geography and climate of the vineyard, the suitability of the vine varieties grown in it and the yields derived from them are key in viticulture, as are – on the winemaking side – the style of wine to be made, its alcohol content and the nature and length of any ageing period. All these factors, and more, are intended to be monitored to a greater or lesser extent by the relevant wine regulating authority with a view to maintaining standards but surprise, surprise – and whatever the label may say – they are never in any sense a guarantee of quality.

In the case of beer and spirits, although they are heavily regulated in terms of trades-description acts and health-and-safety laws there are seldom any meaningful appellations and conventions of description are voluntarily applied. In all cases, quality will depend upon the individual producer and, while price is often a reliable indicator, in the quest for value there is no substitute for knowing who the good ones are (or knowing somebody such as a reliable merchant who does).

quinta – Portuguese term for farm, applied to a wine estate.

red lion cocktail refosco regent regionality reserva riserva residual sugar resinated wines restaurants

raboso raki rancio ratafia red lion cocktail refosco regent regionality reserva riserva residual sugar resinated wines restaurants

romania rondinella rosé wines roussanne roussette RTDs rum

rancio – tasting term, being the Spanish for rancid, but not generally used pejoratively, to describe overripe, rich, melted butter or cheesy aromas that often derive from oxidation or maderization, and from lactones sometimes present in wines as diverse as Champagne, sherry, *vins doux naturels* and *vin jaune*.

Red Lion – two parts each gin and Grand Marnier to one part each lemon and orange juice shaken over ice and strained into a sugar-rimmed cocktail glass. Make mine a pint!

Refosco – group of black-grape varieties in north-eastern Italy and the Slavic states. The best wines are made mainly in Friuli-Venezia Giulia, especially the Colli Orientali from the red-stemmed (peduncule) Refosco del Peduncolo Rosso in a bosky, darkly fruity, savoury and quintessentially northern-Italian style. Well-made examples get (and can take) the big oak treatment, and the deep damson fruit over time develops soft tannins ideal for game in fruit-based sauces.

regionality – the New World take, on a big New World scale, of the concept of terroir. Specifically the soil, the weather and the vines' exposure to it as the significant influences on the resulting wine. Particularly important in Australia, where in a manly and completely non-French way people are finally planting the right grapes in the right places – Pinot Noir in the coolest regions and Syrah in the warmer, for example.

reserva/riserva – meaningful terms in southern Europe, generally denoting wines from a good vintage, which must have a higher alcohol content and are required to be aged for longer (sometimes both in barrel and subsequently in bottle) than the regular bottlings. Largely meaningless in France and entirely bogus in the Anglophone world, where bottles labelled with terms like 'family reserve' are to be avoided.

residual sugar – measure, in grams per litre, of the unfermented sugar in a wine (but not the sole determinant of how sweet it is as acidity is also a factor). Nonetheless, most fully dry wines – red or white – have less than 2g/l; off-dry wines may have mid- to high-single figures; noticeably sweet *demi-sec* wines are likely to be in the 10–30g/l range; sweet wines – including port – can easily top 100g/l while Hungary's viscous Tokay Essenzia and the sweetest German wines can run to several hundred grams per litre.

resinated wines – resins were used to seal amphorae and flavour wine in antiquity. The Greek retsina – often made from Savatiano, the most widely planted variety in Greece – is both a survival of this and a potent example of the importance of subjectivity and circumstance in the enjoyment of wine.

restaurants and wine – many restaurants make a substantial proportion of their profit from their mark-up on wine (and on bottled water and coffee) and this is often resented by customers to the extent that a huge section of the wine trade is devoted exclusively to supplying wines to the 'on-trade' that are not readily available in the off-trade where customers would be able to compare prices and calculate the cost of those mark-ups, which are traditionally between 200 per cent and 400 per cent and typically in the middle of that range. In essence, nobody wants to pay £15–20 for a bottle of Jacob's Creek, do they?

Meanwhile, a small but growing number of restaurateurs are experimenting with different practices, much to the benefit of (and with the intention of making) happy customers. Many are offering wine-inclusive menus, with the benefits to the consumer entirely dependent on the selection of the wines (which are mostly pretty good in my experience – there's no advantage to the restaurateur if it backfires); some, especially those also having wine-retail operations, operate on fixed mark-ups of £10 per bottle (for example), making their more expensive wines a much better deal; some have greatly (and riskily) extended their offering of wines-by-the-glass (sometimes using new inert gas storage systems to retard deterioration of wine in the opened bottles); still others are offering the flexibilty of carafes of 250ml, 375ml or 500ml at the pro-rata price of a full bottle (removing the problem of poor-value half-bottles) and then selling the remainder by the glass.

Wine is inconstant, cruel and not to trust, it lets all men down and casts them aside wantonly. To live daily with, and so close to, these facts may explain why so many sommeliers have a rather haunted look about them: one of perpetual disappointment that, with time, hardens into lugubriousness. Nonetheless, most (and happily there are an increasing number of the less lugubrious sex entering the profession) are trustworthy as long as the parameters – especially the budget – are clearly defined at the outset.

Assuming the practice of ordering the second-cheapest bottle on the list is unsatisfactory, what is best to look for? In general Bordeaux and Burgundy are to be avoided – in fact in this instance it's a good idea to forget you've ever even heard those names. All of France is tricky really but if it just has to be, then – for whites: Alsace (especially versatile, food-friendly Pinot Gris); the Loire for Chenin Blanc (especially Savennières) and for reds; and the south-west for everything (especially for Jurançon whites and reds from Faugères). Italy off-the-beaten-track can be good value (forget Barolo and Barbaresco and much of Tuscany) especially the north-east for light, fresh reds as well as whites, Campania for big-boned whites and at the lower end (geographically and budgetarily), Sicily and Puglia. The up-and-coming Spanish regions (such as Bierzo, Campo de Borja and Jumilla), Germany, Austria (especially for reds), Argentina and South Africa are also good sections in which to forage for value and, remember, it may well be the sommelier who has selected the wines and they're often thrilled when people go off-piste with them.

Two more pieces of advice – go to the pub beforehand to avoid any madness of aperitifs (God forbid, Champagne!) and only ever drink dessert wines or digestifs at home. Vigilance in respect of these guidelines may be somewhat relaxed in the unlikely event that somebody you don't like is paying.

Riesling – (pronounced 'ree-sling') noble white-grape variety originally in Germany, Alsace and middle Europe, now widespread. I suspect that if I were to be stuck on a desert island and allowed only one wine to comfort me, I might well choose a Riesling. Good ones have everything – sweet fruit partnered with steely acidity, a lusciousness, weight and complexity that can be appreciated either in glorious isolation or equally as a partner to foods from scallops through to Stilton and most things in between. (I realise this makes certain assumptions about provisioning arrangements on the island, but fingers crossed.) Riesling makes everything from haunting, spine-tinglingly dry wines through to the sweetest of the sweet and distinguishes itself at every turn. All of them can age gracefully and sometimes, it seems, indefinitely. Its naturally high, but, when fully ripe, seldom excessive acidity is what puts the straightness into its spine, while the ability of its roots to tease up from the good earth all manner of minerals and mysteries puts the strength into the narrow shoulders upon which the fruit so elegantly drapes itself. People like me who love Riesling tend to bang on like this, leaving sceptics to wonder why, if it's so fantastic, is it so comprehensively overshadowed by blowsy Chardonnays, shrill Sauvignon Blancs and faceless, tasteless Pinot Grigios?

German winemaking in the second half of the last century – at least as far as exports were concerned – was a catalogue, but seldom a comedy, of errors: Liebfraumilch, the wretched Müller-Thurgau grape, Blue Nun – must I go on? Even Riesling's pure, unsullied heart found itself dragged into the mire as the grape most readily associated with Germany. Perceived guilt-by-association with the unrelated Yugoslavian Laški Rizling and the hideous Lutomer brand of sugar-and-scheiße water which was ubiquitous in the 1970s and 1980s made things worse.

The golden dawn of the new world of wine shone harshly on an aspect of Riesling that again put it out of step with the march of fashion. Riesling has no interest in plastering the make-up of oak-ageing on to her perfect features. She makes lean, clean wines with a flash of metal and high-octane exhilaration, which are the opposite of the fat, buttery, oak-chips-with-everything Chardonnays that took over the world overnight while we were sleeping. Never one to make a fuss, Riesling has quietly waited her turn with modestly downcast eyes and now it seems that she shall go to the ball. Amid the babble of voices of the anything-but-Chardonnay drinkers the clear tones of Riesling are beginning to make themselves heard and with the scintillation of that acidity and the perfect roundness of those ripe, alabaster-white fruits that, once held, are never forgotten, she will not have need of a second chance.

The dizzying slopes of blue-slate soil that tumble down to the snaking bends in the river Mosel north of Bernkastel are where Riesling's most ardent accolytes have built their fantastically named temples – Ürziger-Würzgarten, Graacher-Domprobst, Erdener-Treppchen and Wehlener-Sonnenuhr among them. Out from the Saar, to the Nahe, the Pfalz and all along the Rhine her name rings pure and true through the valleys and across the plains.

Her Alsace cousins treat her with due reverence – the humble cooperative producers of Turckheim, Pfaffenheim and Bebblenheim are among her most devoted followers and will provide a modestly priced glimpse of her charms that is perhaps the most fitting introduction. Onward, ever onward spreads her fame from Austria to Australia's Eden Valley, and to New Zealand and New York state and thence to Washington state this goddess among grapes shall have her dominion.

ripasso – north-eastern Italian style of wine used to make some Valpolicella and named for the winemaking technique of adding some of the semi-dried grapes (similar to those used for making

Amarone) for a second fermentation to add extra flavour and body. Works for me.

Romanian wine – Romania is a large wine producer with nearly half-a-million acres under vine, the majority of which are for white wine consumed domestically. Some promising indigenous grapes include whites Tămâioasă Românească and Fetească Albă (the white maiden) and Fetească Neagră (the black maiden) – it's not going to be easy, is it? The white-grape variety Grasă (meaning 'fat') makes sweet wines in Cotnari that were once as celebrated as those of Tokaji. Predictably, though, it's the international varieties that are seeing a little export activity and sadly it may be the Transylvanian producer of Vampire Red who is being the most sanguine.

rosé wine – in 2003 one of the largest UK supermarket chains reported a mere two per cent of wine sales from rosé; by the end of the decade it was thirteen per cent and still rising. So, when the big wine winners of the noughties (among them Sauvignon Blanc and the Pinots Noir and Grigio) and the big losers (Chardonnay and Merlot spring to mind) counted their chips they will have been as a hill of beans compared to that decade's rollover lottery winner: rosé.

In 2006, Sogrape, producers of Mateus, launched a new rosé with the gilded legend across the front of the bottle proudly announcing it to be 'A Taste of Spam' and the jokers said that it *was* pink, therefore it must be. A closer look revealed it to be a 'Taste of Spain' and it's no joke now. But why rosé, and why now? It seems simplistic to speculate that in the move away from over-oaked, over-alcoholic wines – applying equally to whites and to reds – where better to go than down the middle? But it also seems reasonable, as it does to suggest that rosé gives you a bit of everything.

Some rosés are white wines blended with a small percentage of red wine (usually under five per cent) and, although the EU banned this practice in 2009, it is common practice elsewhere. The majority of rosés are made from red grapes with skins removed soon after they are crushed so they don't colour the juice as much they do red wine – the timing is critical in determining the depth of the colour. The number of grape varieties being used to make rosé is growing all the time and sceptics might care to look for ones that are made from a favoured red-wine grape and give them a try. Grape varieties that make fuller-bodied reds make bigger rosés, so Shiraz and Cabernet Sauvignon will generally make more full-on rosé than, say, Pinot Noir or Grenache. In turn, the darker the colour of a rosé, the more full-bodied and full-flavoured it's likely to be. Pinot Grigio is a white grape with a pinkish skin so, strictly speaking, pink wines made from it are not really rosé – but who wants to be strict where rosé is concerned? Champagne is another exception, as a little local red wine is blended with the white to enhance the colour. There is no wine-producing country that isn't making rosé these days. Australia and Chile make big, bold reds and the pink wines tend to follow suit. The relatively cooler climates of France and Italy produce wines with a lighter, more gluggable feel.

In the days when Rosé d' Anjou was about the only pink option, most was made from the despised and declining Grolleau, a grape so bad that people who make red wine with it – even the careful growers such as Cousin-Leduc [2], who does excellent things with low-yielding, biodynamically-managed sixty-year-old vines – are only ever allowed to call it *vin de table*. The point of chilling it hard back then was to deaden the frequently less-than-fabulous flavours. Most rosé wines still want a good hour in the refrigerator, and on a hot summer's day in the garden they should be served cold enough to send a trickle of condensation running down the outside of the glass. Good rosés are versatile food-matching wines and the fuller-bodied examples are fun to surprise people with – nothing need be off limits – and they often work well with Indian, Chinese and Thai foods. The year 2009 witnessed the arrival of rosé Chardonnay (which smacked of desperation) and rosé Sauvignon Blanc (which smacked of hubris) and both were blended with some red wine to achieve pinkitude. When one sees this sort of thing it's a fair sign that it's all going to end in tears, but a look at the top winemakers who've turned their hands to producing rosé – and the prices they're charging – suggests it's more than a passing fad.

The southern Rhône (Yves Cuilleron [2], Dom des Escaravailles [1], Guiot [1], Jaboulet Aîné [1]) stretching down into Provence is rosé's original home, and the Tavel appellation is the only one in France to specify rosé as its sole authorised wine (d'Aqueria [2], Prieuré de Montézargues [2], Rocaliere [2] and de la Mordorée [2] – often cited as the world's best rosé). Provence makes more than anywhere else (Montaud [1], la Moutète [1], Sainte Marguerite [2], Rimauresq [2]) and some of the best are from Bandol (Lafran-Veyrolles [2], Château de Pibarnon [3], Tempier [3]). Along the Loire classy stuff is made from Pinot Noir in Sancerre (Bailly-Reverdy [2], Henri Bourgeois [3], Dezat [2], Henri Pellé [3], Sautereau [2]) and from mainly Cabernet Franc in the Cabernet d'Anjou AOC (Mauny [1]). In Bordeaux they have their own term *clairet* (the origin of our word claret) for a dark style of rosé that is seldom exported, as well as making – without it seems any great appetite for it – the 'regular' stuff (Larcis Ducasse [2], de Sours [2]).

The best rosé I've ever had was a fortuitously purchased case of a barely pink, toastily oaked 1995 from a serious grower in Auxey Duresses (it was christened at home as the rosey dozey) but so askance do the Burgundians look at rosé that this producer never deigned to make another vintage of it as far as I can tell. The frustrating few that one comes across, such as Jadot [2], Mortet [2], Roty [2] and Simonnet-Febvre [2], prove that Pinot Noir is one of the best grapes for rosé – as well it might be when one considers that some of the lightest reds it makes are borderline pink anyway.

In the far north-east, in the tiny Côtes de Toul they make *vin gris*, the palest of the pale pinks, and good wines are being made all over the south-west as well, in Bergerac (Clos d'Yvigne [2], Tours des Gendres [2]) and out in the wilds of the Languedoc (du Poujol [1], Massamier La Mignarde [1]), the Pays d'Oc (Paul Mas [1], Gayda [1]) and Corsica (Fiumicicoli [1]).

Italy has been something of a latecomer – even though there's no great tradition of *rosato*, nobody can afford to ignore the surging statistics for consumer preferences. In Tuscany the renowned Brunello di Montalcino producer Biondi-Santi [3] probably does have the honour of producing the world's most expensive *rosato* (also in Tuscany: Tenuta di Cappezzana [3], Guado al Tasso [3]). Hereabouts rosé is sometimes called *vin ruspo* (stolen wine), because the sharecroppers would take their last load of grapes home at night and collect the free-run juice of the Sangiovese grapes – naturally making a rosé – before delivering the grapes to the landowner in the morning. The north-east is more generally the place to look, especially in *le Tre Venezie* (Alpha Zeta [1], Ancora [1], Ca dei Frati [2]) and for *ramato* wines made from fully ripe Pinot Gris, the skins of which turn pink and make lovely, smoky copper-hued wines (Ponte Pietra [2], Specogna [2]).

Portugal is making intensely flavourful wines – in the Douro they're made from the traditional port grapes so how could they be anything else? Try Casa de Mouraz [2], Churchill [2], Quinta da Giesta [2],

Niepoort [2], Quinta do Portal [2], Quinta de la Rosa [2] or Tagus Creek [1]). Spain is also impressing, often with old-vine Grenache (Borsao [1], Centelleo [1], Gran Tesoro [1], Macià Batle [2], Muga [1], Navajas [2] or Viñas del Vero [2]). Greece isn't missing out (try Moraitis [3]), and England I suspect will prove to be better for rosé than red (try Chapel Down [2]).

In the new world, California is tricky territory despite (or maybe because of) the fact that it supplies half of the UK's consumption. 'Banish blush' has been my policy but there are exceptions even among the white Zinfandels such as Cecchetti [1]. In the southern hemisphere there are some good wines to be had from everywhere: lots from Australia (Bridgewater Mill [2], Innocent Bystander [2], Magpie Estate [1], Charles Melton [2], Geoff Merrill [1], Paxton [2], Stella Bella [2], Taltarni [1], Turkey Flat [1]), a smattering from New Zealand (Kim Crawford [1], Villa Maria [1]) and South Africa (Boschendal [1], Fairview [1], Slowine [1]). Across the Pacific, Chile (Chocalan [1], Montes [1], Torres [1]) and Argentina (Crios [2], Pulenta [1], Santa Rosa [1]) don't disappoint.

Roussanne – unshouty white grape instrumental in making some of the world's finest white wines in northern Rhône (also bringing its acidity and fine-boned, herbiferous finesse to blends – often with the heftier Marsanne) in Crozes-Hermitage, St Joseph, Châteauneuf-du-Pape and, most illustriously, in Hermitage. Also quietly making influential friends in the wider world, be it in France's New World of the Languedoc or the 'real' one in South Africa, Australia and the USA. Back home again, it is also aka Bergeron in the Chignin appellation of Savoie, where it makes the region's quintessential, bracing 'skiing' wine.

RTD – (ready-to-drink) the grown-up versions of alcopops, for example, pre-mixed gin and tonic or bourbon and cola in a can or small bottle. Try as I might, I can't imagine a set of circumstances to make such a thing necessary. If one were able to assemble glasses, ice and slices of lemon, why would one not be capable of screwing the tops off bottles of gin and of tonic?

rubbish drinks – hard to think of a more accurate term for the small category of drinks distinguished (if that's the right word) by having neither function nor, hopefully, future. They are neither the cheap alcohol-delivery systems that are park-bench drinks nor, being generally the cheapest industrial 'wine' loaded with artificial-fruit flavours, do they taste nice.

Regulation in the USA has required the makers of 'bum wines' to lower their alcohol content, generally to around 13% abv. This applies to brands such as MD 20/20 (widely known as 'Mad Dog' although the initials are those of the producers Mogen David), Night Train Express and Thunderbird (both of which are skeletons in the Gallo cupboard), Cisco and Wild Irish Rose (both brought to the table, or – more likely – upturned crate, by Constellation Brands, the world's largest wine company). This is roughly the same as most table wine and raises the question of why anyone in their right mind (could be a clue there) would turn down a decent, basic jug wine in favour of 'Mad Dog' Blue Raspberry, for example. Who knows what evil lurks in its murky, toxic-blue depths but the taste hangs around like a bad smell (as does the smell, which is even worse). Thunderbird seems to be on its way out in the UK – it took me some time to find a bottle and it was the last one on the shelf – maybe it was the last bottle on the planet. Let's hope so, because whatever it's made of smells of melons and tastes so horribly chemical and bleachy it's probably not something anybody should ingest.

With regard to the peach-flavoured wine category, in the incalculably unlikely event that anyone ever asks, 'Can I give you some Canei?' Just say, 'No. You cannot.'

rum – Caribbean spirit distilled from fermented sugar-cane juice, its reduction to syrup or – mostly – the further reduction of that to molasses. If a drink expresses the place where it is made then rum says warmth and sunshine and a slow pace of life. Its origins confirm the fact that people will make booze with whatever is close to hand and easily fermented.

The fermented sugar that rum is distilled from was probably in itself the earliest form of booze (known as arrack), but, unusually, it is possible to trace the development of the modern drink to a single event: when Christopher Colombus (Cristobal Colón) took sugar-cane cuttings to Hispaniola (Haiti and the Dominican Republic) in 1493. The first rum was made early in the sixteenth century and subsequently became a link in the 'triangle trade' that took slaves from West Africa to the New World, replaced the human cargo with one of spices, tobacco and molasses for rum, for the markets of the Old World and then back to Africa with mixed cargoes to barter for yet more slaves.

As with all spirits the first product is colourless and fairly neutral – some white rum is rectified and bottled straight away and is used mainly for mixing and cocktails. Some is aged for one to three years (generally in oak for dark rum and in steel tanks for white) and sometimes the golden (aka *oro* or *ambré*) rum will have been coloured with caramel. Still more will undergo longer ageing in oak barrels and become premium (aka *añejo* or *rhum vieux*) dark rum, although some of this will be charcoal-filtered to remove the colour. Most rums are blended before release and the skill of the master blenders is equal to the skill of their Scottish and French counterparts.

The former Spanish islands of Cuba (Caney, Havana Club, Palma Mulata, Paraiso, Santiago de Cuba), Puerto Rico (Bacardi, Don Q, Del Barrilito, Llave), Dominican Republic (Barceló, Bermudez, Brugal, Palo Viejo, Matusalem – especially Red Flame 151 Proof), Nicaragua (Flor de Caña, Plantation), Venezuela (Santa Teresa) and Guatemala (Zacapa) traditionally tended towards producing a higher percentage of white, silver or light rum. Bacardi, which started in Cuba, is the world's second-most-valuable drinks brand, with sales in 2009 of nearly 250 million bottles and, surprisingly, remains – after nearly 150 years – a family affair and a product of reasonable quality, certainly when compared to its equivalents in the other white spirit categories. The big booze companies own the rest of the largest brands but many of the medium-sized companies remain independent. To continue with a generalisation that is becoming blurred by producers' responses to market forces, the former English strongholds of Antigua (English Harbour), Barbados (Cockspur, Doorley's, Old Brigand Mount Gay – specifically Extra Old and Sugar Cane), Bermuda (Gosling's – especially Black Seal), the Virgin Islands (Cruzan, Lamb's Navy, Pusser's – especially Nelson's Blood), Guyana (El Dorado, OVD, Wood's), Jamaica (Captain Morgan, Conquering Lion, Hansen, Lemon Hart, Myers, Plantation, Appleton Estate – including Wray & Nephew) and Trinidad and Tobago (Angostura, Fernandez 19, Royal Oak, Ten Cane) have a predilection for the dark (aka black) versions that have such a long association with the Royal Navy and its favourite pastimes (allegedly according to Winston Churchill) of 'rum, sodomy and the lash'.

The former French islands of Guadeloupe (Damoiseau, Karukera), Haiti (Barbancourt – especially the fifteen-year-old, which is often cited as the finest of all rums), Martinique (Bally, Duquesnes, Clément, La Mauny, St James, Trois Rivières) specialise in '*rhum agricole*, which is distilled only from fermented, fresh sugar-cane juice and prized over the cheaper molasses versions the French sniffily refer to (and make) as *rhum industrielle*. The white rums in the former style, and which are essentially the same as Brazil's cachaça, can be wonderfully complex – especially the aged ones – like a fine old Grave white wine with a jigger of Malibu. *Sacré bleu*!

Rum is made in small quantities elsewhere in the world, in Australia (Bundaberg), various countries in Asia, and on Mauritius (Green Island), though one wonders why when there's not exactly any shortage of the 'real' stuff.

Spiced rums have a long history but the current trend for making flavoured versions seems a slavish following of fashions in other spirit categories and undermines the noble heritage of a drink, which, when expressed at its best in complex, long-aged and often vintage-dated, small-batch production of single mark 'sipping' rums such as the ones listed above, richly deserves its place at the tasting table next to the finest brandies and whiskies.

Rusty Nail – two parts whisky to one part Drambuie stirred with ice in a rocks glass within sight and smell of the blooming heather and garnished with a stag's head.

Sack Sagrantino Sake Sangria Saperavi Sauvignon blanc Savagnin Savatiano Scarlett O'Hara cocktail Scheurebe Schioppettino Schnapps Screwdriver cocktail Sec Secondary fermentation Second wine Semillon

sack – archaic term for a sweet, fortified wine from Spain (including the Canary Islands) very popular in England in the sixteenth to eighteenth centuries, much referenced in literature to the extent that Britain's Poet Laureate is salaried with '£100 and a butt of sack yearly'. (The sack reference is now largely symbolic and has fallen into neglect: however, the Spanish government awarded one to an incumbent in the 1990s. He had it bottled and was dissuaded from selling it as 'Laureate's Choice' only by a certain firm of antiquarian booksellers who pointed out the crass folly of the enterprise to his agents, and kept a couple of bottles.)

saké – (aka saki) Japanese beverage (usually 15–20% abv) fermented from rice. If that sounds a bit vague, it's intended to as I hope to avoid joining either the beer writers who insist it is wine, or the wine writers who say it is beer. These rejections perhaps reflect the fact that the drink's umami notes put it at the flavour margins of the usual spectrum of either. The nearest comparator in wine is sherry, particularly those exposed to the effects of flor yeasts and which develop *rancio* (see p. 321) flavour characteristics; in beer perhaps the turbid, wine-like lambics of Belgium are closest. Much saké is cloudy and very sensitive to light, most is intended to be drunk young either chilled, at room temperature or warmed, depending on the season and the quality (the best, aged types are not heated).

Sangría – has endured a tough time of it these past thirty-odd years – it has been difficult to shed the image of outsize, sombrero-topped straw donkeys and peeling, pink flesh. However, it can be the essence of summer if well made, with the addition of brandy (the quantity depending on your plans for the rest of the day) and abundant chunks of apple, pear, orange and lemon, which are steeped for an hour in a jug of respectable red before adding copious ice and more or less the same quantity of good lemonade.

Sauvignon Blanc – it is often said that, while there are many good Sauvignon Blancs, there are no great ones. This is not true – it's more the case that people look for them in the wrong places. The grape is now so closely associated with the pungent, aromatic, 'cat's-pee-on-a-gooseberry-bush' wines that originated in the Loire and have now spread throughout the southern hemisphere – and to which the aperçu correctly applies – that its best, oak-aged manifestations are thought of as being somehow something else.

The Sauvignon Blanc grape, in its green, up-front-and-in-your-face incarnation, appeals more immediately to the nose than the palate, which it assaults with piercing, nervy, short, prickly things like cut-grass, nettles and blackcurrant bushes. Along the Loire – most famously in Sancerre and Pouilly-Fumé and less expensively in Menetou-Salon, Reuilly and Quincy – the wild green things are offset by flint and gunsmoke depth and minerality.

The grape plays an important supporting role (with the help of a little Muscadelle) in most of the great sweet wines of Bordeaux where it provides acidity and zest to the dominant and, when fully ripe, rounder Semillon. In the dry whites of Entre-Deux-Mers, and for preference those of Graves and Pessac-Léognan, the roles are reversed and some of the greatest (Pavillon Blanc du Château Margaux, Smith Haut Lafitte) are made from up to ninety per cent Sauvignon (and as such would qualify to be labelled as a single varietal under most New World appellation systems). The expensive influence of new-oak barrels is essential and adds a grilled edge to the pineapple fruit that is itself a counterpoint to the profound mineral side of these wines, which age into extraordinary complexity and richness – doesn't sound much like Sauvignon, does it?

There is a small outpost of northern Burgundy – Saint Bris – that is forever Sauvignon and good things are done wherever yields are kept low in Bergerac and across the south-west. In north-eastern Italy, in Friuli and Alto Adige top-class cooler-climate styles are made.

In California it is sometimes called Fumé Blanc, a term coined by the late, great Robert Mondavi to lend a bit of Loire cachet to his unfashionable white wine. How times change – imagine Sauvignon Blanc being unfashionable! South Africa has embraced it and has benefited from the investment with interest; Chile flies the flag of zing in the face of the sophistication thing (for now).

The southern-hemisphere country that has picked up the ball and run with it is New Zealand, where Sauvignon Blanc has underpinned the rapid development of an entire wine industry (which is wisely now diversifying). Cloudy Bay, who started it all, make Te Koko, an oak-aged wine that can stand shoulder-to-shoulder with the best of Bordeaux's grandes dames. *Plus ça change*.

Scandinavian beer – interesting things are brewing up here and independents thrive: in Norway Hansa Borg Brewery has twenty-five per cent of the market, Aass and Nøgne Ø need new names and HaandBryggeriet has a brew called Norwegian Wood, which seems to promise aid for sufferers from brewer's droop; Sweden has the independents Gotlands, Närke and Krönleins amongst many others. Denmark isn't really Scandanavia, I know, but it's convenient to mention that Carlsberg have their specialist brewer Jacobsen there on their home turf (also Ceres).

Finland has some decent beers, almost all Big Beer-owned except Olvi – the third biggest – of which Heineken-owned Lapin Kulta is made in a brewery staffed mainly by women. But that's boring compared to sahti. No, it's not the homophonous Hindu practice of widows throwing themselves on their husbands' funeral pyres but another barbarous activity with mediaeval roots – that of home-brewing. The results are a primitive, turbid, multi-grain beer – sometimes made from bread – flavoured by juniper branches and apparently with a pronounced banana flavour. Some is made commercially by Finlandia.

Scarlett O'Hara – four parts each Southern Comfort and cranberry juice to one part lime juice shaken with ice and strained into a cocktail glass – after a couple, frankly you won't *give* a damn.

Scheurebe – hybrid white grape developed in Germany. When fully ripe it can make excellent sweet and *Trocken* styles in Franken, Pfalz and also in Austria.

Schnapps – (from 'to swallow') the term for the fruit-brandy family of drinks distilled from fruit wines, therefore including eaux de vie and slivovitz (and by extension grape brandy) but not American schnapps, which are liqueurs.

Screwdriver – one part vodka to two parts orange juice stirred with ice in a highball glass (but I seem to remember that drinking some of the juice out of the carton and replacing it with vodka works – if you're sixteen and/or camping).

Sea Breeze – over ice in a highball glass build two parts each vodka and cranberry juice with three parts grapefruit juice. What would you do with a drunken sailor?

sec – French term for dry, except when it means quite sweet, as it would in reference to Champagne.

secondary fermentation – one taking place after the initial alcoholic fermentation and desirable for a number of purposes, for example the malolactic fermentation that takes place in the original fermentation vessel to soften the malic acid in some wines. Other fermentations take place after bottling, for example to put the fizz in Champagne and for the bottle-conditioning of some quality beers.

second wine – many of Bordeaux's best chateaux – and quite a few elsewhere – make a wine from the newer plantings of vines and/or parcels that are not quite up to scratch for the *grand vin*. Some are very good and sometimes very good value – especially from lesser vintages when maybe smaller quantities of the big 'un are made.

Semillon – underrated white-grape variety originally of France (where it has an acute accent on the 'e'), now widespread (and pronounced with the double 'll' silent, so gentlemen! remember never to say 'I've got a nice little semillon here'). Semillon doesn't get the attention that Sauvignon Blanc enjoys though they are often blended together, and more people have probably heard of Château d'Yquem, its most famous incarnation, than of the grape itself. It's a versatile variety that by no means restricts itself to sweet wines from Bordeaux's Sauternes and Barsac areas. It's the mainstay of most of Bordeaux's dry whites from everyday bottles of Entre-Deux-Mers through to Sunday-best wines from Graves and Pessac-Léognan. (Taken together, Yquem's Bordeaux neighbours – near and far – deserve a group hug for the dramatic improvement in their white wines over the past few years.)

Semillon has made its quiet way to most corners of the world. South Africa has a long and successful history with it – to the extent that it had a near-monopoly position a couple of hundred years ago – and it crops up all over the Americas too. But its home-from-home in the New World is Australia's Hunter Valley, where since the 1870s it has made deeply distinctive, wonderfully detailed, age-worthy wines with steely minerality tempered by floral scents. Semillon's future prospects are rosy here – they are also making good-value botrytised sweet wines in the irrigated, semi-desert inland zones and – thank heavens – the attempts to force Semillon into an ill-conceived union with Chardonnay seem to be less frequent these days.

Sercial – white-grape variety of Madeira, where it produces the driest of the island's fortified styles. Also grown in mainland Portugal, where, in reference to its high acidity, it's called Esgana Cão, which means 'dog strangler' – those mediaeval marketing guys just didn't *get* it, did they?

serving wine – a lot of hoo-ha surrounds the serving of wine, some of which seems to become an end in itself rather than being the means to a specific end, which is to give the wine you've bought and paid for the best possible chance to shine. With this is mind, the questions to ask about a wine are: Is it the right temperature? Is it likely to improve with some exposure to oxygen? Does it have any sediment? What sort of glasses should it be served in?

First things first, though, and in the matter of getting the bottle open it may be the case that the only small fiddly mechanical device that has caused more pain and suffering than the average corkscrew is the average thumbscrew. The only one actually worth buying is a lever-pull (sometimes called a 'rabbit' but, no, not *that* sort of rabbit – it doesn't need batteries). The lever-pull looks as if it's a sledgehammer to crack a nut – it takes up too much space in a drawer and isn't very good with artificial corks (so don't throw your old corkscrew away). But, like all things that are supremely fitted for their purpose – the Hoover, the Blackberry and, so they say, that *other* sort of rabbit – once used, there is no substitute.

It's hard to overestimate the importance of temperature when it comes to getting the most out of any wine. I think of temperature as the fourth dimension of wine, after smell, taste and texture, and it affects all those three in turn. On the whole, we serve our white wines too cold and our red wines too warm. It's a reasonable generalisation that the lighter the wine, the longer the time (in the fridge). Muscadet, for example, and lighter Italian and German wines should be around 8–10°C, medium-bodied wine in the 10–12°C range and the biggest Chardonnays and Alsace Pinot Gris in the 12–15°C range.

Most people know that Loire reds and Beaujolais benefit from chilling – in fact, the lightest reds should be served a good deal cooler than the biggest whites. Pinot Noir also has a lot of the crisp (even sort of crunchy) characteristics that appreciate just a little kiss of coldness to bring out their smoky, sophisticated side. The act of putting a bottle of red wine in a refrigerator seems to cause many a strong hand to tremble but most red wines aren't meant to be drunk at much over the mid-teens °C because the smell of the alcohol can mask the bouquet. A glass of a big Aussie Shiraz that's been left standing in the sun for an hour or two makes the point pretty well.

Those Pinots, from Burgundy in particular, are among the most responsive to a change in temperature. The low teens °C should be good for lighter wines and around the middle to high teens °C mark should do the trick if you're pushing the boat out with a *premier* or *grand crû*. I'll admit to the possibility of a slight tremor in my own hand at that level and would recommend a wine thermometer – the types that fit round the bottle are convenient – and, most importantly, a timer to remind you to check how things are going every ten minutes or so for more venerable (and fragile) vintages.

If you're chilling wine in quantity forget about the fridge – unless you put them in the night before, a bunch of bottles will give you a warm fridge, not a cold wine. Buy in lots of ice – life is too short to make it – and mix it with water in a bucket, in a bin, in a bath for all I care. The addition of water makes it four times faster than using just the ice. If you really have to, and nobody's watching, you can chill an emergency glass of white wine in two minutes by pouring it in to a Ziploc plastic bag and sliding it into the freezer.

When it comes to decanting and 'breathing' I'm not talking about butlers and crystal and silver salvers. I'm talking about getting some oxygen on to a wine to let the flavours open up. Ever noticed that big, young reds often taste better the next day? When people take the cork out of a bottle to let a wine breathe they're headed in the right direction but it only makes sense if you then sloosh your reds – all of them – in to a jug and then back into the bottle. It's called 'double-decanting' and it works wonders. (I can't tell you how pleased I was at a tasting to see a top winemaker pour out a glass and then give the bottle a really good shake up and down – always good to find out you're not the only one . . .) In the meantime, have a beer to give it that vital half hour to get the process going. Of course, if you've a bottle of something venerable with a deposit of lees (sediment) in the bottom then a bit more care is called for – pour the wine out steadily, without stopping and against a strong light so that you can see when to stop pouring (i.e. when the sediment starts to go into the neck) – and remember to rinse the bottle before returning the wine to it.

Glasses should be big – the bigger the better – with a turned-in, or tulip-bowl shape to prevent as much as possible of those precious aromas from disappearing into thin air. Don't fill them more than one third full – but refill often if you fear looking mean – to give plenty of swirling room. With special wines these days I seem to spend so much time swirling and sniffing that I can almost forget to actually drink it. (I did say 'almost' . . . it's never actually *happened*.)

Much of the time, subtlety is what distinguishes a special wine and marks it out from the common herd, but there are other times when more is definitively more, and you want a wine that leaps out of the glass like a Mae West impersonator jumps out of a cake and drawls, 'Is that a Pinot in your pocket or are you just glad to see me?' Drinking outdoors is more often than not one of those times.

A bit of air is a good thing for a wine but a lot is not and most of the subtlety gets quite literally blown away in an English country garden, where you need powerful wines. Aromatic whites – southern-hemisphere Sauvignon Blanc or Alsace Gewürztraminer and Muscat, for example – and heavily oaked Chardonnays do the trick. For reds, bear in mind that the airlines don't serve up all that Syrah for no good reason. Your sense of smell suffers in a pressurised cabin as much as in a pressurised-barbecue scenario but big, bold, black-fruit flavours and those in-your-face liquorice and wintergreen aromas of Australian and South American 'shizz-bangs' still get through. Big-boned Malbecs from Argentina have the same effect when you're firing up the barbie of Olde Ingerlund.

Sex on the Beach – build over ice in a highball glass three parts vodka, one part peach schnapps and three parts each cranberry and orange juice. If you're on a crowded beach put some of the ice down your Speedos.

Shandy – roughly half-and-half mix of lager and lemonade, somewhat neglected in the UK – except in innuendo – but is a serious business in Germany where it is called Radler or Russen in the south, where it solves (for me) the problem of what Weissbier is actually *for*.

Shiraz – black-grape variety grown in every major wine-producing country. Aka Syrah in its French heartland of the northern Rhône, but, since more French people could tell you the names of the villages where it is the only grape used before they could tell you the name of the grape itself, I have gone – after much deliberation – with shizz-bang as that is the name most Brits would know it by (and, increasingly, the choice of name reflects the style of the wine being made).

Always bold, often with black-fruit flavours and, as Shiraz, frequently with either a twang of something medicinal or, as Syrah, a twist of something peppery. And if you're prepared to brave that journey up the Rhône Valley, with the prices following you steeply upwards, the flavour will evolve into a rich savouriness with black olives and something – trust me – remarkably like bacon.

Obviously, you won't see the name Syrah on the labels of those Rhône wines though – oh, no, that would be far too simple – you *will* see it on wines from elsewhere in France (*Vins de Pays d'Oc*, for example) or rather you would (and you may need to take a big swig at this point) except that producers often now use the name Shiraz because that's the one we're used to seeing on bottles of our favourite rambunctious Aussie reds. Those wines took us by storm in the 1990s and the rest of the world soon wanted to get a piece of the Shiraz action, with California's 'Rhône Rangers,' Chile, Argentina, South Africa and New Zealand leading the charge. 'The bigger the better' seemed to be the idea, although, for my money, 'too big for their boots' was a better description of some of the oppressively alcoholic, wintergreen or, worse, burnt-rubber scented wines of a few years ago.

A move in recent years towards lighter, fresher, more balanced styles – often made from grapes grown at cooler, higher altitudes – has come as quite a relief, I don't mind telling you. What goes around comes around and some of what would have been high-testosterone Aussie examples are now showing their feminine side as a result of being blended with some Viognier, just like they do in . . . no – go on, have a guess.

Recently, succulent, food-friendly rosés have started to appear and – although I dare say there were a few raised eyebrows up and down the Rhône when Australia started making sparkling Shiraz – they're more than just an oddity.

Side Car – five parts brandy to two each of Cointreau (or triple sec) and lemon juice shaken with ice and strained in to a cocktail glass with a sugared rim and a sheepskin umbrella.

Silvaner – (aka Sylvaner in Alsace) white grape of Germany, notably Franken, where it makes full-bodied wines that at their best subtly blend bracing acidity in a harmonious marriage with ripe, white fruits. Sadly struggles for recognition in a market that threatens to ignore all but the loudest shouters.

Simple syrup – slowly and completely melt twice the volume of sugar to water, being very careful not to burn it; cool and bottle for use in cocktails. It should keep for a few weeks in the fridge.

Singapore Sling – shake one part each cherry brandy, Cointreau, Bénédictine and lime juice with three parts gin, six parts pineapple juice and dashes of bitters and grenadine. Strain over ice in to a highball glass, top up with soda water and wait for Suzie Wong to come along (in a thong).

Sloe Comfortable Screw – two parts Southern Comfort built over ice in a highball glass with four of vodka, filled with orange juice and a float of one part sloe gin. Geddit? Additional float of Galliano to make it Up Against the Wall (as in banger). Witty, or what?

sloe gin – I've never understood why it has this naughty image, as examplified by my mum – hello, Mum! – who made it in her youth and reminisces about it with a bit of a nudge and a wink, like they do, because, surely, if a person were going to be naughty with a bottle of gin they wouldn't put sloes in it and bury it in the ground for six weeks, would they? They'd neck it. Originating in the Basque Country, but now popular throughout Spain, pacharán – ate *patxarán* to the picky Vascos – is a strongly addictive version using sweet anis instead of gin.

Slovakia – wouldn't rate a mention but for three things: the top German winemaker Egon Müller's investment in a project to produce fine Riesling (Château Belá [2]); some Tokay-style wines on the Hungarian border (Ostrožovič) and a vodka called Double Cross (for the name alone).

Slovenia – that part of former Yugoslavia bordering Italy and Austria and often confused with the previous entry (which calls itself Slovenská – what are they *like*?). Produces some very good, mainly white wines from Kerner, with their Faust label [2] and including some fine, late-harvest wines from Curin-Prapotnik. Especially good whites from Renski Rizling, which is the 'real' Riesling (try Dveri-Pax [2], Jeruzalem Ormož [1], Marof Estate [2], Simčič [2]) as opposed to the dire Laški Rizling (aka Welschriesling, although no more Welsh than it is Riesling), which we oldies suffered with so egregiously in the UK in the 1970s and early 1980s.

snakebite – half lager, half cider – mixed. Nobody seems to know how the snakebite earned its fearsome reputation as an inebriant though I for one have always been impressed by the seriousness of intent shown by people who order one; however, something seems to happen that makes everything go cloudy in the jar and many pubs refuse to serve it.

Snowball – advocaat and a squeeze of lime stirred with ice in a rocks glass and topped up with lemonade to taste. The pygmy bottles of it – hideous, stunted throwbacks to the cesspool that was the seventies – can still be found in odd corners and (whisper it) are really rather nice.

Solera – system of ageing wine, specifically sherry, in a series of barrels where, year by year, a quantity of wine is bottled from the oldest and replaced with wine from the second-oldest and hence in sequence to the youngest barrel, which receives the new year's wine. The solera is dated with the year of the first vintage, some of which – albeit eventually in homeopathic proportion – will still be present in the oldest barrel.

South African wine – to describe the product of a vineyard that has 350 years of documented winemaking history as 'New World wine' is, surely, a load of old Grobbelaars. Admittedly, the conquistadores were planting vines in Chile 150 years before, but we don't know their names and where they lived; here, it's all very personal: old St Paul's Cathedral was still standing in London when Jan Van Riebeeck, the founder of Cape Town, produced the first wine at the Groot Constantia estate in 1659 and Simon van der Stel, the second governor of the Cape, built the white-painted mansion that stands at the heart of it in 1685, twenty-five years before the new St Paul's was completed.

Whatever, the three South African candidates I have for 'best New World Chardonnay' (Hamilton Russell [3], Jordan Estate [2] and

Rustenberg [2]) along with a proliferation of reds jostling for 'best value New World this or that' are in many cases examples that SA is the New World country with the most in common wine-wise with the old. Nowhere is the pace of change in wine faster than in the world's ninth-biggest producer and nowhere else is quality radically improved across the board. South Africa has been the fastest growing part of the UK market in the late noughties and there is now a blizzard of brands (the biggest of which are First Cape [1], Fish Hoek [1], Constellation's Kumala [1], run by leading Cape light Bruce Jack, bag-in-box Namaqua [1], and Company of Wine People's Arniston Bay [1]. Other big SA wine companies are Distell's Fleur du Cap [1], Nederberg [1], Neethlingshof [1], Plaisir de Merle [2], DGB's Cape Mountain [1], Bovlei Co-op's Peaks View [1], and the once much-boycotted – and now partly black-run former national-wine co-op KWV. Black-owned Ses'Fikile [2] is an all-women operation, by the way. The UK's hyperactive Paul Boutinot has False Bay [1] and Paarl Heights [1], and then there's Alliance Wine with Aloe Tree [1].

DRINK LIKE A KING with ...

Aloe Tree
Cape Diamond
Cape Mountain
Fairview
False Bay
Gordon's Bay
Paarl Heights
Peaks View
Porter Hill Station
Winery of Good Hope

... FOR THE PRICE OF JUST DRINKING

For richer, for poorer, Pinotage is South Africa's own red grape, and increasingly it's for the former as growers great (Beyerskloof [2], Kanonkop [2]) and small (Gordon's Bay [1], McGregor [1], Swartland Co-op [1] and Winery of Good Hope [1]) have worked out how to deflect the green and burnt-rubber aspects (and I've heard worse terms that are unsuitable for repeating in a family guide to booze). A new style of 'coffee' Pinotage (try Diemersfontein [2]) is emerging and polarising growers – clearly this is not a grape for the quiet life.

Many top growers eschew Pinotage and pursue Bordeaux and Rhône blends, and if there is one thing that marks SA out for even greater future success it is its winemakers' skill and savvy (and boldness) in blending. *Méthode cap classique* is the winemaking term for classic-method sparkling wine, some of which is very good (Graham Beck [2], Krone [2], Pongrácz [2]).

For still whites, Chenin Blanc – the most widely planted of all grapes here (try Daneel [2], Kanu [1], Ken Forrester [2]) – and Semillon (Eikendal [2], Nitida [2]) have a long history, but, despite an uptick, seem to have been passed over currently in favour of the glamour of Chardonnay, now less clumsily oaked, and Sauvignon Blanc. Growers have recently persuaded the bureaucrats to abandon the name Cape Riesling for the rubbish Crouchen grape so that the coming rage for Riesling doesn't get held up.

South Africa has a precise, if clunkily named, geographical appellation system – Wine of Origin – descending in four levels from vast and pointless to precise and useful. A good example of the vast and pointless is Western Cape, which covers more or less everything, but because winemakers move faster than bureaucrats, some excellent wines are designated thus (AA Badenhorst [2], Hermanuspietersfontein [2], Luddite [3], Schaal [2],) along with the more basic Clear Mountain [1] or Zidela [1]). The next level is regional, (for example, the Coastal Region where you'll find Miles Mossop [3]) and the third and most useful level is district names like Stellenbosch and Paarl. Then we're back to largely useless again in the fourth level of tiny wards.

The whole Springbok wine effort is concentrated on the coastal strip 100-odd miles north or east of Cape Town and, conveniently, the jewels are respectively a hop, step and a jump from that most miraculously sited city. (None of that: 'Stonehenge was nice but why did they build it so far from the airport' stuff here.)

The sweet Muscat wines of Constantia – one of those jewels mentioned above and now a southern suburb of Cape Town – were world-famous in the eighteenth century before falling into neglect; however, the style has been resurrected and – if quality is a guide – is heading for similar renown again, with dry whites from Sauvignon and Semillon in support (Buitenverwachting [1], Klein Constantia [1], Steenberg [1] and neighbouring eponymous one-vineyard district Cape Point).

Stellenbosch is the Cullinan diamond among the geezers. It's South Africa's Napa, its Barossa, its Saint Émilion. Good wine is made everywhere now but Stellenbosch is HQ and the tourism side of things is racing ahead with great style. Cooled by the breezes from two oceans, which shape the character of many of the best South African wines all the country's favoured grapes shine here. The choices are plentiful: Alto Estate [2]; De Trafford [3]; Ernie Els [3]; Flagstone [2]; Foundry [2]; Hartenberg [2]; Haskell [3]; Kaapzich [1]; Laibach [1]; Le Bonheur [1]; MAN [1]; Marklew [2]; Meerlust [1]; Morgenhof [1]; Morgenster [2]; Mulderbosch [2]; Mullineux [2]; Quoin Rock [1]; Raats [1]; Le Riche [1]; Rust en Vrede [2]; Saxenburg [2]; Simonsig [2]; Spier [1]; Teddy Hall [1]; Thelema Mountain Vineyards [2]; Tokara Zondernaam [2]; Uitkyk [1]; Warwick [1]; Waterford [1]; Villiera and Vergelegen [2] (pronounce it with an initial 'f' and then as much guttural gusto as you can muster as their excellent and disputatious winemaker does, Vergelegen is one of the oldest and grandest producers they don't grow any Pinotage and their Bordeaux-blend 'Red' is one of the jostlers – and one of the world's great wine values).

The vines spread largely uninterrupted to the north, into Paarl (Avondale [1], Boschendal [1], Fairview [1], Glen Carlou [1], Joostenberg [2], Vondeling [1]) and to the west, to the former French-Huguenot enclave of Franschhoek (Boekenhoutskloof [1], Cape Chamonix [1]).

As in every country where people are passionate about wine, the search is on for cooler, more elevated sites for the creation of cooler, more elevated wines. To the south-east, Elgin (Paul Cluver [1], Iona [2], Catherine Marshall [1], Shannon [2]) is catching up with Walker Bay (Ataraxia [2], Beaumont [1], Bouchard Finlayson [1], Creation [3], Crystallum [3], Hamilton Russell [3], Newton Johnson [2]) and southernmost Elim shows promise with Agulhas [2] and Lomond [2].

To the north of Cape Town in the Coastal Region there are pockets of excellence in its sub-zones of Durbanville (De Grendel [1]), Philadelphia (Havana Hills [1]) and Darling (Groote Post [1]). Further north the districts of Swartland (Allesverloren [2], Charles Back of Fairview's Spice Route [2], Lammershoek [2], and outperformer Sadie [3]) and Tulbagh (Tulbagh Mountain Vineyards [2] – aka TMV, Tulbagh Co-op [1]/Porter Mill Station [1]) are developing fast. Northernmost in the Olifants River region vast quantities are made in Citrusdal (Ormer Bay [1], Liberty [1], and other fair-trade brands including Fairhills [1], Thandi [1] and Stellar [1]) and Lutzville (Cape Diamond [1]). The inland Robertson (Bon Cap [1], Bon Courage [1], De Wetshof [1], Robertson Winery [1]/Klippenkop, Springfield [1]) and Breedeskloof (Deetlefs/Stonecross [1]) districts are on a roll and Klein Karoo does a nice line in port-like wines (Axe Hill [3], De Krans [1]) while another sweet style is mistelle-like jerepigo (Rooiberg [1]).

South Africa leads the world in terms of dealing with biodiversity issues related to wine: compulsory measures have been introduced for producers and organic and biodynamic practices are spreading fast. This is good news, for even a cursory look shows they have a great deal to protect.

***GET A HANDLE...**

THE SPRINGBOKS ARE ADAPTING THE LESSONS OF THEIR LONG HISTORY OF MAKING OLD WORLD-STYLE WINES, ESPECIALLY

BLENDS, TO FIT THE CALL FOR LIGHTER, FRESHER, BRIGHTER STYLES – THEY'VE EVEN HOUSE-TRAINED PINOTAGE RECENTLY!

South and Central American beer – craft-brewing is springing up to offset Big-Beer sameness in Brazil (Eisenbahn) and Mexico (Moctezuma – a minnow compared to the likes of Corona – in bed with AB InBev and the world's fifth-biggest beer brand; Sol and Dos Equis – both swallowed by Heineken in 2010; and Tecate), all of which are OK with a wedge of lime, else you're in a taste-free zone.

Spanish beer – with the very recent exception of Italy, brewing in southern Europe naturally takes a distant second place to winemaking and the beers tend to be straightforward pilsner-style thirst-quenchers. The Spanish love adulterating things though, which I'm sure was the cause of the hangovers I used to get from drinking draught beer (or maybe I should have tried going to bed before 3AM now and then). Heineken-owned Cruzcampo is the biggest, but the Spanish still have more big independent brewers than most other countries (Estrella Damm, Mahou-San Miguel make some good stuff, including a handful of excellent dark beers) and a small but growing bevy of micros to keep them on their toes.

Spanish wine – in the mid-1980s, when I lived there, it was all a lot simpler. If you were flush, there was Rioja but if you didn't have 50p to spare, there was ho-hum Valdepeñas or maybe a leathery, jousting red from Jumilla. Below that, things got a bit dodgy and you were generally better off with a San Miguel or going native and, like one of the locals, glugging their fantastic sherries served straight from the barrel.

There was also the wine from some bloke called Torres, who'd made a name for himself when his best wine beat Château Latour in a blind tasting in Paris in 1979. In addition, I was vaguely aware of mythical Vega Sicilia, which cost a week's wages if you could find any, given that it was all spoken for by the bishops and the bigwigs. Travelling around was the only way to try other regional wines and, though a lot of them were dull – oxidised whites and dried-out reds – every now and then I'd find a gold nugget such as the graceful whites made from Alabariño found in Galicia or the tangy Ribeiro served there in a stubby-stemmed handmade ceramic bowl.

DRINK LIKE A KING WITH ...

Borsao

Castaño

Cruz de Piedra

Juan Gil

Luis Cañas

Marqués de la Villa

Olvena

Peique

Telmo Rodriguez

El Seque

... FOR THE PRICE OF JUST DRINKING

OK, it may have been simpler then – but better? not on your nellie. Today there is no more dynamic wine country in the world than Spain and all for the simple realisation that making smaller quantities of better wines is the way to go. Spain has more land under vine than anywhere else and a lot of those vines are well-established. All they needed was a change of mindset – difficult after generations of assuming more was better – and an awful lot of secateurs to prune those vines and lower the yield for more concentrated, characterful wines.

The appellation system follows the familiar model with a vacuous top tier that adds 'Ca' – for 'Calificada' (meaning 'qualified') – on to the end of the established Denominación de Origen – DO– level for some Rioja and Priorat, and a relatively recent category *vino de la tierra* (VdT) – the equivalent of France's *vin de pays* – not just for the best *vino de mesa* but for ambitious producers who can plough their own furrows free from too much restriction.

The Rioja system releases wines of different quality-levels after incremental periods of maturation: *sin crianza* or *joven* (young) gets none; *crianza* gets two years of which the first is in oak; *reserva* gets an extra year in bottle and *gran reservas* get two years in oak and three in bottle and often much more. This system is replicated, at least in part, in other regions and is a useful, but by no means a foolproof guide.

***GET A HANDLE...**

> SPANISH WINEMAKERS HAVE REALISED QUANTITY ISN'T EVERYTHING AND ADAPTING SOME OF THEIR WELL-ESTABLISHED VINEYARDS TO MODERN PRACTICES HAS THEM MAKING WORLD-CLASS WINES, ESPECIALLY TEMPRANILLO REDS AND A VARIETY OF FRESH WHITES THAT CAN BE STUNNING VALUE (ALMOST AS GOOD VALUE AS SHERRY).

North-west

Galicia – Spain is a continent masquerading as a country and in its green, Celtic part, the bit on top of Portugal, whites rule. The westernmost Rias Baixas DO fjord-scape is home to those elegant, enigmatic mollusc-friendly Albariños (of the three export trailblazers, of which only Pazo de Señorans [2] remains independent, Martin Códax [2] – which, to avoid embarrassment, is the name not of a winemaker but of a fourteenth-century troubador of local renown – is now owned by Gallo, as Lagar de Cervera [2] is owned by La Rioja Alta; neither of these have compromised too much on quality despite vastly increased production). Outperformers include Condes de Albarei [2], Fefiñanes [3], Galegas [3], La Val [2], Terras Gauda [2], Valminor [2] and Viña Nora [2]. As across the border in Portugal, Galicia's 'other' whites are mostly blends, and increasingly sophisticated Ribeiro (Docampo [2], Pazo do Mar [1]) uses some of the same grapes – Loureiro and Trajadura – and adds Torrontés and Godello, with or without some Alabariño – while Monterrei (Gargalo [2], Pazo das Tapias [1]) substitutes Doña Blanca for

Albariño. Valdeorras puts Godello centre stage to great effect.

Reds begin their long march across Spain in earnest a little further east in Bierzo, where firm, aromatic wines from the Mencía grape are a hot tip to go supernova (Dominio de Tares 2, Peique 1, Pittacum 2, R Sanz 2, Burbia 2, local figurehead Raul Perez's Castro Ventosa 1 and the catchily named Descendientes de José Palacios 2). The pace picks up in the province of Castilla y León, which boasts two strutting red DOs in the high Duero (Portugal's Douro) valley, some very fine VdT de Castilla y León (Abadía Retuerta 2, Dehesa de Rubiales 1, Dostares 2, Finca Coronado 2, Mauro 3, Monte La Reina 1 and Uribes Madero 3), VdT Zamora (Viñas del Cénit 3) and one of Spain's best DOs for whites, Rueda, where Verdejo makes succulent, sappy wines sometimes with help from Sauvignon Blanc or Viura (Alvarez y Diez 1, Antano 1, Arco de la Viña 1, Belondrade y Lurton 3, Naia 2, Nava Real 1, Palacio de Bornos 1, Pariente 2, Javier Sanz 2, Sitios de Bodega/M&R Sanz 2, TorresManur 1, Ventosilla 2, Veracruz 2, Viños Sanz 2 – a common name round here – and the influential Telmo Rodríguez).

The intense, long-aged but finely delineated wines of Vega Sicilia, Spain's grandest reds, have been made in the Ribera del Duero DO for knocking on 100 years. The place is booming now but you do wonder, what took them so long? At over 900 metres the cool nights mean these finest expressions of Tempranillo (aka Tinto Fino here) have freshness and plenty of acidity as well as depth and concentration. It now stands shoulder-to-shoulder with Rioja, and has benefited from the investment that has journeyed over the mountains separating them. The number of producers has risen ten-fold in the thirty-year existence of the DO and careful selection is necessary (Aalto 3, Alión 3, Arrocal 2, Astrales 3, Briego 2, Cillar de Silos 2, Ébano 2, Fescenino 2, O Fournier 2, Jaro 3, Codorníu's Legaris 2, Monasterio 3, Moro 3,

Pago de los Capellanes [2], Pago de Carraovejas [3], Sastre Villacreces [3], Pesquera [3] from Alejándro Fernández who kicked the whole thing off in the 1980s and then Dane Peter Sisseck, who picked up the ball and ran with it to make his Pingus [3], Spain's most expensive wine).

Toro is another Tempranillo town (here it's a particularly intense local clone aka Tinta de Toro), where the wines have less finesse but are supposedly better for their raw, rustic power, but some people think that's a load of bull. Expansion has been explosive here too – a five-fold increase in wineries since 1998. Things really got going when Vega Sicilia set up Pintia [3] and the icing on the cake was the LVMH purchase of Termanthia [3] in 2008 – although for my money their second wine Numanthia is better at a fraction of the price. Try also Campo Eliseo [3], Marques de la Villa [1], Quinta de la Quietud [2], Toresanas [1], Villabuena [3], Maurodos [2] and Paciencia [3] – owned by Bordeaux's Bernard Magrez in partnership with Gérard Depardieu. The Cigales DO is also worth investigating for stylish Tempranillo, although it's in its infancy export-wise (Cesar Principe [3], Traslanzas [3]).

North-east

It's not so long since Rioja – comprised of its three sub-regions of Alta, Baja and Alavesa – *was* Spain as far as wine goes and although ten bob doesn't take you very far these days, a supple, toasty *reserva* can still be among the best-value wines to be had anywhere. The problem is finding one. All that extended ageing in American oak doesn't fit so well with the moneymen's plans these days so they've been trying to market the merits of young Rioja – an oxymoron in my book. With a vastly increased 1,200 producers making all sorts of wines there seems a risk that the region may go the way of Chianti and risk losing any meaningful identity. The grapes remain the same – predominantly Tempranillo, blended with Garnacha and sometimes Graciano – it's what is done with them that's changing.

There are still established producers making good everyday wines (Faustino [1], Luis Cañas [1], Marqués de Cáceres [1], Navajas [1], Olarra [1], Valdemar [1]) and some of them compete with the poshest firms (Contino [3], Lopez de Heredia [3], Marqués de Murrieta [2], Marqués de Riscal [1], Marqués de Vargas [3], Muga [2], Palacios Remondo [2], Remelluri [2], La Rioja Alta [2], San Vicente [3], Urbina [1]) in making the fine, traditionally crafted *reservas* and *gran reservas* full of the pale, silky, stewed fruit and rich, vanilla tannins that made Rioja's name. Meanwhile, there are some very good, intense wines, some aged in French oak (Artadi [2], Bagordi [1], Baigorri [3], South African Bruce Jack's La Báscula [2], Roda [3], Romeo [3], Pernod Ricard's Ysios [3]) that would be hard to identify as Rioja and, in contrast, a complacency and mediocrity in some of the established brands that is shocking. One of the biggest producers – none of whose wines is up to scratch – thinks that *sin-crianza*-level varietals are the way ahead; the boss of another top-ten firm has told me that: 'It doesn't matter what's in the bottle.' ¡Dios mio! The UK should be more demanding as it is by far the biggest export market, but at least there's no shortage of suitable stuff for Haro's annual *batalla de vino*, when large crowds of people gather to spend the day spraying each other with wine.

Some traditions deserve to be left behind and, although I've always had a sentimental (or just mental) soft spot for the leathery, over-oaked and oxidised white Riojas of the past, tasting the best of the new wave – still made from Viura, sometimes with Malvasia, but fresh and intense – has been a revelation, especially Baron Ladron [1] de Guevara, CVNE [1] and Allende [3], Spain's best white.

Navarra's dark-pink *clarete* wines are said to have been the model for Bordeaux's reds and are still among the best in this varied region, which always seems something of a 'nearly man'. The fact that one of the best producers (Guelbenzu [2]) has now taken the VdT route can't help. The reds are a mixed bag of Spanish and French grapes and in the right hands (Artadi [2], Inurrieta [1], Nekeas [1], Ochoa [1], Principe de Viana [1], Zorza [1], and Chivite [1] – the leading light, and continuing to shine) are good value but buying at random is not advisable. Spain's prickly *vinho verde*, Chacolí, is made along the coast to the north (Ametzoi [2], Txomin Etxaniz [2]) – the Basques call it Txakoli but then they call a poached egg a *galdarraztatutako arrautzarekin* so best leave them to it.

Some of the same things might be said about Penedès, which has perhaps suffered from having one man – Miguel Torres, who has possibly done more for Spanish wine (from everyday bargains like Viña Sol [1] to those Bordeaux-beaters) than any other – be such an out-of-scale figure. Catalonia wanted above all to be modern and got stuck halfway there when everybody else got lucky with the move to making better wine from the traditional grapes. There are other good people (Albet i Noya [1] and Jean León [1] – although León is owned by, um, Torres) but the newer, catch-all Catalunya DO is taking over and, more importantly, things are starting to look up big time for the big thing here: Cava.

Cava can be made anywhere in Spain but the ball really started rolling here in Sant Sadurni d'Anoia in 1872, when Don José Raventós i Fatjo made a wine called Codorníu, and it's taken until now to start getting the quality sorted (quantity was never a problem). Preferably made from lots of Parellada and not much Macabeo or Xarel•lo, they're lighter, fresher, zestier and altogether less burpy than before (Gran Gesta [1], Hill [1], Jaume Serra [1], Juvé y Camps [2], Mas Maciá [1], Miret [1], Portaceli [1], Raventos i Blanc [1], Recaredo [2], Torre del Gall [2] and Freixenet [1] – Codorníu's great rival) – but of course they could never be in the same league as Champagne . . . could they? Try Gramona.

On the French border, the happening Empordá-Ampurdán DO (Castillo Perelada [1], Espelt [1], Gran Recosind [2], S'Alqueria [3]) and further south Alella (Parxet [2], Roura [2]) are ones to watch. Behind the city of Tarragona, the best bits of its eponymous DO have set up shop on their own in Costers del Segre (Castell del Remei [1], Cérvoles [3], Cusiné [2], Raimat [1]) and Conca de Barberá (Clos Montblanc [1], Torres [3]) for juicy, modern styles; in Terra Alta (Artesano [1]) and in Montsant for dense reds (Can Blau [3], Capçanes [1], Clos dels Codols [2], Falset-Marçá [1], Jaspi Negre [2], Masroig [1], Portal del Montsant [3]).

Montsant encircles the best bit of all – Priorat(o) – transformed in two decades from a backwater into a powerhouse, where some of Spain's most mineral-laden, most intense, most expensive (and now some of her most overpriced) reds are made from Garnacha and Cariñena. Try these: Buil & Gine [2]; Clos Erasmus [3]; Clos del Portal [3]; Combier-Fischer-Gerin [3]; Costers del Siurana [3]; Fuentes [3]; Ithaca [3]; Mas Alta [3]; Mas d'en Gil [3]; Mas Doix [3]; Mas la Mola [3]; Pasanau [2]; Torres [2]; Vall Lach [3]; and Clos Mogador [3] – started by René Barbier in 1979 to set the whole thing in motion, along with Mas Martinet [3] and Alvaro Palacios [2].

Other new-fangled north-eastern DOs making good wines in the absence of any particular distinguishing characterisitics or history include mountainous Somontano (Enate [2], Viñas del Vero [1], Olvena [1], and Pirineos Co-op [1] made with local Moristel and Paralleta and maybe the way ahead), and, in Aragón, all the 'C's: Calatayud for strong Garnacha (Alarba [1], Jorge Ordoñez's Ateca [1], Cruz de Piedra [1], Escoces Volante [1], Jalón [2], San Alejandro [2]); Campo de Borja for many a juicy bargain (Alto Moncayo [3],

Aragonesas [1], Borsao [1]) and Cariñena, the place – not the grape (San Valero [2]).

South of Madrid, although they've been making wine for centuries, is Spain's New World, but a new world with some seriously old vines. Living on the south coast in the mid-1980s, I used to drink – with much pleasure and trivial expense – a leathery Monastrell (Mourvèdre) from Jumilla called El Tio de la Bota ('the old boy with the wine-bag'). Now Jumilla's hour has arrived at last to the extent that one wine (El Nido [3]) got a 99-point mark from Robert Parker for their 2004. OK, it was Parker's chum Jay Miller, and it is made by Jorge Ordoñez, prime mover-and-shaker of the new Spain, but ¡REALLY! – ¡99 POINTS! ¡from JUMILLA! Join me in reminiscing with Casa Castillo [2], Casa de la Ermita [1], Juan Gil [1], Luzón [1] and San Juan [1].

There's a cluster of adjoining DOs here in the Levante, centred around Valencia, all with some stars-in-the-making to look out for (including the promising red grape Bobal), in the improving Alicante (El Seque [1], Enrique Mendoza [2]) Gutiérrez de la Vega [2] – still making traditional sweet red *fondillon*), and in Almansa (Piqueras [1], Tintoralba [1]), Manchuela (Sandoval [3]), Valencia (for the cheapest dry and sweet whites – not all to be despised – and some outperformers including Cambra [2], Marqués del Turia [1]), and especially Yecla (Castaño [1], La Purísima Co-op [1] and La Báscula [3]) and Utiel-Requeña (Casa del Pinar [3], Fuenteseca [1], Mustiguillo [2], Rozaleme [1]).

Heading towards the capital means saddling up the donkey and crossing the aching, baking spaces of La Mancha (Campos Reales [1]) and Valdepeñas DOs (Félix Solís [1], Los Llanos [1], Navarro Lopez [1]) and the broader Castilla-La Mancha VdT (Castillo del Moro [1]) where standards are creeping inexorably upwards. The laggards clustered around Madrid have churned out plonks for yonks but there are stirrings even here in Méntrida (Jiménez Landi 2), Mondéjar, Vinos de Madrid (Tagonius 2), Uclés (Fontana 1) and the Pagos – a new category of single-estate DOs – of, for example, Domínio de Valdepusa (Marqués de Griñón 3) and there will be more. The last frontier is towards the one with Portugal and even here – in the Spain of silence and siestas – in Ribera del Guadiana (InViOSA 1 Co-op), the Extremadura VdT (Mirabel 3) and down to the coastal VdTs of Cadiz (Huerta de Albalá 2) and Granada (Calvente 2) there is perceptible movement.

Fortified wines

Spain's fortified wines are some of the world's best. Of the sweet *vinos generosos,* Málaga – like Marsala – nearly died out, but there are one or two determined souls who have refused to let this unique style of fortified wine go gently into that good night (Telmo Rodríguez 1, Lopez/Málaga Virgen 2 and Jorge Ordóñez 3). In my day a cheap source of fino lookalikes, Montilla-Moriles, fifty miles north of Málaga, is now a source of some of the best, blackest treacliest Pedro Ximénez. There's good sweet stuff in the islands too but mostly it stays there – Malvasia in the Canary Islands (El Grifo 2) and good dry reds from local Manto Negro on Mallorca, especially in the Binissalem and Plá i Llevant DOs (Ánima Negra 2, 4 Kilos 3, Macía Batle 2).

Used and abused but unbowed – even amused – sherry, from Jerez (pronounced 'herr-ETH'), Sanlúcar de Barrameda and declining El Puerto de Santa María – is the greatest gift Spain brings to the world's table. Sherry's always just about to go mega: new producers (Navazos 3, Rey Fernando de Castilla 2, Tradición 3, Valdivia 2) come along and take old soleras to new heights, and London gets its first sherry bar in 2010 (Pepito – a few square metres of Jerez, transplanted) . . . the people who love it go on quietly loving it.

The fine-boned Palomino Fino grape expresses itself in the pale essence of dryness that is *fino,* made using the solera system (see p. 352). Fino is as dry as the chalk it grows in but the joy with which it is sploshed around hereabouts is anything but dry. The locals drink it young, cold and fast and sometimes mix it half-and-half with lemonade and ice to make a *rebujito*. Mysterious things happen during their minimum three years in barrel as these – the best – wines cover themselves with a thin veil of yeast, called *flor*, under which they develop umami-like, slightly rank, *rancío* characteristics. These are the ones to drink fresh and cold but, as with Manzanilla – the 'other' Fino – made with a salty, seaside tang in Sanlúcar (Argüeso [1], La Guita [1], Hidalgo [1]), longer ageing will bronze and broaden them into the real, nutty Amontillado. Sometimes, when the *flor* doesn't occur, and known as *Palo Cortado* (pale cut), they are aged for decades to emerge as some of the finest of all sherries.

The second-best, more strongly fortified, wines don't do the *flor* thing and are called *Oloroso*. Some go the route of further sweetening into cream sherries and the commercial Amontillado style – which really should have another name. All the biggest houses (Barbadillo [1], Gonzalez Byass [1], Harvey's [1], Osborne [1], Sandeman [1], Valdespino [1], Williams & Humbert [1]) make good stuff and age-dated sherries – twenty-year-old VOS (very old) and, with another decade, VOR[rare]S – can be great bargains and smaller firms (Delgado Zuleta [2], Sanchez Romate [1] and Alvaro Domecq [2] – re-establishing the family name) and stock-holding *almacenistas* (Gutiérrez Colosía [1], Lustau [2]) should also get a look-in.

sparkling wines – sparkle because of the carbon dioxide dissolved in them and kept in place by the pressure in the bottle and which comes out – sometimes spectacularly – as bubbles when the bottle is opened. All of the best stuff is made by the *méthode Champenoise* but which must now be termed either *méthode traditionelle* or *méthode classique* or a Eurocrat will wash your mouth out with soap and water. The term *crémant* now denotes a sparkling wine made by this method pretty much anywhere in France except Champagne. The second-best method (by a long, long way) is called *charmat* (or, unglamorously, 'tank') where everything up to final bottling is done in a pressurised tank. There is nothing at all glamorous about the cheapest method – straightforward carbonation, the bicycle-pump method used for fizzy soft drinks. The French term for fizzy is *mousseux*; the Italians divide theirs between *spumante* for fully fizzy and *frizzante* for half-fizzy.

The physiological bit is clear: bubbles get you drunker, faster. Hence the thrill, the buzz, the squeals of delight . . . the sheer 'ooh! la-la' of it all. The effervescence stimulates the lining of the stomach into a frenzy of digestive action and the bubbles provide a greater surface area of booze for it to work on. Inhibitions are shed more quickly, as are clothes.

Springbank – family-owned Campbeltown distillery dating from 1828 with a serious claim to making the ultimate all-rounder malt. Where once there were perhaps thirty, it is now one of three, with Glen Scotia and the new Glengyle, who will bottle their first liquid in 2014.

spritzer – you only get out of a spritzer what you put into a spritzer, so don't think you can dose up any old rubbish in this way and end up with a nice drink. Use a full-bodied California Chardonnay or an off-dry German wine with some sweetness to the fruit. Lighter Italian whites, for example, will be almost tasteless if you spritz them.

spumante – Italian for fizzy; *frizzante* is half-fizzy.

Stinger – two parts Cognac to one part white crème de menthe shaken with ice and strained in to a cocktail glass. Popular as a nightcap in New York, but, as that's the city that never sleeps, presumably it doesn't work very well.

supérieur(e), superiore – usually indicates a wine of slightly higher alcoholic strength or from a sub-zone of a demarcated area, but it ain't no guarantee.

sur lie – indicates a white wine that has been left in contact with its lees (sediment) to develop more body and often a bready character. Only usually seen on labels for the better Muscadets.

sweet wines – no, not those flabby, sugary, half-sweet (frequently German) horrors that certain aged relatives bought in the seventies – and which, despite their awfulness, could still be made sweatily worse by drinking them at something near room-temperature.

No, not them but some of the gems of the wine world, the miniature works of art that allow dedicated winemakers to showcase what they can do with super-ripe fruit. The key to it all is in the balancing of the natural sweetness of the fruit with the acidity necessary to keep it crisp and prevent it from cloying. When they get it right the results can be spectacular.

The French have a phrase that translates roughly as being

'inhabited' by a fine wine and the first time this happened to me was with a Sauternes. The extraordinarily intense flavours – of apricots and marmalade – seemed to envelop my whole face and linger on my lips for several minutes. Their echo was there next day and they'll remain imprinted on my sensory memory for ever.

There are three types of sweet (or dessert, or – to the Brits – pudding) wines. Fortified wines include port and Madeira and the *vins de liqueur* and *vins doux naturels* of southern France (and similar *licoroso* or *liquoroso* wines in the Portuguese and Italian terms). Fortification is the addition of grape spirit to stop the fermentation and preserve some of the sweetness of the fruit before all the natural sugars turn to alcohol.

Some other local French versions are Macvin de Jura, Floc de Gascogne and Ratafia de Champagne. They are distinct in theory from the *mistelle* wines (aka *mistela* in Spain) like Pineau des Charentes and South African jerepigo, where the spirit is added to the juice before fermentation begins. These are consumed after some ageing while others are used in blending in fortified and liquoreux wines.

The second method is to semi-dry the grapes with the effect of concentrating the sweetness through evaporation, yielding minuscule quantities of intensely sweet wine usually called *passito* in Italy (where red and white versions exist and where *vin santo* can be the exception and actually be dry – only in Italy!). They're called *vin de paille* – literally 'straw wine' as the grapes are laid to dry on straw matting – in France in the northern Rhône and in Jura.

The region with the strongest claim to being the spiritual home of late-harvest stickies – the third sweet winemaking method – is Sauternes and neighbouring Barsac in Bordeaux, although many a German winemaker would dispute my choice. In both places – and now in virtually every winemaking country – for the best wines, the grapes are individually picked at the moment of maximum ripeness, which can be weeks after the first grapes are picked and into December for Germany's *Eiswein* (literally 'ice wine'). In 2010, the EU finally rescinded its mad ban on New Zealand sweeties, opening up still another source of supply for my own sticky habit.

Swiss beer – Switzerland has plenty of micro activity bubbling away beside the lakes of Heineken and Carlsberg (and their Hürlimann) but as you'll have to go there to find it, you may not find it worth it. Yawn. However, you may liven things up with a pint or two or three of Albert Egger, BMF, Schützengarten, Statguet or Sternen.

Swiss wine – Switzerland has the most pampered vines on earth, and some of the highest, and so painstakingly are they tended that it's no surprise that ninety-eight per cent of the wine they make is consumed domestically. Valais (Favre 2) is the main white region with some of the country's most widely planted white grape, Chasselas (unloved, except aka Fendant here), indigenous Petit Arvine and Completer and many of the usual international suspects. Red-wine production has overtaken white with a virtual monoculture of Merlot in southern Ticino, where the grape also makes rosé and white and the quality spectrum is just as wide – try Castello di Morcote 3 and Tamborini 3. Pinot Noir does well and native Cornalan and Humagne Rouge are also making some interesting stuff. Value is a problem but then when isn't it in Switzerland?

tegra mole tinto tinto cão tonic wines torbato torrontés touriga franca trajadura

tannat tarrango tempranillo tequila tequila sunrise terret terroir three penis wine tinta barroca

Talisker – property of Diageo and the only whisky distillery on the Isle of Skye. Inspires fierce loyalty from its devotees.

Tarrango – an Australian cross of the Touriga Nacional and Sultana grapes to make light, tight, cherryish Beaujolais-style wines.

Tempranillo – (aka Tinta Roriz, Aragónez in Portugal, Ull de Llebre – hare's eye – in Catalonia, and Cencibel in Valdepeñas) noble red-wine grape of Iberia. The most widely planted grape in Spain – their Cabernet Sauvignon or Sangiovese in essence, and the silky, deeply coloured mainstay of blends, especially in Rioja, and now spreading in California, Argentina and Australia.

T

tequila – the mezcal made in the Jalisco area of central Mexico, and living testimony to the lengths people will go to to get their hands on some booze, being double-distilled from *pulque*, a sort of beer made from the sap of the slow-cooked and pulverised core of the Blue Weber agave, a type of succulent plant that takes ten years to reach maturity and which, contrary to popular belief, is not a cactus but closely related to the amaryllis family.

There are 9,000 producers of the stuff, most of them in tin shacks making 'mixto' (with up to half cane or other sugar) and presumaby not paying much attention to the official grades of quality: *blanco* or *plata* (white or silver), bottled without ageing, as is *joven* (young) but that is coloured or, better, blended with some *reposado* (rested), which spends two-to-twelve months in barrel. *Añejo* (aged) gets one-to-three years; *extra añejo*, from 2006, a minimum of three.

With very few exceptions, the older, rarer and more expensive it is the more unpleasant it tastes, to the extent that the really fabulous ones are almost undrinkable. The diversity of flavours is remarkable and each seems unique so you might compare them to bat's urine or the small quantity of liquid that eventually collects in the bottom of the fridge – double-distilled of course. Nowadays, nobody seems to do the salt and lime thing that made it bearable – the Margarita performs the same office now I suppose.

Forty per cent of what is produced is consumed domestically but even more than that by tequila nerds in the US, few of whom seemed to notice that a super-premium brand called Porfidio was in fact any old rubbish *blanco* with a bit of colouring and labelled *añejo*. It was banned in 2008 – 'porfidious albino', indeed. As with grappa, I have persevered and found one (Don Julio) that is a many-layered, citrussy good thing to drink and so I suppose I shall return to the fray. If you're wanting to sample a few more of the 9,000, try: Asombroso's del Porto, aged in port barrels; Cabo Wabo; Don Fulano; El Tesoro, Herradura; Chinaco; Corazón – a good *blanco*; Gran Centenario; José Cuervo – the largest by far and still privately owned, the twenty-five-year-old Reserva de la Familia for expensive preference;

Noble; Partida; Patrón; Sauza – the Tres Generaciones, or '3G', is the best; or Two Fingers, which sums it up rather nicely.

Tequila Sunrise – try to build three parts tequila to six parts orange juice and one of grenadine over ice in a highball glass with a straight face.

terroir – much misunderstood term that does have meaning when defined as the soil and climate of a vineyard (and the vines' exposure to the latter in terms of altitude and aspect). The problems arise when it is used more broadly to refer to what the location adds to the grape or, more poetically, to the *genius loci*.

three-penis wine – Chinese concoction including the dried and powdered parts of deer, dog and seal and claimed to be sovereign in the treatment of a flagging libido.

tonic wines – beloved of grannies and Glaswegian teenagers, a dubious category of fortified wine or *mistelle* with additional flavourings. The tonic most likely comprises the alcohol. Buckfast is made in the tranquil surroundings of a Benedictine abbey in Devon, though things are less tranquil where much of it is consumed on the council estates of urban Scotland, notably in Lanarkshire, where it is also known as 'wreck the hoos juice', 'commotion lotion', 'made by monks for drunks' and 'Lurgan Champagne'. Mentioned on average in four crime reports per day in the Strathclyde police district. The ingredients for the perfect storm are 15% abv, caffeine of up to 55mg/l (equivalent of eight cans of cola per 750ml bottle) and bags of residual sugar to keep the mayhem going. Close inspection of the labels of Jamaican versions (Magnum and, er, Mandingo) suggests they are more sensibly offered as an aid to male vigour.

Touriga Franca – (formerly Francesa) most widely planted black grape of northern Portugal's Douro region. Much blended in port, now spreading to the south and *not* French in any way, shape or form.

Touriga Nacional – smouldering black grape of northern Portugal's Douro region, where it is much blended in port and also makes intense, tannic single varietals there, in the Dão region and in South Africa.

Traminer – frumpy white-grape variety, the plain sister of glamorous Gewürztraminer, which is more aromatic. Traminer is grown widely but without much enthusiasm across central Europe; however, she can blossom in northern Italy and in Austria if coaxed out of her shell by skilled winemakers such as the late, great Alois Kracher.

Trebbiano – much-scorned white-grape variety, the most widely planted in Italy and France (aka Ugni Blanc and some seventy-plus other names across Europe). Possibly produces more of the world's wine than any other, much of it dull but which can be refreshing and fruity in the right hands. Has its moment blended with Malvasia in vin santo. Much is distilled into Cognac and Armagnac.

Tunisia – once a major wine producer with a long history of viticulture, but now a declining producer of rosé mostly – around 30 million bottles to slake the thirsts of holidaymakers.

Turkey – of her vast grape production, thankfully only a small amount is turned into wine, the industry being dominated by three big companies making whites preferable to their often baked, over-alcoholic reds. Kavaklidere, Doluca and Tekel's amusingly named Buzbağ might be acceptable to wash down an after-pub kebab but – in the extremely unlikely event that you are given the choice – go for Turkey Flat from Australia's Barossa Valley.

ukraine ullage united states wine uruguay uva di troia uva rara ukraine ullage united states wine uruguay uva di troia uva rara ukraine ullage united states wine uruguay uva di troia uva rara ukraine ullage united states wine

Ukraine – 1894 was Ukraine's winemaking heyday, when Tsar Nicholas II built a vast winery at Massandra. It still houses (and sells from) a million-bottle collection of wines, the best of which are sweet. The country now produces a large amount of wine, especially sparkling, notably from the Crimean peninsula.

ullage – the loss of wine from a container through evaporation or spillage. For venerable bottles of wine there is a precise scale describing the level of the wine, from perfectly fine 'into neck', via 'VTS' (very top shoulder), 'TS' (top-shoulder) to worrying 'MS' (mid-shoulder) and, no thanks, 'LMS' (lower-mid shoulder) and below, where too much oxygen will have made vinegar of it.

Uruguay – they like their wine, but good, strong reds from the south, around Montevideo – mostly from their signature Tannat grape, which is fine but they'll need more than that – are trickling out (the wonderfully named Bouza 2, Castillo Viejo 1, Juanicó Pizzorno 2 and Pisano 2 – the prime moving-and-shaking family).

US beer – without doubt, and to the amazement of all who think American beer as being only ever like 'making love in a punt' – see the section on the brewing industry for details of the USA's Big Beer interests – the Yanks' craft beers are among the best in the world. Irony heaped upon irony's head, they sometimes run the risk of over-achieving, with quite a few rather over-the-top 'extreme beers'. They are impressive, certainly, but too much like an academic exercise and not very gluggable. Some can be so bitter that when people drink them they make a face like my cat Sooty used to when he was trying to sick up a furball. The quintessentially British concept of a 'session beer' is, I suspect, in very many ways a foreign one in US craft-brewing circles (but they might look to Boulder Beer's well-balanced Mojo for a clue – it has a bit, but never too much, of everything).

The keystone for the building of America's 'microbreweries' was set in place as early as 1965 when Fritz Maytag bought San Francisco's failing Anchor Brewing Company – as in Anchor Steam Beer – and began to turn it around. The pioneer of US craft beer is now head of the industry's Brewers' Association (BA), which morphed out of the American Homebrewers' Association, established when that activity was made legal as late as 1978 (the shadow cast by Prohibition was a long one). The following year Anchor was joined in its lonely furrow by Sierra Nevada and Boulder Beer and in 1981 Redhook got going. By the time the east coast woke up and smelled the coffee with the founding of the Boston Brewery in 1985 and the Brooklyn Brewery a couple of years later things were humming nicely nationwide.

Today the BA represents most of the USA's 1,500 or so craft brewers, two-thirds of which are also brewpubs, including Alaskan Brewery, BJ's Brewhouses, Blue Point Brewing Company, Boulevard Beer, Breckenridge, Deschutes, Dixie, Dogfish Head, Elysian, Flying Dog, Flying Fish, Goose Island, Gordon Biersch, Great Lakes,

Harpoon, Iron Hill, Kona, Jacob Leinenkugel, Long Trail, Lost Abbey, McMenamins, McSorley's, Mendocino Brewery, New Belgium, New Glarus, Old Dominion, Pyramid, Rogue, Saint Arnold (the patron saint of brewers so in a way beer really is my middle name), Saranac, Schlafly, Shiner, Shipyard, Smuttynose, Stone, Summit, Sweetwater, Utah Brewers, Widmer Brothers, Wynkoop and from the oldest brewery in the US, Yuengling, though a taste of this strangely watery, but still good, lager might suggest it was the ill-used model for all the less-than-good things that happened to US beer subsequently.

When successful brewers succumb to the inevitable temptation to expand they confront the apparent impossibility of mass-producing a quality product and the inevitable fall in quality usually happens (especially with beers on draught, as two rapidly expanding outfits, New Belgium and Brooklyn Brewery, risk demonstrating). There have been casualties among the pioneers such as the early demise of the influential New Albion; once-cultish, old-style-lager Rolling Rock, which was bought by ABInBev in 2006 and is now just a name, and Pete's Wicked Ale, which ain't so wicked any more.

US wine – there are vineyards in every single, spangled one of the United States of Wine. California's star is of a much brighter magnitude than the rest, of course, but Washington and Oregon, although of a very different stripe in terms of size, hold the banner of quality aloft with pride. The Golden State is in itself the world's fourth-biggest winemaker and the second-ranked supplier to the thirsty UK market, providing three of the top-ten selling brands: Blossom Hill; Gallo and Echo Falls. Yet of all the major winemaking places, the US is the one we know the least about. The one name everybody does know is the place they are least likely to drink wine from because it produces mainly expensive wine: Napa Valley.

The brands are owned by the big winecos that completely dominate an export market that has exploded twenty-fold in the last twenty years to become a billion-dollar industry. As far as booze goes, the UK seems to be just about everybody's biggest customer and the US is no exception – their savvy (some would say cynical) marketing and selling methods make the slickest European efforts look like the work of slack-jawed yokels. The UK supermarkets, with the usual exception of Waitrose, stock only brands from the five or six majors along with their 'own brands' and occasional 'private brands'; and this is the problem for most UK consumers: there is no middle ground in American wine. Their big wine distributors have consolidated themselves into positions of immense power – Southern Wine & Spirits and the wine operations of the warehouse-style supermarket Costco are gargantuan on a scale without an equivalent elsewhere.

Once you go beyond the monolithic, such as California itself and the mega-brands, there is nothing until you hit the atomistic level of the almost 7,000 unfamiliar small producers (up from 2,000 in 1997), few of whom are in need of an export market. Getting to grips with the geography is tricky too because the names are as unfamiliar as those of the producers and there's nothing to hang them on to make them stick. The cattle-stunner-grade imbecility of the American Viticultural Area (AVA) appellation system (no, didn't think so) doesn't help: the North Coast AVA contains the whole of Napa and Sonoma while only twenty-five miles away the Dunnigan Hills AVA contains one winery – RH Phillips [1].

California

California is big – and when we're talking about US wine we are talking about California, as they make ninety-five per cent of the stuff and supply seventy per cent of the domestic market. In fact, it's the eighth-largest economy in the world and the world's three-largest wine companies base their production there: Constellation, who own Mondavi, the world's fourth-biggest wine brand; Gallo; The Wine Group – no, nobody else has heard of them either, but they are big in bag-in-box with their Franzia [1] brand which is sold only in the States and, more interestingly, good-value Big House [1]. Kendall-Jackson [2] remains the largest family-owned company but there's families and then there's families – every slavering corporate-California wine-hound wants to invite you to be part of their 'family' at the moment.

The Californian giants *are* making decent stuff despite the truly industrial scale of production. The geography of it, at least, is simple: it's made in the 300-mile-long Central Valley – California's equivalent of Australia's Riverland. This flat, fertile expanse feeds the state and, as in Oz, the vines (including much Ruby Cabernet, a workhorse red grape produced by crossing Carignan and Cabernet Sauvignon for quantity, rather than quality) are grown almost hydroponically, their every need catered for with scientific exactitude, and the result is that everything looks great but the lack of character or identity is almost clinical, and the temptation to take this metaphor any further must be resisted at all costs.

But *plus ça change*, there has been a monstrous glut of wine that in the mid-noughties saw the phenomenon of Bronco Wines' Charles Shaw brand Two-Buck Chuck, which still sells big-time in the Trader Joe's grocery chain for as little as two dollars a bottle. By hardball buying into the oversupply of a perishable product their competition is with beer rather than with other wines – though the stuff has picked up various prizes in blind tastings. A certain toughness has always been a prerequisite for success in the States and, since the first vineyard was planted there nearly 250 years ago, the pioneers of California wine, among them Agoston Haraszthy in the nineteenth century, André Tchelistcheff and Robert Mondavi (said to have tasted 300 wines every day) in the twentieth – have shown the tenacity necessary to see off everything from endemic phylloxera to Prohibition.

The glut has focussed many a winemaking mind on quality and the somewhat cooler northern part of the valley (known as the San Joaquin Valley in the real world), in El Dorado (Boeger 2), Sierra Foothills (Clockspring 1), and – more importantly – Lodi, is now turning out some serious quality, good-value Zinfandel and other hot-climate, southern French and Spanish varietals (Bogle 2, Delicato 1, Ironstone 2, Lodi Vineyards 1, Scotto 1 and Quady 1 for sweet wines and Constellation-owned Ravenswood 1). But the real upside of California comes from getting to grips with the smaller producers – hard and expensive work but with significant rewards.

I was greeted at the first Napa Valley winery I ever visited by somebody whose business card described their role as that of 'Contemporary Muse'. 'The Pinot's good today,' she told me shortly thereafter. 'It rilly likes sunny days . . .' Welcome to the Napa Valley, the Garden of Eden of wine, where the best acre of vines can cost a third of a million dollars and the average bottle of Cabernet Sauvignon in one Yountville wine merchant is priced at over seventy dollars (although the serpent of recession has finally arrived here too and those figures may now be on a typically strict, California-style diet). And who knows but the muse may be right – something has to account for that grape's exasperating inconstancy.

The thirty or so miles of Interstate 29 from the town of Napa to Calistoga pass through an area very much geared towards high-end tourism. To that end Robert Mondavi 1 in Oakville is excellent for educational and wine-tasting courses and it's worth popping across the road for a quick look at the extraordinary flying saucer of a building that houses the joint Mondavi-Rothschild venture Opus One [3]. Tasting here needn't take long as they do indeed produce just the one opus each year.

Napa can be as inward-looking as sometimes only the States is capable of being. While the rest of the world has been listening out for fresher, lighter, finger-picking styles they've kept the stadium rock blaring, squeezing every last atom of extract from every grape, every last point out of Parker and every last dollar (as if) out of the wallets of their captive (as in rabbits in car headlights) market as if nothing (not to mention everything) in the world of wine had moved on while they were waiting for each other to blink. Nevertheless, some of their Cabernets – now on their way to becoming a unique, antiquated style – can still be show-stopping, albeit at heart-stopping prices (all [3]: Altamura, Araujo, Beaulieu, Cakebread, Caymus, Corison, Dalla Valle, Diamond Creek, Dominus, Dunn, Forman, Frog's Leap, Grgich Hills, Groth, Kathryn Hall, Heitz, Joseph Phelps, L'Aventure, St Clement, Shafer, Silverado, Silver Oak, Spottswoode, Staglin, Stag's Leap Wine Cellars, Togni and Beringer [1] – owned by Foster's and the fifth-biggest wine brand in the world but still making benchmark 'Reserve' Cabernets). But hold on to your hats, because there's a whole other level (of prices, at any rate) above these. Harlan Estate [3] has busted through the $1,000-mark for the most-collectable vintages while Screaming Eagle [3] has flown over three times that – we're talking per bottle here, people – and the foothills of Olympus are well-populated too (Abreu [3], Bryant [3], Colgin [3], Grace [3], Scarecrow [3], Sine Qua Non [3]).

Back in the earthly garden, one of the great aspects of the Edenic thing is that everything thrives, so man need not live by Cabernet alone and there are terrific – even affordable – wines from an ark full of grapes: Chardonnay, *bien sûr* (Château Montelena [3], Clos du Val [2],

Kistler [3], Peter Michael [3], Newton [3], Sonoma Cutrer [2] and insanely expensive Marcassin [3], which is anyway made from pineapples as far as I can tell); post-*Sideways*, but presumably pre-coital, Pinot Noir (Chalone [2], Cuvaison [2], Merry Edwards [3], Morgan [2]), instead of the 'fucking' Merlot (Stag's Leap [3], Duckhorn [3], Martinelli [3], Pahlmeyer [3], Paloma [3]). Some 'Calitalian' winemakers give the impression they've compressed the whole of Italy into a few dozen acres, such is their range (L'Uvaggio [1], Viansa [2]) and Zinfandel (Biale [3], Saddleback [2], Turley [3]), should never be overlooked in the alphabetti-spaghetti.

There is also first-class fizz from Dom Chandon [2], Gloria Ferrer [3], Roederer [3], Schramsberg [3], and excellent-value wines being made from the Loire grapes especially Sauvignon Blanc (Long Meadow [2], Selene [2], St-Supéry [2]) and those of Alsace with Pinot Gris, Gewürztraminer – even Riesling – gaining ground (Claiborne & Churchill [2], Trefethen [2]). Godammit, there are even blends (Viader [3]) and Bordeaux-style 'meritage' – rhymes with heritage (Cain [3], Dry Creek [3]), and the 'Rhône Rangers' (Qupé [2], Bonny Doon [3]), and some Rhône whites (Fetzer [1]) all attest to a somewhat overdue flourishing of diversity.

Those in search of value in Napa need not despair completely (but should probably avert their eyes from Cabernet). Instead try Beaucanon [2], Cartlidge & Brown [1], Constellation-owned Franciscan [3], Folie à Deux [1] or Hess Collection [2]. Thankfully, things calm down further afield, both to the north and south.

Go east from Napa town through Carneros (Cline [2], HDV [2], Saintsbury [3], Schug [3], Sinskey [2]), before heading up into Sonoma itself (Château Saint Jean [1], Clos du Bois [1], Deerfield Ranch [2], Flowers [3], Geyser Peak [1], Hanzell [3], Iron Horse [2], Jordan [3], Laurel Glen [3], Lyeth [1], Rafanelli [3], Saint Francis [1], and Marimar Torres [3]

– daughter of Miguel) and the pounds positively fall off. Further up, in the AVAs of Alexander Valley (Seghesio [2], Sebastiani [1]), Dry Creek Valley (Dry Creek Vineyards [1] for Fume – i.e. Sauvignon – Blanc), Knight's Valley (Peter Michael [3]), and Russian River Valley (Coppola [1], Farrell [2], De Loach [1], Ramey [3], Rochioli [2]), the weather is noticeably cooler with lots of fog from the Pacific rolling regularly in. Northernmost Mendocino (Dolan [1], Navarro [2]), Anderson Valley (Edmeades [2]) and Lake County (Cecchetti [1]) also offer relative bargains (with the emphasis firmly on the 'relative').

South from Napa the Central Coast region between San Francisco and Los Angeles is THE place to find out what California wine is about without the sticker shock, and the string of AVAs of Livermore Valley (Wente [1]), Santa Cruz Mountains (Ridge [3] – the great Paul Draper makes Monte Bello, my desert-island-US wine, very claret-like in style and which in its own way is as good value as a 150-buck wine can be), San Benito (Calera [3]), Monterey (Hawk Crest [2]), Santa Lucia Highlands (Hahn [2], Marmesa [2]), Arroyo Seco (Lohr [2], who grow, among much else, Valdiguié, nearly extinct in its southern French home but making new friends for berryish, Beaujolais styles here – now exported back to Europe), San Luis Obispo (Eberle [3]), Paso Robles (Peachy Canyon [2], Tablas Creek [3]), and Edna Valley (Alban [3]) offer the best value and some of California's most innovative winemaking – some by 'virtual' winemakers using 'custom-crush' facilities for fruit they've cherry-picked from various sources. From here on down there are so many Santas there should have been a cease-and-desist clause (a Santa clause, in fact) as the Santa Ynez (Fess Parker [2], Ojai [3], Zaca Mesa [3]) and Santa Maria Valleys (Au Bon Climat [2]) and Santa Rita Hills (Babcock [2], Sanford [3]) cluster to the west of Santa Barbara itself.

Vintages can't seem to come round fast enough for winemakers in

Oregon, such is the improvement that each one brings (and they weren't bad to start with). The best Oregon producers, many of them in the Willamette Valley, make wines (notably Pinot Noir as good as anything from Burgundy at the price, but everything is getting a go) that have probably met with more critical acclaim than anywhere outside of California. Good ones to try include: Abacela 2; Argyle 3; Beaux Frères 3: Bergstrom 3; Brooks 3; Benton Lane 3; Criston 3; Elk Cove 3; Erath 2; Eyrie 3; Firesteed Cellars 2; Four Graces 3; Lachini 3; Ponzi Vineyard 3 – don't worry, the wine does actually exist; Rex Hill 3; Sokol Blosser 2; Willakenzie 2; Willamette Valley Vineyards 3 and Burgundy *négociant* Drouhin's venture, Domaine Serene 3.

Pacific North-West

You've got to give it up for whoever it was that first cast their eyes across the steppe-like wilderness of Washington state's heartlands and, feeling the winter wind whip straight through them, thought, 'Mmm, cool place for a vineyard.' That was nearly 200 years ago and it's not known if that pioneering soul knew that in the summer the place becomes a blistering dust-bowl, which the US army uses for desert training.

Washington is the second-biggest wine-producing state and knowledge that most of its vineyards are at roughly the same latitude as those of Burgundy – around 47° North – may explain why. It is the key to understanding the balance between the purity and intensity of the New World and the structure and freshness of the Old World that marks them out. Some of Europe's leading wine-makers have caught on, including Dr Ernst Loosen of Germany and venerable Italian firm Antinori who have set up joint ventures with local producers. As in Oregon, the industry is developing at gold-rush speed. At the other end of the scale, many winemakers started out making wine at home and, having recognised the quality of what they're producing, have grabbed the opportunity to do things on a commercial scale.

The desert conditions in summer are a challenge exacerbated by the coastal mountain ranges, which prevent all but the fiercest Pacific storms from making their way inland. At the western edge of the biggest wine-producing area, the Columbia Valley, annual rainfall decreases by an inch for every mile of travel eastwards. The western approaches to the gateway town of Walla Walla are lush and green while the road out to the east is parched and brown. Thus, irrigation here is essential, and gives the best winemakers a level of control over the ripening of the grapes that their more heavily regulated European counterparts would kill for. Another upside of being such a young industry is that sustainability has been high on the producers' agenda from the start. Amazingly, a quality-conscious wine-producing region with an output of around two-thirds that of New Zealand is only just coming to the attention of UK drinkers but more are arriving every year. For now, we'll make do with the likes of Abeja [3], Andrew Will [3], Arbor Crest [2], Badger Mountain [1], Duck Pond [2], Gordon [2], Hogue [1], Kiona [3], Leonetti [3], L'Ecole No 41 [3], Quilceda Creek [3], Woodward Canyon [3] and Château Sainte Michelle [1] – much the biggest, in the top-ten largest US wineries overall, and owned by the Philip Morris fags company Altria, also owners of Columbia Crest [1], Northstar [3], Snoqualmie [2], Stimson [1].

DRINK LIKE A KING with ...

Big House
Calera
Cline
De Loach
Wente

... FOR THE PRICE OF JUST DRINKING

The Rest

I don't know how Alaska and Hawaii are doing – and I've had a couple of stinkers from Colorado (makes up for all those fabulous microbrews) – but there are some excellent wines being made in New York (the state, that is – Manhattan real-estate prices haven't dropped quite that far yet), notably from the Finger Lakes region where fine dry Rieslings (Dr Konstantin Frank [1], Sheldrake Point [1]) can be had at silly prices and from Long Island (Corey Creek [1]). The native American non-vinifera black grape called Norton is still widely grown in the eastern and mid-western USA (especially Missouri, the major wine-producing state for most of the nineteenth century) and makes wines that are, at least, not easily distinguishable from others made from vinifera varieties (Chrysalis [2], Stone Hill [1]). There are only the first stirrings of export activity from Virginia (Barboursville [3], Whitehall [3]) and Texas (McPherson [2]) but if quality is an indication there'll be more to sample soon.

***GET A HANDLE...**

THERE IS LIFE BEYOND THE SUPERMARKET BRANDS AND YOU DON'T HAVE TO PAY NAPA VALLEY PRICES BUT YOU'LL NEED TO SEEK THE GOOD STUFF OUT.

valdiguié verdejo verdelho verdicchio verduzzo vermentino vermouth vernaccia vespaiola vidal vieilles vignes

vin de paille vin gris vin jaune vin santo vintage viognier virtual winemakers valdiguié verdejo verdelho

Verdelho – twangy white-grape variety making the second-driest of Madeira's fortified wines and substantial, lemony varietals in Australia, where it thrived in the nineteenth century but is now most at home in the Hunter Valley.

vermouth – fortified white (for the dry version) or red (sweet) wine aromatised with various botanicals, originally in order to make coarse wine palatable, and named for one that is no longer used: 'wormwood'. Particularly popular during the sozzled seventies, now mainly used in cocktails. The finest of a fine bunch is Dolin, the sole-remaining producer from Chambéry in Savoie, France, and the essence of *savoir-faire* in apéritifs. The other fineries include Cinzano, Dubonnet, Martini and the superior Noilly Prat.

vieilles vignes – 'old vines' therefore with deeper root systems, meaning a more interesting diet for the grapes and, as such, usually a good sign on a label.

vin de paille – 'straw wine', after the fact that the grapes are laid out on straw mats to partially dry (thus concentrating the sugars through evaporation) before being turned into rare sweet wine in France's Rhône and Jura regions. Similar wines made in Italy are called *passito*.

vin gris – 'grey wine', very pale rosé of the Côtes de Toul in eastern France's Lorraine region.

vin jaune – fino-sherry-like 'yellow wine' of eastern France's Jura region.

vino cotto – sweet, Marsala-like 'cooked' wine of Italy's Le Marche. Made domestically by severely reducing a quantity of grape-must through boiling, then adding fresh juice before fermentation and topping-up solera-style.

vin santo – Tuscany's *passito* 'holy wine' and certainly made in a catholic variety of styles, from fully sweet to decidedly dry – the only constants are the grapes (Trebbiano and/or Malvasia), the drying of the grapes – the longer, the sweeter – and the ageing in small barrels.

vintage – much-abused term, the confusion arising because it refers both to the year in which a wine is made and to the process of making it during and after the harvest. A 'vintage wine' means nothing more than that it is the product of a single year's harvest (aka – guess the languages – *Jahrgang*, *cosecha*, *vendange*, *vendemmia*).

Viognier – enigmatic, apricot-scented white grape originally of tiny (except the price) Condrieu in France's northern Rhône, now widespread across the globe and often barely recognisable. Its other role in the Rhône, blending with Syrah in Côte Rôtie, is now much-imitated in Australia – mostly for the good.

virtual winemakers – the natural and entrepreneurial children of the flying winemakers of antiquity, they buy the best grapes (or juice) they can get their hands on, rent equipment (aka 'custom-crush' facilities) and storage, print some labels, use their reputation or contacts to market the stuff and off they go.

vodka – in the 1860s, when Piotr Smirnov decided to create the finest vodka in all the Russias, he little knew what a wild ride it would be. The drink he put his name to was good. So good that everybody wanted a piece of it . . . including the Tsarist government, who wanted all of it and banned private distilleries. By the time they were themselves overthrown by the revolution of 1917, Piotr's grandson Vladimir had been declared an enemy of the people. Luckily he escaped a Bolshevik firing squad with just his life and the specifications for making the 'dear little water' (of life, of course, like all the rest), which he took to Constantinople, then to Poland and finally to Paris. Hard times saw the company sold to another émigré who took it to the USA and, when he met with blank looks for the colourless, 'tasteless' spirit, sold it on again. A British bar-owner in LA with a lot of unsold ginger beer on his hands got talking to the owner (from the Hueblein company), and with a bit of lime added, the Moscow Mule was born and vodka's star was lit in the West. After all that malarkey, perhaps it somehow deserves to be the biggest booze brand on the planet but

Piotr would spin in his grave if he tasted Smirnoff Red Label today – it's crap.

Vodka has been around a lot longer than that, of course, probably about a thousand years longer, and is the distillate of the grain/seed branch of booze's wonky family tree. Like rum and tequila, it's one of the I'm-gonna-make-some-hooch-out-of-this-shit-if-it-kills-me species. Ninety per cent is made from wheat, corn or barley and is effectively distilled beer (and what are spuds – that comprise the other tenth, mainly in Poland – if not seeds)? Its broad range of bases proved as useful during Prohibition as did its almost undetectable nature on the breath during the three-martini-lunch epoch of the seventies and eighties – happy days!

That very neutrality, also ideal as the fuel for launching a thousand cocktails, is what has made it the world's favourite spirit. We get through around a bottle a head per year, so about seven billion bottles globally, but it has another life as a sipper (or a shooter) and keeping it in the freezer is a must. Most is charcoal-filtered, and the charcoal does the same as Odour Eaters do for smelly feet, but I've never got the 'tasteless' thing. Subtle, yes, ethereal even, but the only thing I'd describe as tasteless are some of the things I've done after drinking too much of it. I'm not interested in flavoured vodkas, although bison grass (Zubrowka) has something about it and, now I think about it, Absolut's pear and apple are good, but most are just taking the old route of masking the flavour of rough vodka. Scandinavian caraway-flavoured akevitts as well as Polish potato and oily Russian grain versions all claim to be the Ur-vodka. Those northern countries take it as seriously as wine as an accompaniment to food both in terms of matching styles with dishes and also precisely how it is consumed (not just with regards to temperature but how many seconds should elapse between swallowing a particular morsel of food and chasing it with the drink – or vice versa).

The premium brands, obviously, are big business. Sweden's formerly state-owned Absolut was sold to Pernod Ricard in 2008 for $8.3 billion and brands a decade or two old such as France's Grey Goose or Holland's Ketel One have changed hands for $1 billion, even $2 billion.

Top voddie is made all over nowadays, in Croatia (Akvinta), France (Ciroc, which is grape-based), Ireland (Boru), Holland (Effen), Sweden (DQ, Frïs), Finlandia (duh!), USA (Fleischmann, Georgi Hangar One, Kamchatka, Rain, Royal, Skyy, Square One, Tito's Handmade, Teton Glacier), Kazakhstan (Snow Queen), Slovakia (Double Cross), Russia (Green Mark, Kauffman, Moskovskaya, Nemiroff, Pyat Ozer, Russian Standard, Stolichnaya), UK (Chase, voted the world's best in a major competition in 2010, Wight, and Three Olives), Poland (Belvedere, Chopin, Luksusowa, Snow Leopard, Ultimat, Wyborowa).

wine welschriesling whiskey sour wine welschriesling whisky sour wine

whiskey sour wine wine competitions welschriesling whiskey wine

wine competitions welschriesling whiskey sour wine competitions

welschriesling whiskey sour wine whiskey sour wine welschriesling

whisk(e)y – they don't like it when I say this, but whisky appears to be oak-aged vodka. There is, I realise, a deficit of swirling Celtic mists, smoking peat fires and blooming heather in this definition but it's preferable to my other, looser definition: beer schnapps. Why? Because a description of the early stages of making whisky could easily be mistaken for a description of brewing beer. It is made from the same grains as beer, exclusively malted barley for Scotch malt whisky but often mixtures of that with rye, wheat or corn – all malted or unmalted – in everything else. And, as with beer, the other ingredients – water and yeast – wouldn't appear to have the potential for producing the multifarious styles and shades they do but there's more to it than meets the eye. The quality of the barley is important, but the most important 'ingredients' of Scotch whisky, its secret weapons, in fact, are smoke and oak. The peat that is burned during the malting process is also encouraged to flavour the barley and, in turn, the nature of the peat will communicate itself to the grain. For example, there are no trees on wind-blasted Orkney and the peat is comprised largely of heather, the fragrance of which imprints itself on the DNA of the whisky; Islay (pronounced

W

'EYE-la') peat is mainly of moss that soaks up the sea-spray over the years and imparts that distinct salty tang to the smoke.

It's pushing it to call smoke an ingredient and even more so to say the same of oak but the barrel-ageing process is known to contribute at least half of the flavours to any whisky, and the better the oak the better the booze. There's a lot of money in whisky and the Scots are a thorough, determined and resourceful breed – it was they who actually built the British Empire while the English were poncing about in various silly hats, after all. So, it seems a small price to pay to spend a lot of time scouring the Ozark Mountains – with all the *Deliverance*-style dangers that must entail – for the finest, 150-year-old American white oaks grown on only the north-facing slopes, which receive less light and moisture and so grow more slowly and produce more 'early wood' (no smut, please). The porous spring growth allows the spirit to penetrate deeper in to the wood and melt down more of the harsh acids of the raw, young liquid into the lovely, nutty multiplicity of warm caramel flavours and intense fruit essences of the mature one.

The toastiness beloved of bourbon drinkers is exactly that, and comes from the toasting of the long-seasoned wood. No, not raising a glass in its honour but carefully charring the inside of the barrels – this also gees up the release of the vanillin, leather, smoke and clove-like compounds in the oak itself, including the coconutty whisky lactones, which sounds like a band that Shane MacGowan might like to be in. The Scottish perfectionists adhere to the standard, symbiotic practice of the barrels being used Stateside for ageing bourbon for four years before bringing them to Scotland.

The flavours of whisky leap into sharper focus with the addition of water, say half as much again. I don't usually do that but with cask-strength whisky at 63.5% abv you can have your cake and eat it and get the beneficial effect of adding the water without losing the fire of the spirit. The whisky writers are not having us on when they rhapsodise over toffee and créme brûlée, menthol and cinnamon; when they feast on coconut, toasted almonds and milk chocolate; luxuriate in pineapple and poached pears; gorge themselves on hazelnuts and fudge and sink back, exhausted, to revive themselves with a little mint. Gas chromatography-olfactometry analysis of a whisky produces a sort of 'whiskypedia' to identify all the different aroma-active compounds (or smells) in them and as many as 140 have been identified in a single whisky. So it seems that when I once blurrily wrote a tasting note for a whisky that simply said, '. . . sheems to tashte of everyfing,' I may not have been that far off the mark.

There are around 100 distilleries making single malts (defined as the product of a single distillery) in the five regions, which are less crisply defined, and some of them have dozens of labels, sorry 'expressions' – ghastly coinage – according to the age and style of the 'liquid' and how it was matured. Recently, a trend for marketing vintage-dated whiskies has emerged, sending the prices up to the thousands of pounds. Some of them are very good, but *that* good? In 1994 a whisky was launched that had been 'finished' with six months in a cask that had previously been used for ageing ruby port. It went down well and other wood finishes followed. Now there are squillions of them. It's the whisky world's altogether classier take on flavoured vodkas and rums.

The vast and varied Highlands region is too diverse to characterise but to get a feel for the range of flavours try Aberfeldy, Dalmore, Dalwhinnie and Glenmorangie. The region illogically includes all of the islands except Islay whose whiskies are noted for being peaty and smoky. Try Isle of Arran, Isle of Jura, Talisker, Orkney's Highland Park and Scapa, and for Islay try Ardbeg, Bowmore, Bunnahabhain, Lagavulin and Laphroaig. The products of the few remaining Lowlands distilleries (Auchentoshan, Glenkinchie) are characterised as being softer and sweeter than most while Speyside is the powerhouse of Scotch with by far the greatest number of producers (Aberlour, Balvenie, Glenfiddich, The Glenlivet, Glen Moray, Glen Spey, Knockando, The Macallan) and many of the blended whiskies are made here. Campbeltown's three remaining sea-girt distilleries on the Kintyre Peninsula are Glen Scotia, Scotia and the revived Glengyle.

There is something of a renaissance of independent bottlers both of single malts (Duncan Taylor, Ian Macleod, Inverarity) and of blends from more than one distillery, sometimes called 'vatted' malts (Compass Box, Douglas Laing, Gaelic Whisky, Sheep Dip). The 2000 brands of blended whisky are made from a mix of malt and 'grain' whiskies (i.e. containing grains other than malt); anything labelled 'Blended Scotch' (or 'blended Irish') whisky will be such and distilleries are not named (especially not those of the industrial plants in such romance-free places as Paisley and Parkhead).

Diageo has the biggest slice of the £3.1 billion Scotch-whisky-export cake (they own Johnnie Walker – the world's third-biggest booze brand – as well as Bell's, J&B and numerous distilleries including Blair Athol, Caol Ila, Cardhu, Cragganmore, Dalwhinnie, Glen Elgin, Glenkinchie, Glen Ord, Glen Spey), followed by French-owned Pernod Ricard (Chivas, Ballantine's). Other big players include India's United Breweries (Whyte & Mackay), Bacardi (Dewar's), France's LVMH (Glenmorangie, Ardbeg, Ballie Nichol Jarvie – aka BNJ), USA's Fortune Brands (Laphroaig), Trinidad's CL WorldBrands (Burn Stewart), Japan's Suntory (Bowmore,

Auchentoshan) and Takara Shuzo (Tomatin and their The Antiquary blend). Oh, yes, and William Grant (Glenfiddich) and the Edrington Group, which are both, er . . . Scottish (The Macallan, Cutty Sark, Famous Grouse – anybody in want of evidence of man's ability continually to improve his lot need only taste the Grouse, now slugging it out with Bell's for the prize of best-selling UK brand, as it differs from previous best-sellers in one crucial respect – it's good whisky, and it tastes nice.)

Whatever Irish whiskey's claims to be the original, among their four remaining distilleries they may have the world's oldest in Diageo-owned Bushmills in the north (the licence to distil in the area dates from 1608). The number of distilleries may be small but the variety of liquids is large and it and the other three (Pernod Ricard-owned Midleton, making Powers, Jameson and Redbreast; and independent Cooley, making Tyrconnell, which also revived the Kilbeggan distillery in 2007) make light, approachable often triple-distilled whiskies, usually from mixed grain, not all of which is malted and only one of which (Cooley's Connemara) is exposed to peat-smoke. Elsewhere in the UK, good whisky has been made in Wales (Pendryn) since 2000 and the first one made in England for 100 years (English Whisky Company in Norfolk) went on sale in 2009 with its three-year-old, and a Cornish one is in production.

US whiskey has a long and proud history reflected in a wilfully confusing nomenclature. To get things straight (if you'll forgive the pun on the term for any whiskey aged for two years or more): bourbon whiskey – mostly from Kentucky – is made from a minimum of fifty-one per cent corn (maize) in the mash (Baker's, Basil Hayden's, Blanton's, Booker's, Buffalo Trace, Bulleit, Elijah Craig, Fighting Cock, Four Roses, Heaven Hill, Henry McKenna, Jim Beam, Jefferson's,

Knob Creek, Maker's Mark, Old Fitzgerald, Old Forester, Old Grand-Dad, Old Rip van Winkle, Woodford Reserve, Wild Turkey) and those from Tennessee must be both charcoal-filtered and 'sour mash', like most bourbon (i.e. from a fermentation started by addition of material from a previous, already fermented acidic 'sour' batch; a 'sweet' mash starts fermentation from scratch). Dickel and Jack Daniels are the only Tennessee charcoal-filtered bourbons being made at present.

The same minimum content of rye is required in spicier, fruitier rye whiskey (Mount Vernon, Beam's Old Overholt, Rittenhouse, Sazerac, Wild Turkey and other big names also make a rye version) and the rarer wheat and malted-barley versions; a minimum of eighty per cent corn is required in 'corn whiskey', which is usually aged only for a few months in uncharred new oak, if at all.

Branch water, drawn from the branch of the stream that a distillery is built on, is the water added to a whiskey before bottling to rectify the alcoholic strength, and is always neutral so as not to affect the character of the end-product. The closest US equivalent of single malt whiskies are the 'single-barrel' and 'small-batch' bourbons.

Canadian whisky has been around since the 1880s (their Seagram company – now broken up – was once one of the biggest names in world booze) and is made by continuous distillation from a mix of grains but can be labelled as rye even if that grain doesn't predominate (Alberta Springs, Black Velvet, Canadian Club, Canadian Mist, Crown Royal, Forty Creek, Glen Breton, Pendleton, Rich and Rare, Tangle Ridge, Wiser's).

The Japanese have been mad for whisky for decades and have been making it since the 1920s although it only got serious in the last twenty years. It is now a very serious business with a Japanese whisky, Nikka's Yoichi twenty-year-old making tsunami-size waves by winning *Whisky Magazine*'s best malt award in 2008. Special mention should also be made of the excellent Suntory. The same will never happen to any Indian or Thai versions although Thailand's Mekong is a drinkable, cheaper alternative to beer. Everybody's at it, of course, and whisky of one sort or another is made in various countries both near – including France (Glann ar Mor), Germany (Blaue Muas), Bulgaria (Hapsberg, Black Ram), Sweden (Mackmyra) – and far: Australia (Great Southern, Lark, Hellyer's Road) and Taiwan (Kavalon).

Whiskey Sour – three parts bourbon, two parts lemon juice and one part simple syrup shaken with ice and strained in to a rocks glass – will while away the time as you wait for the 3.10 to Yuma.

W

xarel-lo xynomavro xarel-lo xynomavro xarel-lo xynomavro xynomavro xarel-lo xynomavro xarel-lo xynomavro xarel-lo xyno

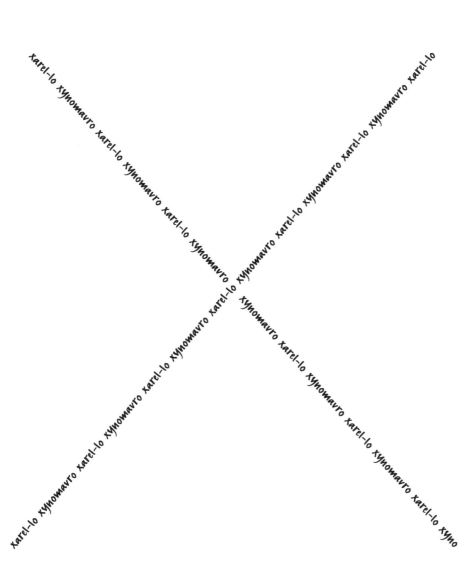

xarel-lo xynomavro xarel-lo xynomavro xarel-lo xynomavro xarel-lo xynomavro xarel-lo xynomavro xarel-lo xynomavro xarel-lo xynomavro xarel-lo xynomavro xarel-lo

Xynomavro – (literally 'acid-black') zippy red-wine grape variety in Naoussa, northern Greece, where it makes good wines, which mellow with age – and included here as I've got to have something beginning with 'X' for heaven's sake, and it was either this or Xarel•lo.

X

Yield Yeasts Yield Yeasts Yield Yeasts Yield Yeasts Yield

Yield Yeasts Yield Yeasts Yield Yeasts Yield Yeasts Yield

Yeasts Yield Yeasts Yield Yeasts Yield Yeasts Yield Yeasts

yeasts – boring they may be, but be grateful to our little fungal friends and their digestive process (we're drinking their waste) because it's as simple as this: no yeast = no booze. The spontaneous fermentation caused by wandering spores is still practised in some wineries and breweries; other strains are kept under lock and key.

yield – the root system of a vine will suck a certain amount of nutrients out of the good earth. The more grapes there are, the less each of them gets. Reduce the number of grapes and you get better wine.

Zinfandel Zombie Zweigelt Zinfandel Zombie Zweigelt Zinfandel Zombie Zwei

Zombie Zweigelt Zinfandel Zombie Zweigelt Zinfandel Zombie Zweigelt Zinfandel Zombie Zweigelt Zinfandel Zombie Zweigelt Zinfandel Zombie

Zinfandel Zombie Zweigelt Zinfandel Zombie Zweigelt Zinfandel Zombie Zweigelt

Zinfandel – robust red-wine grape variety (now known to be what is aka Primitivo in southern Italy, especially Puglia, and, for that matter Crljenak Kastelanski in Croatia), planted over fully a tenth of California vineyards (so it's a very big deal indeed). Makes strap-on, manly reds – top-class in the right hands – and girly, 'white' rosés in the wrong ones.

Zombie – equal (and I suggest small) parts each of light, dark, golden, *añejo* and over-proof rums, maraschino, simple syrup, lime juice and grapefruit juice, two dashes each of absinthe, bitters and grenadine shaken with ice and strained in to a rocks glass with a pineapple spear, orange slice, cherry and sprig of mint to garnish. A bed in the Cocktails Ward of the Betty Ford Clinic awaits those who fail to heed my advice.

Zweigelt – alphabetically challenged red-grape variety, the most widely planted in Austria, where they make good wine with it.

Acknowledgements

Peter Ackroyd – for kind words; David Akrigg – for early doors; Genavieve Alexander – for a straight bat; Dawn Alford – for a big break in a very good mag; John Alleyne – for rum; Hal Andrews – for Rioja; Joxe Mari Arbelaitz – for Navarra; Roger Asleson – for Napa; Fabio Baldo Papini – for Italia (and La Costaglia); Richard Bampfield – for Bordeaux; Rosamund Barton – for Bordeaux as well; Nicolas Bauer – for good value; Anne Beech – for a steady hand; Simon Beesley – for a steady eye; Simon Berry – for sine qua non sampling; Richard Bigg – for sherry; Grigor Bonomo – for Beringer; Adrian Bridge – for port; Dave Broom – for whisky; Pete Brown – for beer; Bruce Cakebread – for Napa; Luca Capodoglio – for vino cotto; Tom Cave – for knowing stuff; Phil Crozier – for Argentina; Tilly Culme-Seymour – for bloggeration; Jonathan Downey – for cocktails; Jim Edwards – for Ticino; Kelly Falconer – for nerveless editing; Elizabeth Ferguson – for Champagne; Nigel Foster – for chills and spills; Peter Gago – for Penfolds; Gina Gallo – for explaining; Natalie Galustian – for encouraging; Sandrine Garbay – for taking the time; Amanda Garnham – for Armagnac; Rick Gekoski – for putting up with me; Mathieu Germond – for a sommelier's-eye-view; Sue Glasgow – for being on the case; Malcolm Gluck – for Persimmon, for example; Alex Goodwin – for despatches; Jamie Graham – for the inside line; Ed Griffiths – for banging the drum; Casilda Grigg – for patience and perseverance; Ben and Joe Grogan – for waiting patiently; Salvador Guedes – for Portugal; Tony Harris – for a long time; Laely Heron – for the USA; Lisa Herriot – for logistics; Karis Hunt – for an early break; Bernard Hine – for Cognac; Merlin Holland – for a magic number; Bruce Jack – for sparking; Jancis – for incomparability; Dan Jellinek – for Scoff!; Hugh Johnson – for unimprovability; Gary Jordan – for South Africa; Louisa Joyner – for buying my book; Alan Kennett – for Australia; Belinda Kitchin – for a KiwiManuel Louzada – for Chile; Bill Lumsden – for whisky; Bérénice Lurton – for Barsac; Rab McWilliam – for my first break; Ed Maggs – for enthusiasm; Helen Maher – for unflappability; Pierre Mansour – for The Wine Society; Louise McKee – for bawling my wares; Sarah Miles – for stepping in; David Miller – oh yes, definitely Mr Miller; Noel McGuinness – for getting me started; Neil McGuigan – for Australia; Charles Metcalfe – for Portugal; Marcin Miller – for spirits; Jim Murphy – for drinking like kings; James Palmer – for restaurateurship; Marcelo Papa – for Chile; Françoise Peretti – for Champagne; Sue Pike – for PR as it should be; Alessio Planeta – for Sicily; Rupert Ponsonby – for more PR as it should be; José Rallo – for Sicily; Jonathan Ray – for more than there is space for here; Marina Ray – for a cool head; Maureen Rice – for keeping an even keel; Max Riedel – for explaining; Lindsay Roberts-Warren – for eagle-eyes; Mary Rochester-Gearing – for getting stuff done; Frédéric Rouzeau – for Champagne; Davina Russell – for moving it along; Kate Sarginson – for efficiency above and beyond; Brad Scott – for Three Penis Wine; Leonid Shutov – for vodka; Olly Smith – for enthusing; Steve Smith – for New Zealand; Aldo Sohm – for daring; Nick Spong – for doing Scoff!; Sarah Standing – for style (and travel); Peter Straus – for kicking things off; Richard Tanner – for Germany (and Tanners); Mark Tower – for cellar times; Tiago Trigo – for the Douro; Andre Van Rensburg – for Stellenbosch; Clare Wallis – for persevering; Chris Williams – for South Africa; Jason Yapp – for brio; Zoom – for the USA; Zoran Jevtic – for cyberthings.

Index

D

N

O

P

Q

R

S

X

Y

Z